SONS OR DAUGHTERS

Volume 31, Sage Library of Social Research

Sons or Daughters

A Cross-Cultural Survey of Parental Preferences

NANCY E. WILLIAMSON

Preface by DAVID M. HEER

Series Editor's Preface by JETSE SPREY

Volume 31
SAGE LIBRARY OF
SOCIAL RESEARCH

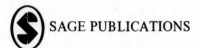 SAGE PUBLICATIONS   Beverly Hills   London

For information address:

SAGE PUBLICATIONS, INC.
275 South Beverly Drive
Beverly Hills, California 90212

SAGE PUBLICATIONS LTD
St. George's House / 44 Hatton Garden
London E C 1N 8ER

Printed in the United States of America

Library of Congress Cataloging in Publication Data

Williamson, Nancy E   1945-
    Sons or daughters.

    (Sage library of social research; v. 31)
    Includes bibliographical references and indexes. 1. Sex of children, Parental preferences for. I. Title.
HQ755.83.W54   301.42'6   76-26888
ISBN 0-8039-0673-0
ISBN 0-8039-0674-9 pbk.

FIRST PRINTING

With special thanks to:

Connie, Elizabeth, Eva, Fay, Jo, Judy,
Leslie, Pat, Roz, Sarah, Terry, and Yvonne.

CONTENTS

PREFACE

In recent years research on parental sex preference has burgeoned. One cause for this has been the belief that very soon highly effective means will be available to allow parents to choose the sex of their child. In fact, already certain physicians have received great publicity for their prescriptions designed to increase a couple's probability of conceiving either a male or a female child. A second cause for the burgeoning research is related to the interest of many Third World nations in reducing their birth rates. In many of these nations couples have a pronounced preference for sons and also a definite tendency more frequently to go on for additional children after the birth of a daughter than after the birth of a son. Hence the birth rate in these nations would be reduced either if there were a highly effective means for parents to choose the sex of their child or if their boy preference could be eliminated. A final cause of the increased interest in sex preference relates to the Women's Liberation Movement. As Dr. Williamson points out, the status of women is inversely related to the degree of son preference in any given society. Hence, the degree of son preference serves as a useful index of the status of women.

Although the earliest research on parental preference for sex of children dates from 1931, there has up to now been no comprehensive survey of the research so far conducted. Since already a very large amount has been published, Dr. Williamson's comprehensive book is able to perform two valuable functions. First, and most obviously, we learn what research has already been conducted and the conclusions we can gather from it. Secondly, we come to understand the gaps in our knowledge and those matters about which it would be useful to learn more. To give an example, we find that there is very little knowledge concerning the fate of a child whose actual sex turns out to be different from that which the mother or father preferred.

One important finding from the existing research is that a pronounced parental preference for sons does not in all societies lead to a higher subsequent fertility among couples having mostly or entirely daughters. Whereas in Taiwan and Korea such son preference does lead to higher subsequent fertility among couples having a preponderance of daughters, it does not have this consequence according to surveys conducted in Morocco, India, or Bangladesh. It may be that there are no behavioral consequences of son preference in Morocco, India, and Bangladesh simply because so few of the women in these nations practice any form of birth control. On the other hand, the reason may lie in the fact that although the rewards for having a son are very high, the penalties for having a daughter are equally great. In this circumstance, the expected gain from the next child (for which the probability of being male is only slightly more than .50) is not particularly high. If this second theory is correct, a preponderance of daughters leads to higher subsequent fertility in Taiwan or Korea, not only because the marginal gain from another son is large, but also because the marginal loss from another daughter is not so pronounced. However, it is still debatable which of these two reasons for this difference between the Taiwan and Korea findings on the one hand and the findings in Morocco, India, and Bangladesh on the other is correct. This gap in our knowledge points to the need for further research.

A second finding which many readers will find surprising is the large number of ways in which son preference can be, and has been, measured and the fact that the various operational definitions of son preference often tend to measure other variables along with the concept they are intended to measure. For example, questions which ask the desired number of sons and daughters if life could be lived over contaminate son preference with rationalizations of the existing sex composition of the respondent's children. Furthermore, questions which ask a respondent to state the ideal number of sons and daughters for someone else (such as one's own daughter) may confound son preference with traditionalism; respondents who cannot conceive that anyone could ever have a choice as to the sex of children may advise an equal number of sons and daughters, whereas respondents who are sufficiently free of traditional thought ways to imagine the possibility of choosing the sex of one's child will advise having a higher proportion of sons. Future researchers on parental sex preference will find they can save themselves much heartache by bearing in mind the methodological lessons to be learned from Dr. Williamson's book.

Finally, the reader will find in this book much valuable information on the social-structural conditions which create pronounced son preference in many agrarian societies, a preference for at least one child of each sex in most industrial societies, and daughter preference in a very small minority of societies. The inevitability of son preference in eighteenth century England's patrilineal kinship system was of course admirably set forth in 1813 by Jane

Austen in her famous novel *Pride and Prejudice*. Dr. Williamson shows that son preference in many Third World nations is still highly associated with the same characteristics as it was in eighteenth century England: patrilocal residence, patrilineality, inheritance only through males, and the payment of a dowry as the prerequisite for marrying off one's daughter. She also shows that in those few societies in which daughter preference prevails it is associated with a matrilineal, matrilocal kin system and with payment of a brideprice rather than a dowry.

If humankind will soon have a method of choosing the sex of its children, we had all better get ready for the possibility. The "future shock" resulting from this event will be minimized for those persons who have already read this book.

David M. Heer
University of Southern California

SERIES EDITOR'S PREFACE

Our knowledge about the institutions of marriage and the family has bene-fitted during recent years from the contributions provided by related specialties within the social and behavioral sciences. Among the latter, the work of social demographers doubtlessly is a case in point. It is a field characterized by a sophisticated research technology and by the formulation of theoretical questions that are of great relevance to the understanding of the structuring of continuity and change in marriages and families across the world.

Because of this, I am quite pleased to see *Sons or Daughters: A Cross-Cultural Study of Parental Preferences* published as part of our N.C.F.R. Monograph Series. Our contemporary society is one in which parenthood is becoming increasingly a matter of choice rather than chance. In this social context the preference of parents for children of a specific gender is likely to become a factor of increased importance in the determination of family size. Furthermore, such a preference—should it exist—may affect parental aspirations and plans for their child's education and further career. Finally, we might hypothesize the parental preference, when frustrated, could lead to the desire for couples to share in the parenthood experience of others. In other words, the subject-matter of Dr. Williamson's book touches base at a wide range of relevant issues within the realms of current marital and familial behavior.

The cross-cultural design of the study, in combination with its substantive focus, also can be seen as a worthwhile addition to our insight and knowledge of the rapidly growing field of sex-role studies. It is obvious that a parental preference for sons, if we see it within a range of different socioeconomic and cultural national settings, reflects a great deal more than a mere manifestation of "sexism" or male domination. Instead, the author's data focus our attention on a range of basic issues which concern the costs and satisfactions of children in human societies. In this manner, her discussion significantly broadens our frequently rather narrow sociological and psychological approaches toward the study of parenthood.

In short, it seems to me that this specific socio-demographic study will be of interest to a wide segment of our N.C.F.R. membership, and other students of contemporary marriage and the family. I hope it will gain the reader audience it deserves.

Jetse Sprey
NCFR Monograph Editor

ACKNOWLEDGMENTS

Any project extending over a span of almost eight years incurs a number of debts. In the first place, I received financial assistance from a number of sources. From 1968 to 1972, I was supported by a predoctoral fellowship from the National Institute of General Medical Sciences of the National Institutes of Health. The Population Council paid for my transportation to Taiwan and for my field work there in 1970. The considerable costs of the Taiwan study itself were borne by the Agency for International Development, Office of Population. Computer money for the data analysis came from the Harvard Center for Population Studies, the Harvard Department of Sociology, the Department of Sociology and the Bio-Medical Sciences small grant program at Brown University, and the East-West Population Institute. A small grant from the National Science Foundation paid for a part-time research assistant during 1971-72, programming and keypunching expenses, and supplies. In 1975, a Ford Foundation Faculty Fellowship for Research on the Role of Women in Society gave me the opportunity to revise the manuscript. The East-West Population Institute made available its excellent facilities and provided an *ideal* climate for the completion of the project.

Many people have been helpful with intellectual contributions. Primary is David M. Heer, Professor of Sociology at University of Southern California, who was the director of the Taiwan project. He has been extremely helpful over the last eight years. Especially valuable has been the experience of working with him on the very competently managed Taiwan project from its inception. He originally introduced me to the topic of son preference and its possible relationship to fertility.

A second person I would like to thank is Dr. Hsin-ying Wu, the director of the Taiwan field work and Professor at the Institute of Public Health, College of Medicine, National Taiwan University. Dr. Wu had the task of finding interviewers, supervising their training and performance, overseeing the coding and keypunching, and making the master tape. Under his direction, over 8,000 male and female respondents were interviewed in 1969-1970 and then over 6,500 of the same persons were interviewed a year later. It was a difficult job.

One member of Dr. Wu's staff, Hsiu-mei Hsieh, was particularly helpful to me during my field work in Taiwan. She acted as a translator when I wanted to talk to respondents or interviewers. She also helped me with several small projects like making lists of the major industries in the two study townships.

Other persons who offered valuable ideas along the way were: Ezra Vogel, of the East Asian Studies Center at Harvard who read and made suggestions for the Taiwan questionnaire and who later read an earlier version of this manuscript; David Armor, now at the Rand Corporation, who made several suggestions about the data analysis; Harold A. Thomas, Jr. of the Harvard Center for Population Studies; Ronald Freedman of the University of Michigan Population Studies Center with whom I discussed evidence for son preference upon several occasions; T.H. Sun whose thesis provided an important model for my work; John B. Williamson of the Department of Sociology at Boston College; and Monica S. Fong of the East-West Population Institute.

Jetse Sprey, editor of the National Council on Family Relations Monograph Series, along with an anonymous associate editor, suggested important revisions which are reflected in the final product. Rhoda Blecker of Sage Publications and Yvonne Tucker, a writer, both provided editorial assistance.

Still more aid, both editorial and typing were given by Roz Reck, Mary Lelwica, and the secretarial and librarian staff of the East-West Population Institute. Claire MacDonald did the library research upon which the second part of Chapter 4, sex preferences of adopting parents, is based. Karin Domnick handled the final editorial revisions, and prepared the indexes.

All these acknowledgments point to one thing: the surprising amount of support—financial, intellectual, and technical—that one needs to get a book of this kind done. I am grateful I had such support.

N.E.W.

Chapter 1

INTRODUCTION

In many societies, the institution of the family is now undergoing change. Students of modernization have long been concerned with how family structures and attitudes impede or encourage economic, social, and political development. This book deals with one cluster of attitudes of parents–preferences for different combinations of sons and daughters. We want to show how parental sex preferences vary by culture, what social and economic conditions affect these preferences, and whether sex preferences affect (particularly, increase) family size. A further connection, between fertility and modernization or development, will not be pursued here. We will assume that for many (not all) developing countries, including Taiwan, which will be considered in detail, smaller families will facilitate economic development. For a more extensive discussion of the relationships between family size, population growth, and economic growth, a good place to begin is Robinson and Horlacher (1971).

The Significance of Parental Sex Preferences

The subject of parental preferences for sons or daughters is important for several reasons. First, in some countries, son preference seems to affect completed family size. Parents may not want a certain number of children so much as a minimum number of boys. Thus, if policy makers want to reduce desired and actual family size, they should understand why parents want sons so badly. Second, if it becomes technically possible for parents to control the sex of their offspring, we might like to know whether boys or girls would be preferred, in what proportions, and by whom. This would help us assess the potentially vast implications of this technological innovation. Third, son preference can be considered one rough indicator of the sexual equality of a society (or an individual). A society characterized by no sex preference is quite likely to be a sexually egalitarian society in which little emphasis is put on sex differences. If policy makers want to increase sexual equality, then it is essential to know under what conditions sons are, and are not, preferred.

Types of Sex Preference

For our purposes, individuals might be classified into six categories, according to their sex preferences. There are those who would like to have (1) all sons, (2) a predominance of sons with at least one daughter, (3) equal numbers of sons and daughters or at least one of each, (4) a predominance of daughters with at least one son, (5) all daughters, and (6) any sex combination. We are excluding here people who do not want any children at all or those who are uncertain about their preferences.

Considering the individual, sex preferences might change over time, perhaps depending on his or her experience with different numbers and sexes of children. Furthermore, an individual may have preferences about birth order in addition to preferences about family size and sex composition (i.e., an individual may want the first child to be a boy and the second a girl). Most people have many more preferences relating to children which we will not explore here (such as feelings about timing of births, multiple births, and physical characteristics of children). We will deal primarily with sex and number preferences, with an occasional mention of order preferences. It should be pointed out that parents have relatively more control over the number of their children than they do over the sex of their children. This distinction will be important throughout our discussion of sex preferences.

Hypotheses About Sex Preferences

As our review of empirical evidence in Chapters 2 and 3 will show, the second category, preference for a predominance of sons with at least one daughter, is very common around the world. It appears to be widespread in developing countries like China, India, Pakistan, Taiwan, and Korea but also is fairly common in the United States, although it is not reflected in

American family sizes. Thus, we might begin by considering the context of this particular preference and then suggest specific conditions under which it might be found. Afterward, we will take up more briefly parental preferences for equal numbers of boys and girls, preference for a predominance of girls, and lack of sex preference. Preferences for all boys or all girls are too rare to be dealt with in any detail.

PREFERENCE FOR A PREDOMINANCE OF SONS

Parental sex preferences cannot be seen as an isolated set of attitudes (often reflected in behavior) but as attitudes which fit into a social setting. We will begin by suggesting that preference for a predominance of sons is one of the attitudes that characterizes individuals who are part of a traditional partriarchal family. Goode (1963) has described the "ideal type" of such a traditional family system as follows. Elder males have considerable authority over other family members through distribution of land, jobs, houses, and spouses. In general, kin members are very important to each other economically, politically, religiously, and socially. Land ownership tends to be an important source of family wealth because holdings may be pooled rather than individually owned.

Marriages, accompanied by dowry or bride price, are often arranged by kin and are based more on economic or political considerations than on love between the bride and groom. The subsequent husband and wife relationship is not primarily one of friendship and companionship but is characterized by a division of labor and lack of equality. Same-sex kin and neighbors are more likely to be sources of companionship than one's spouse.

With marriage a woman leaves her family and village to settle with her husband's family where she is expected to adjust to this new family. At least for some period of the marriage she may be under the supervision of a mother-in-law. Divorce and remarriage are rare, but when they do exist, they are more readily obtained by the husband than the wife. Better-off men may have more than one wife.

Women contribute to the family through home productivity, childbearing, and childrearing, whether or not they work outside the home. A wife's status increases when she produces sons who will eventually inherit the family wealth and carry on the family name.

It is an empirical question just how widespread such a traditional patriarchal family is and whether these elements of the traditional family are always found together. In trying to understand the conditions which foster son preference, we will attempt to find evidence about family structure. But there are other factors which may encourage son preference. Nowhere do families operate in a social and economic vacuum. For instance, families living in a society or community filled with conflict may feel they need sons for protection.

Below we have outlined our hypotheses about the conditions under which parents might want a predominance of boys. We will consider economic, social (including cultural and religious), and psychological situations.

A. Economic

(1) Parents will want a predominance of boys if sons are economically more productive to the family than daughters. This could occur when daughters give their labor to their husband's family upon their marriage, or when females on the average are less suited to certain kinds of important activities (such as plow agriculture, hunting, or warfare) due to disadvantages of childbearing, stature, or strength, or when jobs bringing in money to the family are considered appropriate only for males.

(2) Parents will want a predominance of boys if the parents expect to rely primarily on sons in old age.

(3) Parents will want a predominance of boys if upon marriage sons bring dowries into the family, while daughters require dowries in order to marry.

(4) Parents preferring a predominance of sons will want at least one daughter when daughters participate in jobs such as childrearing, household work, agriculture, or home industries or when they provide companionship to the mother. Also, having a daughter can help maintain the sex role segregation and division of labor within a family (i.e., boys do not have to be asked to do "women's work" if there is a daughter).

(5) Parents will prefer a predominance of boys when boys have more opportunities for advancement in the society.

(6) Parents of lower economic class (or of a racially discriminated group) will be more likely than better-off parents to prefer a predominance of sons if sons are thought to provide economic security or protection.

B. Social

(1) Parents will want a predominance of boys if the residence pattern is patrilocal and the family system is patrilineal. With these patterns, daughters give their labor, loyalty, and children to their husband's family rather than their own.

(2) Parents will want a predominance of boys if it is important to have a male heir and provide continuity of the family line and name. This should be especially the case where ancestor worship is practiced.

(3) Parents will prefer a predominance of sons if they live in an area where there is conflict between significant groups in the community.

Sons, in this case, may be desired for protection of the family or group.

(4) Parents will desire a predominance of sons if there are social or religious customs which require having sons.

(5) Parents will prefer a predominance of sons if they are living in an extended family and subject to pressures for family continuity.

(6) Parents will be more likely to want a predominance of sons if the family is living in a rural area rather than in an urban area. The reason may be that the traditional patriarchal family is less influential in urban areas or that individuals in cities may be exposed to new ideas about sexual equality, opportunities for women, new roles for women, and freedom of individuals from family influence. Or finally, sons may be less advantageous in urban areas.

(7) Certain cultures and religions have traditionally encouraged a preference for sons. Parents who are part of these cultures or religions may prefer a predominance of sons. Examples of such groups are the Chinese, Moslems, and Orthodox Jews. By extension, parents from other more traditional religions may be more "son-preferring" than parents in more individualistic or more recently-founded religious groups.

C. Psychological

(1) Men will be more likely to prefer a predominance of sons rather than daughters if having sons is a sign of masculinity, or if sons provide men greater companionship than daughters.

(2) Women will prefer a predominance of sons in order to obtain greater status, security, or influence. Related to this hypothesis is the idea of Freud that women may want sons to compensate for the fact that they were not born male.

(3) Parents will want a predominance of boys if boys are viewed as easier to raise.

In our review of the empirical literature, we will attempt to see whether there is any support for these hypotheses dealing with the preference for a predominance of boys.

PREFERENCE FOR EQUAL NUMBERS OF SONS AND DAUGHTERS

Parents may prefer an equal number of sons and daughters either because of an acceptance of what fate tends to bring or because of some perceived advantage of an equal number. The reasons given for wanting an equal number may be based on psychological needs and sex role ideas more than on economic or social needs. Below we list several hypotheses about conditions under which parents will prefer an equal number of boys and girls. The last two hypotheses mention the preference for at least one of each sex.

(1) Parents who believe that one must be happy with what God or nature sends may express preferences for an equal number of boys and girls, considering this the most natural, and hence best, combination.

(2) In a society with sharp sex role segregation, parents will want children of each sex to fulfill the appropriate family responsibilities. Furthermore, in such a society, it may be considered proper for boys to spend their time with boys and girls with girls. This may lead to a preference for at least two of each sex so that each child has a same-sex companion.

(3) Parents may desire at least one child of each sex for variety, based on the notion that the sexes will have different traits, strengths, leisure activities, and interests. If these same parents believe that an odd number of children is undesirable, then they may prefer an even number of children and of boys and girls. The objection to an odd number of children may be that one child may be left out or "ganged up upon" (i.e., "Three's a crowd").

(4) If boys are seen as having a special tie to their father and girls to their mother, then parents may desire at least one of each—one for each parent. The preference could be based on the opposite notion—that girls have a special relationship to their father and boys to their mother.

The first hypothesis should be considered separately from the others. It may reflect a traditional or fatalistic orientation toward family size and sex composition. The other hypotheses deal with positive reasons why parents might want equal numbers (or at least one of each sex). Parents expressing these reasons may be more likely to limit their family size after the desired balance is achieved.

PREFERENCE FOR A PREDOMINANCE OF DAUGHTERS

As our cross-cultural review will show in Chapter 4, there are very few societies characterized by many individuals having preferences for daughters. This makes the examples of deviant societies or individuals with daughter-preference all the more interesting. We will also consider one other situation where daughters may be preferred—adoption. In the United States at least, there is some evidence that daughters are preferred by adoptive parents.

As with the hypotheses about son preference, we have organized the hypotheses about daughter preference into economic, social, and psychological reasons. Following these are hypotheses about why daughters might be preferred for adoption.

A. *Economic*

(1) If women are considered wealth or if they are the medium of exchange in a society, daughters may be preferred.
(2) If women are more economically productive than men in the society, then parents may prefer daughters.
(3) If the parents' support in old age depends on daughters, then daughters may be preferred.
(4) If girls bring in a bride price, parents may prefer daughters.

B. *Social*

(1) If the kinship system is organized matrilineally, families may prefer daughters to carry on the family line.

C. *Psychological*

(1) If parents consider daughters easier to raise, then daughters may be preferred.
(2) Parents will prefer to have a predominance of daughters if they believe that daughters will be more rewarding companions or helpers as children or as adults.
(3) Men may prefer a predominance of daughters in order to avoid competition which might occur with sons.

D. *Adoption*

(1) An adopted girl might be thought to be more adaptable to a new family and less disruptive than a boy.
(2) In a patrilineal society, a girl would not carry on the family name which might be an advantage if the parents had misgivings about an "outsider" perpetuating the family line.
(3) If the adopted child were Oriental (which is common in the U.S.), a girl might be preferred because of the notion that Oriental women are beautiful. A girl might find a marriage partner more easily. Furthermore, if the child grew up to be short in stature, it is easier to be a short girl than a short boy due to sex role ideals.

In Chapter 4 we will investigate these hypotheses by looking at five daughter-preferring societies and some evidence on adoption. Instances where sons are preferred for adoption will also be discussed.

LACK OF SEX PREFERENCE

Some parents may not have sex preferences at all. Here are several hypotheses about situations where we might expect to find lack of sex preference.

(1) Parents who have (or expect to have) many children may have no sex preferences, knowing that there is a good chance they will have several children of each sex.

(2) Parents who have already fulfilled their sex preferences (say, they have two boys and a girl) may have no preferences for the sexes of subsequent children.

(3) Parents who are environmentalists and who believe that most sex differences are produced by socialization rather than anatomy will have no reason to prefer one sex over the other.

(4) Parents who believe that the differences between individuals of the same sex are potentially just as great as those between individuals of different sexes will have no reason to prefer a sex "balance." They will assume that sufficient variety can be found among children, regardless of their sex.

(5) Parents who believe in sexual equality will tend to have no sex preference.

(6) Future parents who wish to defend themselves against disappointment may express no sex preferences.

Consequences of Sex Preferences

In addition to describing sex preferences and considering their determinants cross-culturally, this book is concerned with the family size consequences of sex preferences. We will also mention the possible impact on parents (who do or do not realize their preferences) and on children (who are or are not the ones preferred). We will be investigating whether sex preferences are related to approval of family planning, ideal family size, the propensity to continue childbearing, and the use of contraception. One of our goals is to specify under what conditions sex preferences may influence family size. Anticipating our results, some of these conditions appear to be: low and predictable infant and child mortality; considerable skill in the use of contraception (so that the couple can stop producing children when their preferences are met); strong sex preference; and a desire for a moderate-sized family (three or four children). For a society characterized by individuals living under these conditions and having strong sex preferences, the demographic transition from high fertility to low fertility may well be slowed down. If these conditions are *not* met, we would not expect sex preferences to affect family size. For example, in the United States parents now strongly desire small families (around two children) and do not have strong sex preferences. Currently, the size considerations seem to have overwhelmed any sex preference. Thus the effect of sex preferences should be slight in the U.S.

Contribution to the Field

This study will make several contributions to our knowledge. First, its extensive cross-cultural review of the literature on sex preferences is unique and ought to be useful to other researchers. Second, we will consider the problems of measuring sex preference. As the review of the literature will make evident, most past studies of sex preference have been quite simple, often using only a single survey question to measure sex preference, sometimes on a small and unrepresentative sample. In contrast, we will be testing our hypotheses using data from a great variety of cultures. We will also present findings from a large study done in Taiwan which included many questions on sex preference.

Third, a study of sex preference is important because of the possible contribution of sex preference to population growth. Only when sons and daughters are equally valued or when only one or no son is required is it likely that fertility will approach replacement levels.

Fourth, the Taiwan study provides a little information on the reliability of survey data on sex preference since the survey was repeated a year later and several sex preferences questions were asked twice. About 6,500 of the same respondents were found and successfully interviewed again.

Finally, few previous studies of sex preference have felt it worthy of considerable study in itself. One exception to this is the work of Chung, Cha, and Lee (1974). In our book we will be using sex preference as one indicator of the egalitarianism of the society or the individual. Thus, when we are searching for determinants of different types of sex preference, we are really looking for determinants of egalitarianism, an important problem quite independent of fertility behavior. It is likely that a society with high son preference is one with a low status of women, few women in powerful positions, less favored treatment of girls, and feelings of inferiority on the part of women (and superiority for men). This broader issue is illustrated by a recent advertisement on behalf of the Christian Children's Fund, Inc. which showed a picture of a three or four year old Taiwanese girl. Below was this caption:

Little Mie-Wen in Formosa already knows many things . . . the gnawing of hunger . . . the shivering of fear . . . the misery of being unwanted. But she has never known love. Her mother died when she was born. Her father was poor—and didn't want a girl child. So Mie-Wen has spent her baby years without the affection and security every child craves.

It would be most superficial to think of sex preference only in terms of its fertility implications.

Limitations of the Study

The limitations of such a cross-cultural review of the literature are several: the lack of comparability of the data, the inadequacy of many of the studies, the complete lack of data for many countries, and the inadequacy of some of the measures of sex preference. Nevertheless, there is a good deal we can learn from the previous studies that we have pulled together.

Considering the Taiwan data which we present in Chapter 5 and analyze in Chapter 6, there are several shortcomings. Except for some information on reliability, data for only one time period will be used here because too few of the son preference questions were asked a second time. This means that we may appear to be making longitudinal inferences from cross-sectional data—a hazardous enterprise. Thus, if we discover that respondents in the more urban townships have more son preference, we might be tempted to conclude that as more people move to urban areas, there will be an increase in son preference. This implication goes beyond the data and is merely speculative.

Another limitation is that our sample is not representative of Taiwan as a whole. We covered only one urban township (Hsinchuang, 5,000 respondents) and one rural township (Kungliao, 3,170 respondents). Both were located in northern Taiwan. Furthermore, since we attempted to interview all ever-married women (and one-fifth of their husbands) in the two townships, responses may lack complete independence. Some respondents may have discussed the interview with other respondents. In addition, our response rates were not as high as we might have desired (around 75%)

Due to limitations on the length of the Taiwan questionnaire, several possibly relevant background variables had to be omitted (such as history of farm background, history of the family structure, and nature of extended family relations). Furthermore, not all aspects of son preference were adequately measured. Religious aspects of son preference, attitudes of parents toward sons and daughters during times of economic depression or war, cultural traditions about sons, psychological aspects of having sons versus daughters, and usefulness of daughters were all slighted in the questionnaire. However, even with these limitations, we can still learn a good deal about the nature and causes of sex preference.

Plan of Presentation

In Chapter 2 we review the empirical literature on the sex preferences of American parents, with some attention to changes over time. Only for the U.S. do we have data from different time periods. Included in this chapter is information from several European studies as well. Chapter 3 deals with sex preferences in four geographical areas, Latin America, the Middle East, India/Pakistan/Bangladesh, and the Far East. Omitted are the countries of sub-Saharan Africa, Eastern Europe, and the Soviet Union. For these areas, the data were either insufficient or nonexistent. Evidence of daughter preference is presented in Chapter 4, where the focus is on five small matrilineal societies and on the phenomenon of adoption.

Findings from the Taiwan study are presented in Chapters 5 and 6. Here we further test the hypotheses just listed and deal with some of the problems of measuring sex preferences. In the final chapters, we expand the topic to include other possible relationships between sex roles and fertility and discuss public policies dealing with sexual inequality. Two case studies—the Republic of Korea and the People's Republic of China—are examined to consider what policies to counteract boy preference have been tried or might be tried. Given how engrained sex preferences are, and how little most countries are doing to counteract sex preferences, it seems likely that it will be a long time before boys and girls are welcomed equally. In the last chapter we review our findings and discuss the more general issue of modernization and son preference.

Chapter 2

PARENTAL SEX PREFERENCES IN THE UNITED STATES AND EUROPE

The sex composition preferences of Americans have been quite thoroughly documented—in contrast with the situation in other societies. In this chapter we will consider these questions: What preferences about the sex combinations of their families do Americans have? Do sex preferences influence fertility attitudes or behavior? Besides fertility consequences, are there any other consequences, for parents or children, of sex preferences? For example, do sex preferences lead to children being rejected by the parents whose desires are unrealized? And finally, what economic and social and psychological conditions tend to be associated with these preferences? Are any of the hypotheses given in Chapter 1 borne out?

In order to discover whether the preferences, their consequences, or determinants have changed over time, we will look at the evidence chronologically. We will begin with attitudinal data measuring sex preferences without reference to fertility behavior.

Description of Parental Sex Preferences

The very first study of sex preference attitudes done in the U.S. was reported by Winston (1932-1933). He asked fifty-five male undergraduates, presumably at his own institution, North Carolina State, how many boys and girls they wanted for their future families. The sex ratio of preferred boys to girls was 165. This is the first of many studies which show pronounced boy preference among American college students and especially among males.

The next attempt to measure sex preferences was in the Indianapolis study which collected data on fertility attitudes and behavior from 1,309 "relatively fecund" white couples who were living in Indianapolis in 1941. Of the many interesting findings reported by Clare and Kiser (1951) on sex preferences, the more important will be cited. First, the husbands, but not the wives, seemed very concerned that if they had an only child it be a boy. Among husbands who already had a boy first, 66% preferred a hypothetical only child to be a boy. Among those husbands who had a girl first, only 15% would prefer an only child to be a girl. A majority of the women had no sex preference for an only child, with the remaining group slightly more in favor of having a girl than a boy. In contrast, the husbands either had no preference (42% of the total sample) or wanted a boy (48%) rather than a girl (10%).

When respondents were asked about preferences for a two-child family, about 70% of the wives and 80% of the husbands chose the one-of-each-sex family with 12% of the wives and 9% of the husbands giving no preference. Of those remaining, women were slightly more likely to prefer the two-girl over the two-boy family, while with the husbands it was definitely the reverse. Again, men showed more son preference.

Clare and Kiser presented ample evidence that the parents in their sample often rationalized what they got, hence complicating the measurement of their sex preferences. However, in our view the two questions asked in the Indianapolis study, one on preference for an only child and the other on preferences regarding a two-child family, seemed designed to elicit rationalizations. All the couples in the subsample in which sex preferences were studied had already had at least one live birth. Almost all had one or more living children. When asked about their preferences for an only child, they naturally tended to respond in terms of their own experience. Similarly, many couples already had two children and their responses reflected this reality. Had the question been worded, "What would be your preference for an additional child?," the rationalization effect would have been much less. Rationalization is also less of a problem when a nonparent sample is being studied or when sex preferences are very strong as they are in several of the developing countries to be discussed in the next chapter. The Clare and Kiser conclusion that there is a "strong tendency for parents to be satisfied with the sex of the children they have" (1951: 464) may apply more to American parents than parents in other cultures. However, until more approaches to the measurement problem have been tried, even this conclusion is premature.

The next study (Strunk, 1947-1948) did try a different question and found more evidence of boy preference. Respondents in a national poll in 1947 were asked whether they would prefer a boy or a girl if they had a (another) child. More respondents preferred a boy (40%) than a girl (25%) with 27% having no preference, and 8% no opinion. Most of this boy preference was due to the responses of men, 45% of whom wanted a boy. Women were evenly distributed among those wanting a boy (34%), a girl (32%), while 34% gave no preference or no answer. No further analysis of this national poll was published in 1947 although recently, Westoff and Rindfuss (1974) reanalyzed these data.

Another college student study (Dinitz et al., 1954) was done in the early 1950s. The authors administered a questionnaire to 380 Ohio State University students (185 males, 195 females) who were enrolled in introductory and advanced sociology courses. Students were asked their preference for the sex of their first child (with the option of "either") and for the sex of an only child (with no option for "either").

The authors concluded that the male was still the strongly preferred child among these students. When they were asked about the preferred sex of an only child, 92% of the males and 66% of the females specified a boy. When given the option of "either," 62% of the males and 59% of the females specified a boy for a first child. A third of the males and females took the option of "either." Almost none of the males (4%) and females (6%) chose a girl. Almost twenty years later, Peterson and Peterson (1973) replicated this study. Jumping ahead in our chronology, we will discuss it here. At Northern Illinois University, 262 students were asked the same two questions above. For an only child, 81% of the males and 64% of the females still wanted a boy. This represented a 10 percentage point decline for the males and a 2 percentage point decline for the females compared with the Dinitz study. When asked about a first child, again a third specified "either." Of those remaining, over 90% or more of both men and women wanted a boy, the same as in the Dinitz study. This particular pair of studies shows little change in college students' sex preferences over the period, assuming the samples are roughly comparable.

A study done with college students (Markle, 1969) in the late 1960s also found pronounced boy preference. Two hundred and eighty-three students from three different Florida colleges responded to questions about the preferred sexes of their first, second, third, etc. children. For a first child, 80% of the men and 79% of the women wanted a boy while 16% of the men and 9% of the women listed no preference. This study (published as Markle and Nam, 1971) found fewer people with no preference. However, the very small percentages of respondents wanting a girl (4% to 10% in all three studies) as a first child remained constant. Markle did not ask about preferences for an only child so comparisons cannot be made here.

Markle and Nam (1971) also reported that the ideal sex ratios of boys to girls preferred by their college students was 122. In response to a question about preferences for a first, second, third child, many respondents alternated their preferences (a boy first, a girl second, a boy third, and a girl fourth) with the percentage of those with no preference increasing with additional children.

Three other college student studies, all done in the early 1970s, might also be cited here. Largey (1972a: 12) did a pilot study of 222 State University College at Buffalo students. He found that 63% of the students preferred a boy for the first child, 7% preferred a girl, and 30% had no preference. Compared with Dinitz's (1954) finding that over 55% of his sample wanted an equal number of male and female children, 53% in Largey's sample wanted this balanced family. In these and other results, Largey's findings were almost identical to those of Dinitz, although they were collected more than sixteen years later.

A recent study of University of Michigan students (reported as an illustration of new scales for measuring sex and size preferences in Coombs, 1974; Coombs and Coombs, 1974, and Coombs et al., 1975) found only slight evidence of boy preference. Whereas first choices were overwhelmingly for a balance of sexes, further choices revealed a mild boy bias when respondents were asked about sixteen size and sex combinations. The Michigan students had slightly more boy preference than an unspecified U.S. sample which showed only very slight boy preference on their scale, which is based on conjoint measurement theory (Coombs, 1964; Krantz and Tversky, 1971). Unfolding theory gives the technique for obtaining the size and sex preference scales, derived from a theory of preferential choice. On the sex bias scale, which goes from 1 (girl preference) to 7 (boy preference), males had slightly stronger boy preference than females (Coombs, 1975: Table 4).

Using a completely different technique, the author (Williamson et al., 1975; Williamson, 1975) asked college students at Brown University to write future autobiographies, imagining it was their eightieth birthday. They were to describe their life since high school, all the way up to age eighty. The 166 codable essays were read and coded for sex and size of family preferences, among many other topics. Over three-quarters (77%) mentioned having children. Of those expecting children, three-quarters (76%) again, mentioned the specific number of children desired. The average number of children mentioned was 2.7. Half (51%) of those mentioning children also specified the sexes for those children. Of those who included the sexes of their children in the essays, 46% preferred an equal number of boys and girls, 37% preferred a predominance of boys, and 17% preferred a predominance of girls.

In general the preference in this study was for one of each sex if an even number of children were specified but generally for more boys if an odd number were desired. Overall, 39% of our students spontaneously mentioned preferred sexes of children in their essays. There may have been some underreporting since some students with sex preferences may not have thought to write them down. On the other hand, the questionnaire approaches of the other college student studies may have created the impression that sex preferences are more salient or more important than they really are, by asking specifically about sex preferences, by legitimizing the topic, and sometimes, by not giving the option of "no preference." Also, the approaches of the college student studies just reviewed did not tap the intensity of the preferences of individuals. When we hear that 90% of students wanted a son for a first child, we do not know how strongly the respondents feel about this, although we are tempted to infer a strong opinion (after all, practically *everyone* felt that way). The essay approach may be better at tapping salience of sex preferences. Also, with this technique, family size desires must be put in the context of one's expectations about marriage, careers, and leisure.

Summarizing more than forty years' research on the sex preferences of U.S. college students, we are justified in asserting that the preferences are for a boy for a first or only child, for a balanced number of boys and girls if an even number of children is desired, or for a slight predominance of boys if an odd number is desired. Preferences for a single or first girl or for a predominance of girls are rare. Relatively more common is the response of "no preference," chosen by up to a third of the samples, depending on the question. There seems to have been little change in these attitudes over the last twenty years.

Turning now to studies on adults in the U.S. done in the 1960s and 1970s, we will analyze those first which have special (usually small) samples. For example, Heer et al. (1969) reported on a study of very poor couples in Kentucky in 1968. One hundred and eight persons (mostly husbands and wives) were interviewed as part of the pretest for the Taiwan study to be described in Chapters 5 and 6. Using a variety of measures of sex preference, these respondents registered very little sex preference. There was a slight tendency for people to prefer children of their own sex when asked about ideal numbers of boys and girls for themselves or for a son or daughter. This was a highly fertile population whose childbearing was completed in most cases. The mean number of pregnancies to women in the study was 9.5. With such high fertility, there was little concern about sex composition of families. Almost all families had had at least two of each sex. Furthermore, neither sons nor daughters were very helpful in supporting parents (otherwise, these couples might not have been so desperately poor). Thus there seemed to be little reason to prefer one over the other.

Another study using adults was done by Rainwater (1965). As reported in *Family Design,* Rainwater wanted to discover what social characteristics tended to vary with sex preferences of parents. Four hundred and nine individuals were interviewed about marital sexuality, family size, and family planning. Included in this group were most of the sample from Rainwater's book, *And the Poor Get Children* (1960), 152 additional couples, and 50 men and 55 women not married to each other. The sample cannot be considered representative of the U.S. population.

Rainwater found evidence of sex preferences among his respondents, indicated by spontaneous mention of the subject during the open-ended interviews. Considering only married couples in the sample, either the husband or the wife spontaneously mentioned being concerned about sex of children in 18% of the upper-middle class white couples, 37% of the lower-middle class white couples, 64% of the upper-lower class whites, and 33% of the lower-lower class whites. Among black couples, in 41% of the upper-lower class couples and 47% of the lower-lower class couples, either husband or wife mentioned concern about sex of children. For the sample as a whole, there was no consistent tendency for men to be more concerned than women, although for whites in three out of four social classes men were more likely to express concern. Similarly there were no consistent differences between blacks and whites. Overall, for about a third of the couples, one partner spontaneously mentioned a concern for sex of child. Rainwater did not analyze the types of sex preferences volunteered by his respondents. This study is useful in showing that for some couples at least, sex of children is a concern independent of response to a questionnaire.

Another study measured the sex preferences of twenty-five New Jersey teachers (Rotter and Rotter, 1972). The findings were that a sexual balance was critical for most respondents although the most preferred family size was three children. The authors concluded: "Obviously, what people want [but cannot have] is a three-child family consisting of two boys and two girls" (Rotter and Rotter: 403). The authors criticized the usual ideal family size and the ideal number of boys and girls questions because they felt, "preferred number of children and preferred number of boys and girls are not synonymous variables and may obtain different numbers of children" (Rotter and Rotter, 1972: 404). The question which we will be answering in the next section of this chapter is whether sex or size preferences tend to win out in family decision making.

In a recent study, Largey (1972a) investigated the acceptability of sex control. He sent questionnaires on attitudes toward sex control, sex preferences, and innovations to 187 randomly selected couples in the Buffalo, New York area. Sixty-eight percent of the couples responded. He asked five questions on sex preference and came up with the familiar results that couples wanted a boy first, then a girl. Looking at those who approved of sex control, 54% would prefer a boy for an only child, 14% would prefer a girl, with the rest having no preference. Depending on the question asked, the percentages of all respondents having no sex preference varied from 18% to 42%. Responses tended to be influenced by the sexes of previous children. Based on the finding for this sample, that couples wanted one boy and one girl, Largey (1972a) felt that the impact of sex control on the sex ratio would be slight.

Markle (1974) collected sex preference data on Tallahassee residents. Receiving questionnaires from only 43% of his desired sample of 1,000, Markle elaborated on his earlier college student study (Markle and Nam, 1971). He found that "all standard demographic subgroups of the population have strong preferences that their first child be a male. For their first child, respondents currently at zero parity would choose about 20 males for every female" (Markle, 1974: 134-135). For those who had completed their families, the ratio was lower—3.6 males were mentioned for every female for a first child. Even a fair number (34%) of those having a girl first would have preferred a boy as a first child whereas almost none of those having a boy first would have preferred a girl. The overall sex ratios for expected and desired families (for those who currently did not have children) were 116 and 113, lower than the 122 found in his earlier study (Markle and Nam, 1971).

In one of the few studies on the sex preferences of an American ethnic group, Wood refers to a pilot study of sex preferences of Mexican Americans:

> An analysis of 348 married couples included in the Austin Family Survey in 1969 indicates that 72 percent of all respondents desired a son as their first child and these preferences persisted after controlling for education, religion, and occupational status. While this study was based on a small and nonrepresentative sample of the total Mexican American population in the United States, the findings nevertheless suggest that this ethnic minority is characterized by the same overall patterns exhibited by the majority group [Wood and Bean, 1975: 3].

Husbands more often had boy preference than did their wives—80% of the husbands and 62% of the wives wanted a boy for a firstborn. When respondents' preferences were compared with the sex of their first child, Wood found some evidence of rationalization, especially among wives.

Mexican Americans in the Austin Family Study also showed a balance preference. Half (51%) of the sample preferred balanced numbers of boys and girls (usually two of each) although boy preference showed up when odd numbers of children were desired (Wood, 1975).

The only other adult study which did not involve a national sample was one done on Caucasians, Japanese Americans, and Filipino Americans in

Hawaii (Fawcett et al., 1974; Arnold and Fawcett, 1975). In this study of 620 husbands and wives living on the island of Oahu, the preferred sex ratio was 120. Two-thirds (67%) of the respondents thought it was very important to have at least one son, while 58% thought it was very important to have one daughter. When asked about preferences for a first child, about half of the respondents had no preference (a larger percentage than most studies). Of those with a preference, however, sons were preferred over daughters by more than 3 to 1. A few parents said they would go to great lengths to get a son if they had all daughters. About a quarter (23%) of the sample said they would not stop childbearing until four daughters, and another 13% would continue no matter how many daughters it took. This project also investigated reasons for wanting sons versus daughters. These results will be discussed in the last part of this chapter which deals with social, economic, and psychological conditions related to sex preference.

Several recent national studies have asked questions about sex preference. Excluded from this discussion are the Princeton Study reports (Westoff et al., 1961; Westoff et al., 1963; and Bumpass and Westoff, 1970), and the first Growth of American Families study (Freedman et al., 1959), which did not include any attitude questions on sex preference. Excluded also is the study by Ryder and Westoff (1971) which asked only one attitude question on sex preference, the results of which were not published.

We should note here that considerably more information on sex preferences of Americans will soon be available from two new sources. L. Hoffman (1975) is analyzing data from the U.S. national 1975 Value of Children project which interviewed 1,569 married women under forty years of age and 456 of their husbands. Among other questions, respondents were asked about their reasons for wanting boys and for wanting girls. They were also asked questions about size and sex preferences so that each could be assigned a score on the two Coombs' scales (IN for number preference and IS for sex preference). In addition, W. Pratt and L.C. Coombs are presently analyzing sex preference data from a very recent national fertility survey which included 5,990 respondents who represented the U.S. childbearing female population. These respondents were also given the Coombs' size and sex preference questions. These two studies will greatly add to our knowledge of American sex preferences.

This leaves only two national studies which contain attitudinal information on sex preferences (Whelpton et al., 1966 and Westoff and Rindfuss, 1974). The first report analyzed data from the second Growth of American Families (G.A.F. II) study and the second from the 1970 National Fertility Study. Both included only women. G.A.F. II interviewed 3,322 married white and nonwhite women aged eighteen to thirty-nine in 1960. These women were asked, "How many boys and how many girls would be ideal for the average American family?" The responses indicated a strong preference for children of both sexes with very little preference for boys:

> About two-thirds of the wives said they thought the ideal family should include an equal number of boys and girls but 64 percent of the remaining third described an ideal in which boys outnumber girls. The average ideal of all wives included 1.8 boys and 1.7 girls. Interestingly enough, this ratio of 106 boys per 100 girls is quite similar to the actual sex ratio of newborn infants. In answering the question about the ideal number of boys and girls, many wives were probably influenced by the sex of the children they had already borne. The non-whites stated a somewhat larger ideal than the whites . . . but the sex ratio of their ideals is not significantly different [Whelpton et al., 1966: 35].

As was pointed out in the discussion of Clare and Kiser (1951), the question about ideal number of girls and boys, when asked of respondents who already have children, tends to elicit rationalizations. Had the question been "If you had a (another) child, would you prefer a girl or a boy?," probably more sex preference would have shown up.

The other national study (Westoff and Rindfuss, 1974) also found little sex preference beyond a preference for an even number of boys and girls and a desire for a first born male. Analyzing data from a 1970 national probability sample of 5,981 currently married women, they found that the sex preference ratio of ideal number of sons to ideal number of daughters was 110. For women who wanted an even number children (two or four), the ratios were about 105 but for those wanting an odd number of children (three), the ratio was 125. Currently pregnant women had slightly higher preferred sex ratios.

The only instance of widespread boy preference was found when women with no children were asked about their preference for a first child. Their preference ratio was 189. The alternating (boy, girl, boy, girl . . .) pattern found by Markle (1974) was present in these data as well.

More pronounced son preference might have been registered if men and unmarried persons had been included in these national samples. Furthermore, the question asked influenced the amount of sex preference found.

Before leaving the section in which we cite U.S. national studies for the U.S., we should cite Coombs' international study. In an attempt to make cross-cultural comparisons of sex preference, Coombs (Freedman and Coombs, 1974) included data from the U.S. 1970 fertility study and from national studies in Hungary and Belgium in 1966. All three studies included only women. The ideal sex ratios for the three samples were 115 (U.S.), 86

(Belgium) and 83 (Hungary). The 115 figure for the U.S. differs slightly from the 110 reported for the same data by Westoff and Rindfuss and is probably due to the use of different subsamples from the original data. These latter two ratios are especially interesting since they are the only ideal sex ratios under 100 which we have come across. Data in Table 1.4 of the Freedman and Coombs paper include ideal numbers of children and sons by age. From these data, we can infer a mild boy preference and balance preference for the U.S. sample with a similar pattern for Hungary and evidence of girl preference for Belgium. In Hungary the older women (thirty to thirty-nine) were more likely to be boy preferring than the younger women (twenty to twenty-nine).

At a conference at the East-West Population Institute in 1975, L.C. Coombs (1975) presented additional cross-cultural material on sex preference, this time using the Coombs' "IS" scale. In terms of amount of son preference for samples from six countries, the highest values to lowest values went from Korea to Taiwan to Malaysia to Hungary to the U.S. and finally, to the Philippines which showed strong balance preference. The U.S. and Hungary had similar values, showing mild boy preference. Only the Hungary sample included men (bridegrooms, in fact, as will be discussed below) as well as women.

By way of contrast with these studies on college students and other adults, we might conclude this section with a brief mention of two studies measuring the preferences of adults as seen by children (Hartley et al., 1962 and Hartley, 1969). Do children's perceptions correspond with our picture of adult preferences? Moreover, are children's own preferences similar to those of adults?

In a 1962 study, Hartley questioned 132 children, eight and eleven years old, about a hypothetical couple wanting to adopt and having a choice of a girl or a boy. The children were given the option of "no preference." Almost all the children thought that the husband would choose a boy and the wife, a girl. When asked about their own preferences for a future family, more children gave the no preference response (40%). But of those who did give a preference, again, the girls chose a girl and the boys chose a boy. There was no evidence of boy preference. Replicating her study cross-culturally, Hartley (1969) found that the American sample (Caucasians and Japanese Americans in Hawaii) of children five and eight years old either showed equal preference for each sex or a slight preference for girls for themselves or for hypothetical adoptive parents. When asked about their own parents' preferences in different situations, there was a tendency to attribute to them a preference for girls.

This finding held for the European background New Zealand children, and to a lesser extent, for the Maori background New Zealand children who were part of the study. The notion that parents probably prefer girls (held by a majority of most subsamples in the study) may be due to the observation made in connection with Fawcett et al. (1974) that girls are valued for their contributions and traits as children while boys are valued for the adults they will become. This could very well be perceived by children. Children may get the message that parents think girls are "good," obedient, neat, and quiet among other traits. (See Fawcett et al., 1974 and Arnold and Fawcett, 1975.) Thus children could very well get the idea that girls are preferred by parents, the children being oblivious to parents' longer range concerns which favor boys.

Although this completes the review of the major attitudinal studies which describe the sex preferences in the U.S., at this point we will mention several studies from Europe since there is no special section on Europe included in this book. The sex preferences of Europeans have not been well studied or when they have been, the results have been difficult to locate (for example, Gini, 1956; Giurovich, 1956; and Erba, 1956). The first attitude study for a European sample (women in Uppsala and Malmo, Sweden) was done by Dahlberg (1948/1949). He asked over 900 women (who were having babies in either of two Swedish hospitals) which sex they would prefer and which sex they thought their husbands would prefer. These preferences were cross-classified by the sexes of previous children. About a third of the women expressed no preference for themselves, and a third expressed no preference for their husbands. For those without previous children, slightly more women (36% versus 30%) wanted a girl than a boy, with the remaining 34% indifferent. The women attributed to their husbands a boy preference: 49% of the wives said their husbands would want a boy for a first child, 21% a girl, and 30% indifferent. For women with children already, the preference was for children of both sexes. When the woman already had an equal number of boys and girls, she was likely to express indifference. However, of those expressing a preference when they had an equal number, a girl tended to be preferred by the women and, according to the women, also by their husbands. In short, this study did not indicate much boy preference. Only for the first child was a boy preferred, and this was true only for the husbands (as reported by wives).

A more recent Swedish study with a smaller sample (Uddenberg et al., 1971) also found little evidence of boy preference. Women with children wanted their next child to be the opposite sex of their youngest child with only 10% having no preference. Confining the rest of their analysis to those women expecting their first child (N=81), 46% wanted boys, 32% wanted girls, with 22% having no preference. The number of women wanting a boy is lower in this sample than in U.S. college student studies although about the same as the Westoff and Rindfuss (1974) study. Of those expressing a sex preference for a first child, Uddenberg et al. (1971) found 59% wanted a boy while Westoff and Rindfuss (1974) found 63%. The Swedish women attributed more boy preference to their husbands than to themselves.

In the early 1950s, several studies on sex preferences of European parents were done and published in 1956 (Gini; Giurovich; and Erba). Gini (1956) observed, according to Largey (1972), that "The son-preference [in Italy] and also in Switzerland and Belgium is much stronger than in the United States. He [Gini] concluded that the higher the male status and/or dominant position in the society, the greater the male sex preference among both men and women" (Largey, 1972a: 19). Giurovich (1956) also found evidence of son preference among Italian couples, especially among lower class couples who felt that sons were an asset for the family's upward mobility.

The only other studies from Europe are: Bollen (1962), Riley (1968), Peel (1970), and Klinger (1975). Bollen studied the sex preferences of an unrepresentative group of Belgian (Flemish) college students. As reported by Coombs et al. (1975), sex preference data were obtained from each of the forty male and forty female students sampled. In terms of the Coombs' sex bias scale, 82% of the University of Leuven students showed boy preference, 10% showed preference for a balanced-sex family, and 8% showed girl preference. Compared with the Coombs' University of Michigan sample, the Belgian students had more boy preference. But compared with Coombs' Taiwan sample, the Belgian students showed less.

British evidence of son preference in the eighteenth and nineteenth centuries was gathered from the literature of the time by Riley (1968). According to her,

From the three hundred novels [reviewed], only three instances can be marshalled in which something like a preference for a girl is felt, one from an eighteenth-century novel, and two from nineteenth-century ones, two by women novelists, and one by a man. Of these only one portrays a person with a whole-hearted preference for a girl, and this preference is evinced not by a father or mother, but by a famously eccentric aunt, a prototype of the wayward English spinster who takes a pride in being a law unto herself; the desire for a great-niece is yet another example of her eccentricity. In the other two stories, in one the wife defends the birth of a daughter while being obliged to note her husband's disdain for females; in the other, the parents are overjoyed with their daughter at once, but it is admitted that they had, during the pregnancy, hoped for a son [Riley, 1968: 12-13].

The usual justifications for wanting a boy, in these novels, are to continue the family line and name, to attain a certain immortality, and to please the husband. An especially interesting dilemma is faced by the character, Soames, in John Galsworthy's *A Man of Property* (1906):

> His is a case where extreme possessive love overcomes extreme disappointment over the birth of a daughter. In the novel Soames has married in order to have an heir. The birth of a boy is therefore of the utmost importance for him, so that when, after a complicated labour during which he has had to decide whose life should come first, his wife's or the child's—and he has chosen the child's, influenced by his obsessive desire for a son—when, after all this, the doctor tells him that his child is a girl he feels cheated, swindled.... Soames is too disappointed to be able to face seeing his wife [who survived] and new daughter. He goes to see his father who is dying and there tells him a lie rather than disappoint the dying man by letting him know that the child is the wrong sex [Riley, 1968: 10-11].

Whether the British desire for a firstborn son is still at the level portrayed by eighteenth and nineteenth century novels, we cannot say. One recent empirical study found some evidence of boy preference and balance preference. Peel (1970) collected data from 350 newly married couples in contemporary Hull, England. Respondents were asked about their preference for a particular distribution of boys and girls in their intended families. The preferred sex ratio was 116. Almost half (46%) of the 350 families wanted one boy and one girl. The next most popular family was two boys and one girl (15%), then two of each (13%), and two girls and one boy (7%), overall showing only slight boy preference. The rest of the choices were rarely selected.

One very recent study from Hungary should be added. Using the Coombs' measures of sex preference, Klinger (1975) concluded, based on a preliminary analysis of 2,619 questionnaires from men and women planning to marry, "among the present Hungarian marrying couples boy preference is in the majority" (Klinger, 1975: 16). Sixty percent of the respondents showed boy preference on the Coombs' scale, 19% preferred a balance, and 21% showed girl preference. (It is not clear from Klinger's report how many showed no sex preference.) Boy preference was more common among the men. The sex preference scores (which range from 1 to 7) were identical for only half (54%) of the couples. There was more agreement among couples interviewed jointly than among those interviewed separately. Since this is a longitudinal study, it will be possible to assess the importance of sex preferences on future fertility and to ascertain to what degree husbands and wives influence each other's preferences.

In summary, based on these few European studies, we might conclude that the preference is for a balanced number of boys and girls with the amount of boy preference varying by the sample (with college students having more boy preference and husbands, according to wives, having more boy preference) and the country (with southern European countries possibly having more boy preference than northern European countries). Other than one Belgian study (Freedman and Coombs, 1974), we did not find much evidence of daughter preference in any of the European data.

Parental Sex Preferences and Fertility in the U.S. and Europe

Using a variety of approaches, American demographers have tried to assess the effects of sex preferences in fertility attitudes and behavior. Most popular have been the techniques of examining the sex ratios of last-borns, of comparing the number of single-sexed families to the number theoretically expected, and of investigating what proportion of families go on to have more children, cross-classified by the sexes of previous children. Anticipating our conclusions, we will show that for American parents, the desire for sexual heterogeneity does compel a small number of couples to continue child-bearing. But now with the U.S. birth rate at an unprecedented low (the crude birth rate for 1975 dipping under 15/1000), there may not be much leeway for sex preferences in the near future. Preferences for small families are presently widespread and may overwhelm the sex composition preferences of many American couples.

Whether this will be the case in the long run, it is hard to say. The U.S. Value of Children study (Hoffman, 1975) found that economic considerations were most often cited as the primary reason parents were not having more children. Hoffman (1975) and others have suggested that family sizes could well increase with improved economic conditions. Then perhaps more parents would be able to act on their sex preferences by continuing child-bearing until they have one of each sex or a desired son.

After discussing the fertility consequences of sex preferences, we will review the very few studies of other consequences of sex preferences or sex composition, ending this chapter with a reconsideration of the hypotheses about determinants of sex preferences proposed in Chapter 1.

BEHAVIORAL STUDIES

In Table 1, we have cited all the available behavioral evidence of the effect of sex preferences on fertility for the U.S. and Europe. The studies are ordered chronologically. Several conclusions can be drawn from this table. First, the study of this topic began with *elite* samples, for the most part. From the 1930s until the mid-1950s, the sample typically was from *Who's Who in America*. These elite studies generally found some indirect evidence

TABLE 1: Behavioral Studies: Evidence on the Effect of Sex Preferences on Fertility for the U.S. and Europe

Study	Sample	Technique for Assessing Effect	Result	Comment
Winston (1931)	5,466 completed families in *Abridged Compendium of American Genealogy*	Compared sex ratios with those of the U.S. population	♂	Found an overall sex ratio of 112.0 for these families. Sex ratios were higher in smaller families than in larger ones.
Winston (1932-1933)	Same as above	Computed sex ratio of last-born children to see whether families were stopping after having boys	♂	Found sex ratio of 117.4 for last-borns and a sex ratio of 121.3 for completed two-child families. Speculated that boy preference plus birth control could increase the general sex ratio.
Harper (1936)	a) Families from *Burke's Peerage;* b) *Who's Who in America* sample; c) 11,937 families in Wisconsin	Computed sex ratio of last-borns. Compared proportion of families with first two of opposite sex who limited families to two versus those who had three	a) ♂ b) ♂ c) ♀+♂	Found inconsistent results for the sex ratios of last-borns for sample c).
Rife and Snyder (1937)	1,269 middle class families of Italian origin in Ohio	Comparison of observed and expected unisexual sibships	♀+♂	Found excess of two-child families with one boy and one girl.
Myers (1949)	999 *Who's Who in America* families	Compared observed and expected unisexual sibships	♀+♂	Found excess of two-child families with one boy and one girl.

♀: evidence of girl preference   ♀+♂: evidence of desire for one of each sex
♂: evidence of boy preference   o: no effect found
                                X: no effect tested

TABLE 1: (continued)

Study	Sample	Technique for Assessing Effect	Result	Comment
Clare & Kiser (1951)	1,309 couples living in Indianapolis	Attitude questions on sex preferences for an only child and for two children	X	Authors found evidence of rationalization of what parents had. They speculated that this reduces effect of sex preferences on fertility.
Thomas (1951)	Medical students' families (U. of Glasgow). Data on present and parents' families. N=230.	Parity progression ratio (% at x parity who go on to x + 1 parity)	♀+♂	One boy and one girl: 43% went on. Two of same sex: 61% went on. These results for present generation. Comparable figures for parents' generation were 94% and 86%.
Bernstein (1952)	7,616 Who's Who in America families, including those of Myers (1949)	Parity progression ratio	♀+♂	One boy and one girl: 45% went on. Two boys: 52% went on. Two girls: 54% went on.
U.S. Bureau of Census (1956) Thomas (1951)	Families in a Current Population Survey	Comparison of observed and expected unisexual sibships	♀+♂	Differences between observed and expected values were small.
De Wolff & Meerdink (1957)	Births in Amsterdam from 1948-1955	Parity progression ratio	♀+♂	Effect not found for Catholics.
Westoff et al. (1961)	1,165 wives in seven of the eight largest Standard Metropolitan Areas	Analyzed length of birth intervals after boy compared with girl	♂	Found three-month longer intervals after boy. Interpretation: parents are more pleased with a boy and postpone next birth longer. Other interpretations of data are possible.

TABLE 1: (continued)

Study	Sample	Technique for Assessing Effect	Result	Comment
Westoff et al. (1963)	905 wives from the sample above who could be located for second round	Parity progression ratio	♀+♂	Not found for some Catholics and the small sample of Jews.
Loyd & Gray (1969)	Students' families in Kentucky. N=1,018	Parity progression ratio	♀+♂	One boy and one girl: 56% went on. Two of same sex: 62% went on.
Bumpass & Westoff (1970)	Same as Westoff et al. (1963) minus those not located for third round N=814	Parity progression ratio	♀+♂	"Births of a third, fourth, and even fifth order are more likely to occur if the preceding births were also of the same sex." (Bumpass & Westoff, 1970: 93)
Dawes (1970)	5% probability sample of women between 35-44 from 1960 U.S. Census	Parity progression ratio	♀+♂	One boy and one girl: 37% went on. Two boys: 42% went on. Two girls: 41% went on. Smaller effect at third parity. Results sign. at .001 level.
Ayala & Falk (1971)	Students' families from R.I. and nearby states. Predominantly Catholics. N=425.	Parity progression ratio	o	No effect found for either the younger or the older families.
Ben-Porath & Welch (1972)	1967 Survey of Economic Opportunity. 4,796 families with 2+ children	Parity progression ratio including those who have expectation of having another child	♀+♂ ——— ♂ (weak)	One boy and one girl: 61% went on or expected to do so. Two of same sex: 67% went on or expected to do so. Weaker effect at higher parities. Families without sons more likely to go on (or expect to) (58%) than families without daughters (54%) at 3rd and 4th parities.

TABLE 1: (continued)

Study	Sample	Technique for Assessing Effect	Result	Comment
Gray (1972) Gray & Morrison (1974)	Students' families samples from Kentucky plus one non-student group	Parity progression ratio	♀+♂	Effect did not hold for group of black Job Corps trainees' families. Other results sign. at .05 level.
Welch (1974)	1 in 100 Public Use Sample of 1970 Census. N=132,000	Parity progression ratio	♀+♂	No difference found for 1st parity. One boy and one girl: 51% went on. Two boys: 56% went on. Two girls: 56% went on. Diminished effect after 3rd parity and no effect after 4th.
Freedman & Coombs (1974)	National fertility studies for Great Britain, Hungary, and U.S. Large (2,000+) samples	Parity progression ratio	o	Similar results for the Netherlands, according to the text. For U.S. women (1965 study), only for the younger women (20-29) of 2nd parity was the "♀+♂" effect indicated.
Wood & Bean (1975)	a) 1 in 1000 Public Use Sample of U.S. 1970 Population for Anglos b) 1 in 100 Sample for 5 southwestern states for Mexican Americans	Parity progression ratio and regression analysis	a) ♀+♂ b) ♀+♂	"... couples whose previous children include a sex mix are consistently less likely to bear an additional child at each parity than those whose children are all of the same sex." (Wood and Bean, 1975: 12) Stronger effect for Anglos. "For Anglos it is apparent that the dummy variable for the sex composition of previous children is the most important predictor of the probability of having either a third or a fourth child." (Wood & Bean, 1975: 13)

of boy preference, judging from the high sex ratios of last-born children. (However, there might be competing biological or nutritional explanations for this phenomenon as well.) These results could not be replicated for the whole U.S. population, although preference for one of each sex *has* been found in almost all recent studies with more representative samples. Looking at these studies as a group, we can see a general increase in the sophistication of the research, with later studies using control variables, large and representative samples, and better (but still indirect) measures of sex preference. The results consistently show that many parents desire one child of each sex. The parity progression ratio studies show that after two children (but usually not at higher parities), families with unisexual sibships are more likely to go on. Interestingly, there is little evidence that families with girls are more likely than families with boys to go on. Thus, boy preference is not evident from these behavioral studies, even though we found it in the previously discussed attitude studies. The strongest boy preference we found was for a first-born boy. But we did not find behavioral evidence of this, since there is not much parents can do to realize their desires for a first-born son until sex control becomes widespread.

ATTITUDE STUDIES

Turning to Table 2, which includes major studies which measured attitudinal (rather than behavioral) consequences of sex preferences and sex composition, we note again the evidence for "one of each sex" preference, especially in the early studies. Yet in the two most recent ones, the effect is gone. An advantage of this attitudinal approach is it helps us to anticipate change in behavior in the future. Thus, for instance, the women in the Cutright et al. (1974) study said they did *not* expect to go on for more children depending on the sexes of previous children. This warns us that the effect found for so many behavioral studies (Table 1) may not hold for the future. We are in a period of unusually low fertility and it may be that parents do not feel they can afford to continue childbearing just to fulfill their sex preferences.

If these recent two attitude studies (Freedman & Coombs, 1974; Cutright et al., 1974) are taken as a guide, we might predict that the "one of each sex" effect will weaken in the next five years. This might be detectable in the 1980 census, especially for younger wives.

Whether sex composition experience combined with preferences for one of each sex will, in the long run, result in further childbearing is difficult to say. Under adverse economic conditions, Americans could probably get used to very small family sizes (including the one-child family) although apparently they do not desire to do so.

TABLE 2: Major Attitude Studies: Evidence on the Effect of Sex Preferences on Fertility for the U.S. and Europe

Study	Sample	Technique for Assessing Effect	Result	Comment
Clare & Kiser (1951)	1,309 couples in Indianapolis	Couples with children were asked whether considerations of sex combination had affected their family size	♀+♂ (only for some couples)	Some of their couples (6% or less) reported that they continued childbearing to fulfill sex preferences. More (16%-49%, depending on the measures used) said that having a child of each sex was a reason to *not* have more children.
Freedman et al. (1960)	889 women in the first Growth of American Families study (1955). A national sample.	Expectation of more children, cross-classified by the sex composition and number already in family. Also parity progressions.	♀+♂ (weak)	One boy and one girl: 59% expected more. Two of same sex: 61% expected more.
Westoff et al. (1961)	1,165 wives in seven of the eight largest Standard Metropolitan Areas	Number of children desired, cross-classified by whether families had children of both sexes	♀+♂ (weak)	Effect still held with controls for social class and religion and for wives and husbands (as reported by wives). Effect not found for Jews or mixed-marriage wives.
Westoff & Rindfuss (1974)	5,981 married women in the 1970 National Fertility Study	Number of children desired, cross-classified by whether families had children of both sexes	♂ (weak)	One boy and one girl: 19% intend to have more. Two of same sex: 25% intend to have more. Some tendency for women with only daughters to intend and have more subsequent children than those with only sons.
Freedman & Coombs (1974)	National samples from the U.S., Great Britain, Belgium, and Hungary	a) % wanting no more children by number of living children and sons	♀+♂	Not found for Belgium but found at 2nd parities in other three samples.

TABLE 2: (continued)

Study	Sample	Technique for Assessing Effect	Result	Comment
		b) number additional children wanted by number of living children and sons	o	Slight effect at 2nd and 4th parities for U.S. data (1965).
		c) % who expect more children than they consider ideal by number of living children and sons	o	Slight effect for 3rd parities for Hungary (1966) and U.S. (1965).
Cutright et al. (1974)	Subsample of 273 wives with just two children. From larger study of wives living in five North Central states.	Multiple Classification Analysis, predicting the mean % intending to have more than two children and mean number of children intended.	o	Sex composition of first two children was a poor predictor of the two dependent variables, relative to the other background variables used. Authors speculate that now that actual and expected fertility are so low, sex preferences are not showing up.
Norman (1974)	412 college students, including subsample of parents	Cross-tabulation of sex composition of families of students who were parents, by satisfaction with sex of children	♀+♂	Slight evidence that men not wanting more children had achieved their "boy quota."

Based on the examination of past sex preference studies and on our hunches about the future, we make the following predictions about the relationship between sex preferences and fertility in the next several decades. We have assumed sex preferences will not change, observing that they have not changed over the past twenty years. (1) Most families will have two children with small proportions having none, one, and three or more. (2) There will be a stronger tendency for families with first-born daughters to go on more frequently than those with first-born sons as the one-child family gradually becomes more popular and more families seriously consider having one child. Assuming the widespread bias (Westoff and Rindfuss, 1974) for a first-born boy remains, families not having a boy first may go on at the same time it is more acceptable for families with one boy to stop at one. (3) Very few families with one of each sex among the first two children will go on for more. For these couples, there will scarcely be any socially legitimate reason for going on (unless they remarry or there is something wrong with one of the children). (4) A few families with two of the same sex will go on to three but any higher order effects will disappear. (Families going beyond three will be members of subgroups which provide special social support for high fertility. Such families will not be continuing childbearing just to satisfy individual sex preferences.) Thus we expect the second parity "one of each sex" effect to diminish as the two-child family becomes a standard. Because of the diversity and lack of data for Europe, we will not explicitly make predictions for Europe except to say that the above predictions for the U.S. may also apply there.

A third approach, after the behavioral and the attitudinal, to the assessment of the relationships between sex preferences and fertility, is that of mathematical modeling and computer simulation. We turn to this approach now.

MATH MODELS AND COMPUTER SIMULATIONS OF THE RELATIONSHIP BETWEEN SEX PREFERENCES AND FERTILITY

A number of scholars have investigated the probability of different fertility outcomes given different sex preferences, the possibility of sex control, different possible "stopping rules" parents might use, and different assumptions about the probability of families to have boys or girls. Winston's (1932-1933) speculations about the possible effects of birth control and sex preferences on the general sex ratio began the controversy which is not yet resolved. His work was evaluated by Robbins (1952) and later, Weiler (1959). More general contributions to the problem were added by Gittlesohn (1960), Goodman (1961), and Sheps (1963). There was a lull of interest for almost a decade, then an outburst of interest (Serow and Evans, 1970; Mitra, 1970;

Keyfitz, 1971 and 1972; Ben-Porath and Welch, 1972; McDonald, 1973; Pathak, 1973; Jones, 1973; Waheed, 1973; Smith, 1974; Welch, 1974; and Talwar, 1975). Computer simulations and new bodies of data encouraged new approaches to the general problem of sex preferences and fertility. Several papers (Serow and Evans, 1970; Jones, 1973; McDonald, 1973; and Smith, 1974) pursued the question of the possible demographic results of sex control capability.

One general conclusion from these papers is that, unless sex control is available or the probability of having a boy varies by families at a given time, or varies for families over time, selective use of birth control to achieve sex preferences will not affect the overall sex ratio. Very interesting data of Welch (1974), based on the 1970 U.S. Census, indicate that the probability of having a boy may vary according to family.[1] This again raises the issue of the effect of selective use of birth control on fertility. In his Table 1 based on 1970 U.S. Census data he demonstrates that families with four daughters had a .451 proportion of boys for their fifth child (for families which continued childbearing) while families with four sons had a .573 proportion of boys for their fifth child. The other data in the table were generally consistent with this pattern—which indicates some tendency for boy-proneness or girl-proneness in the U.S. population in 1970. If families who were boy-prone tended to stop early in childbearing (assuming a boy preference) and families who were girl-prone continued, the long-run result might be a slight decrease in the overall sex ratio. This might be more significant in the developing countries with stronger son preference and increasing ability to control births, assuming similar degrees of boy-proneness exist (which remains to be tested). On the other hand, improved nutrition might contribute to a slight increase in the sex ratios, as more males survived the fetal stage. Thus, the two trends might cancel out. More research is needed in this area, especially in the countries now going through the demographic transition.

Consequences of Sex Preferences and Sex Composition for Behaviors Other Than Fertility

Five American studies (Sloman, 1948; Farber and Blackman, 1956; Elder and Bowerman, 1963; Sears et al., 1957; and Largey, 1972a) and one European study (Uddenberg et al., 1971) deal with sex preferences and sex composition as independent variables relating to nonfertility behaviors. We will summarize their conclusions briefly.

Sloman (1948) examined case records of 62 children with emotional problems who had been planned for by their parents (i.e., were not accidents) but were, nevertheless, later rejected by the parents. These children were selected out of a caseload of 500 emotionally disturbed children. In this study, parental sex preferences were found to be a factor influencing some parents to reject their children, ultimately harming the children's mental health. In nine cases out of the 62 planned children, their rejection seemed to be attributed to their parents' unfulfilled sex preferences. However, we have no idea how widespread this phenomenon is, in the general population. Hartley (1969; Hartley et al., 1962) warns us that children do not necessarily perceive their parents' sex preferences accurately. Her samples of boys and girls from five years old to eleven reported that women prefer girls and men prefer boys. Although a few studies have found this same-sex preference among adults (Dahlberg, 1948-1949; Heer et al., 1969), most have found that, for only children and firstborns at least, both men and women in the U.S. show some boy preference. By contrast, three of the four samples of children (for both boys and girls) showed some evidence of girl preference. Unfortunately, Hartley did not have data on these particular children's parents' attitudes; hence, we cannot conclusively say there is a discrepancy between the attitudes of children and those of their parents. But her work does caution us from assuming children will be aware of their parents' attitudes.

The second study (Farber and Blackman, 1956) looked at the possible effects of different sex compositions on marital tensions investigated three and fourteen years after marriage. The authors found that "the sex of the children (all boys, mostly boys, same number of boys and girls, mostly girls, all girls) has no effect on either the fourteen-year tension scores or shifts in tension scores from three to fourteen years of marriage" (Farber and Blackman, 1956: 6). Unfortunately, for these parents nothing was known about their sex preferences so it was not possible to see whether parents whose preferences were fulfilled had lower marital tension scores. Therefore, this study was not very conclusive.

In the next study, Elder and Bowerman (1963) wondered whether there was any effect of sex composition on how parents raise their children. For their North Carolina sample of children, they did find some support for the idea that in families composed of boys rather than girls, there is more parental involvement (and especially involvement of the father) and more external behavioral control such as physical punishment. It would be interesting to see whether this finding might hold up cross-culturally as well.

In another U.S. study, Sears et al. (1956) found that mothers' warmth towards a new baby son, but not daughter, depended to some extent on the sexes of existing children.

When it was a boy, the mother's warmth toward him appeared to depend somewhat on the sex of her existing children. If she already had boys only, she was relatively cold toward the new baby boy (p = less than .01). If the new baby was a girl, however, the sex of the older children made little or no difference in the mother's attitude toward it; she was just as warm toward the baby whether she already had boys or girls or both sexes. The same thing was true when the new child had reached kindergarten age [Sears et al., 1956: 58].

The same research project also found a mild preference for sons combined with a preference for one of each sex so that "there was a tendency for the mother to be happier about a new pregnancy if her existing children were girls only rather than boys only, or both boys and girls. Indeed, she was very likely to be least enthusiastic if she already had children of both sexes" (Sears et al., 39-40).

The final U.S. study dealt with sex preference and sex control. Studying the acceptability of sex control among 152 couples in the Buffalo New York area, Largey (1972a) found that those with strong sex preferences were more likely to approve of sex control than were those with weak or no sex preferences. The strength of sex preferences was measured by recording how many answers to the five sex preference questions elicited some specific sex preferences; scores went from 0 to 5.

The only European study (Uddenberg et al., 1971), dealing with several consequences of sex preferences which were realized or not, was a complex one done in Sweden. Using a prospective design, 152 randomly selected women attending a prenatal clinic in southern Sweden were interviewed three times—during pregnancy, right after birth, and six months later. Since one of the goals of the study was to ascertain some of the psychological and social determinants of sex preferences of women expecting a child, women who already had children were eliminated, leaving a sample of 81 women who were having their first child. This was done because the sex preferences of women with children seemed to be so strongly conditioned by the sexes of their previous children that the authors felt that the results from them would be less interesting.

Two results from this study are relevant here. First, the women who came from families with brothers (rather than being only children or having only sisters) were more likely to consider themselves the dominating partner in their marriages, were more likely to prefer girls or have no preference, and were less likely to be "field-dependent" on the Rod and Frame test. (For a discussion of this test, the reader is referred to Witkin, 1962.) This effect is, then, one of sex composition among siblings on various attitudes and psychological traits of women. Presumably additional research has been done on this which might be well worth following up. Second, Uddenberg et al. (1971) found that women having daughters were less likely to have postpartum mental disturbances than women having sons. Even more frequently disturbed after birth were those women who had wanted sons during pregnancy and had gotten sons.

The authors' explanation of this second paradoxical finding was that for some of the women expressing son preference, this was a bow to conventionalism and especially the perception that the baby's father wanted a son, rather than an expression of the woman's own inclination. Rather than believing, as Freud did, that son preference was somehow "natural" for women, these researchers felt that a preference for one's own sex was more healthy (and we, not the authors, might add that this perhaps indicates more self acceptance). They found that women who thought that the father wanted a son but still expressed a preference for a daughter themselves were less likely to have had neurotic symptoms and less likely to be field-dependent on the Rod and Frame test—compared with women who thought the father wanted a son and said they also wanted a son.

This study was small and limited to only one relatively egalitarian society (Sweden). Hence, any generalizations would be hazardous. Yet it is still valuable since it explores a few of the consequences of sex composition of siblings on the behavior of adult women and the consequences of sex preferences (and the actual sex of the child) on women's mental health. Its exploratory conclusions were certainly not what Freudian psychology would lead us to believe.

Given the vast literature on fertility consequences of sex preferences and sex composition, it is remarkable that there have been so few studies of other consequences. There are no studies of fathers whose desires are, or are not, met; no studies following over time children of the "wrong sex"; no studies of how parents with conflicting sex preferences deal with this problem;[2] no studies of consequences of being the "right sex"; and no studies of how parents deal with disappointment when chance goes against them. Such studies might be especially important in those particular developing countries where sex preferences are strong and, we might guess, the consequences for both parents and children are more severe than in a country like Sweden.

Determinants of Sex Preferences

Summarizing the material again in a table (Table 3), we now turn to the problem originally posed in Chapter 1: why do parents have sex preferences? What are the economic, social and psychological conditions which encourage different types of sex preference?

If we are trying to predict the sex preferences for an individual with children, the best predictor often is the sexes of her or his previous children. In Table 3, we list the studies which have found this to be significant. It is important to note that this variable, sex of previous children, works better for

TABLE 3: Determinants of Sex Preferences in the U.S. and Europe

Independent Variable	Dependent Variable	Effect Found	Study
A. Demographic factors			
Sex of previous children	Current sex preference	+ + + + + +	Dahlberg (1947-1948) *Clare and Kiser (1951) Uddenberg et al. (1971) Largey (1972a) *Markle (1974) *Wood (1975)
			When asked about preferences for a first child or for the first two children, parents tend to state preferences consistent with what they already have. However, in the starred (*) studies which included husbands, husbands were much less likely to modify their preferences for a first-born boy if they had a first-born girl than were wives.
Total number of children desired	Ideal sex ratio	X X	Westoff and Rindfuss (1974) Wood (1975)
			Respondents wanting odd numbers of children tend to have higher ideal sex ratios than those wanting even numbers. Thus the overall sex ratio depends on the proportions of people wanting odd and even family sizes.
Proportion of sample who have not yet had first-borns	Sex preference for next child	+ (♂)	Westoff and Rindfuss (1974)
			If a sample is weighted heavily with women who have not yet had one child, the overall result will tend to be more boy preference, reflecting the common desire to have a first-born son.
B. Sex preferences in general			
Social class	Mention of concern about sex of child	−	Rainwater (1965) Men and women in the upper-middle class group were least likely to mention concerns about sex of children.
Race	"	o	Rainwater (1965)
Religion	Strength of sex (cont.)	o	Largey (1972a) No differences found for small samples of Catholics and Protestants.

Key: +: positive effect −: negative effect o: no effect X: other (see comment)
♀: girl preference ♂: boy preference ♀+♂: preference for one of each sex

TABLE 3: (continued)

Independent Variable	Dependent Variable	Effect Found	Study
	preference (scale from 0-5)		
Level of Innovative-ness	"	+	Largey (1972a) Those were more willing to accept new technological innovations were also more likely to express sex prefer-ences. Perhaps both of these attitudes reflect a common willingness to experiment with "nature."

C. Son preference

Independent Variable	Dependent Variable	Effect Found	Study
Perceived cost of raising a boy vs. girl	Son preference (for first child)	+	Largey (1972a) Although most of his stu-dent sample (63%) felt that it was equally expensive to raise a boy as a girl, of those making a distinction, almost all said girls were more expensive to raise.
Social class	Son preference (high sex ratios for last-borns)	+ +	Winston (1931; 1932-1933) Harper (1936) For elite samples, there was some evidence of higher sex ratios for last-borns. Not true for nonelite sample (Harper, 1936) of blue collar families.
Social class	Son preference	−	Giurovich (1956) Felt that having a son was more important for lower class than upper class Italian families.
Occupations of husband & wife	Son prefer-ence (for first child)	o	Markle (1974)
Social class	Son prefer-ence for first child	o	Wood (1975) No difference found between white collar and blue collar respondents.
Religion	Son prefer-ence for first or only child	+ (Cath. & Jews)	Dinitz et al. (1954) Catholic and Jewish students showed stronger boy preference than did Protestants.
Religion	Son preference	+ (Jews)	Largey (1972a) Found that small sample of Jews had "a strong male preference coupled with willingness to use sex control." (Largey, 1972a: 76)
Religion	Son prefer-ence for	+ (Cath.)	Markle (1974) Catholics were highest in son preference, then Protestants, and then

TABLE 3: (continued)

Independent Variable	Dependent Variable	Effect Found	Study
	first child		those with no religion. Result applies only to those with no children.
Religion	Son preference for first child	+ (Cath.)	Wood (1975) Catholics had more boy preference than Protestants.
Race	Son preference (ideal sex ratio)	o	Whelpton et al. (1966)
Education	Son preference for first child	−	Markle (1974) Those with higher education were less likely to want boys for a first child.
Education	Son preference for first child	+	Wood (1975) Positive linear relationship found for Mexican American couples. (Higher education, more son preference.)
Sex of respondent	Prefer son for expected child	+ (husb.) + (husb.)	Dahlberg (1948-1949). Reported by wives. Uddenberg et al. (1971). Reported by wives.
Sex of respondent	Son preference for next child	+ (men)	Strunk (1947-1948) According to Westoff and Rindfuss (1974), this sex difference narrowed when only married people and only people with children were included.
Sex of respondent	Son preference for only child & for two children	+ (husb.)	Clare & Kiser (1951)
Sex of respondent	Son preference for an only child	+ (men)	Dinitz et al. (1954) Result did not hold for preferences for sex of first child (when the option of "no preference" was given).
Sex of respondent	Same-sex preference	+ + (boys)	Hartley et al. (1962) Hartley (1969) Found that girls preferred to have girls, boys preferred to have boys. Children also attributed these ideas to adults.
Sex of respondent	Same-sex preference	+ (husb.)	Heer et al. (1969) Found slight tendency for men to prefer boys and women to prefer girls.
Sex of respondent	Son preference for only child	+ (men)	Peterson & Peterson (1973) Norman (1974)

TABLE 3: (continued)

Independent Variable	Dependent Variable	Effect Found	Study
Sex of respondent	Son preference for first child	– (women)	Markle (1974) Women more frequently preferred boys than men did. Found for those with no children and those with completed families.
Sex of respondent	Son preference for first child	+ (men)	Wood (1975)
Sex of respondent	Son preference on Coombs' IS scale	+ (men)	Coombs et al. (1975) Held for unrepresentative sample of U. of Michigan undergraduates.
Sex of respondent	Son preference	+ (husb.)	Arnold & Fawcett (1975) and Fawcett et al. (1974) Husbands were particularly concerned that they have a son to continue the family name. Wives emphasized more the positive aspects of having girls (such as companionship) and the companionship (for husband) reason for having boys.
Sex of respondent	Son preference scores on Coombs' scale	+ (future husb.)	Klinger (1975) In Hungarian sample, prospective bridegrooms were more likely to prefer boys, prospective wives to prefer girls.
Ease of raising a boy	Son preference	+	Strunk (1947-1948) 42% of a national sample said boys were easier to raise, 23% said girls, 24% said no difference, and 11% had no opinion. Similar results when only those with children of each sex included.
Ease of raising a boy	Son preference	+	Largey (1972a) 67% of student sample felt that one sex no easier to raise than the other. But "of remaining 33 percent, twice as many felt boys, rather than girls, were easier to raise." (Largey, 1972a: 20)
Having no siblings or only sisters	Son preference (for expected child)	+	Uddenberg et al. (1971)
History of mental disturbances	Son preference	+	Uddenberg et al. (1971)
Higher field dependency scores	Son preference	+	Uddenberg et al. (1971)

TABLE 3: (continued)

Independent Variable	Dependent Variable	Effect Found	Study
Desire to please husband	Son preference	+	Dahlberg (1948-1949) Uddenberg et al. (1971) Hoffman (1975)

D. Desire for one of each sex

Independent Variable	Dependent Variable	Effect Found	Study
Parents' perception that their children would benefit	One of each sex	X	Arnold & Fawcett (1975) Some parents wanted one of each sex for themselves. Others mentioned that it would benefit the children (i.e., they would learn to be comfortable with the other sex).
Ethnic group	One of each sex (parity progression ratio)	+ (Anglos)	Wood and Bean (1975) The effect was stronger for Anglos than for Mexican Americans, predominantly Catholic.
Religion	One of each sex	+ (Prot.) (no relig.)	De Wolff & Meerdink (1957) Catholics did not tend to go on for more children, depending on the sex of the first two.
Religion	One of each sex	+ (Prot.)	Westoff (1959; 1961). Sexes of the first two children tended to influence fertility behavior for Protestants but not for Catholics or Jews.
Religion	One of each sex	+ (Prot.)	Freedman et al. (1960)
Religion	One of each sex	+ (Prot.)	Westoff et al. (1963)
Religion	One of each sex	o	Ayala & Falk (1971). For their predominantly Catholic sample, no effect of previous sexes of children was found on parity progression ratios.
Social class	One of each sex	+ (blue collar)	Westoff et al. (1961). Blue collar husbands and wives were more likely to have their fertility desires affected by the sexes of the first two than were white collar couples.
Sex of respondent	One of each sex	o	Westoff et al. (1961)

TABLE 3: (continued)

Independent Variable	Dependent Variable	Effect Found	Study
E. Desire for daughters			
Field independence on Rod and Frame test	Daughter preference (for expected child)	+	Uddenberg et al. (1971). The authors speculated that women preferring daughters were less conventional and more attuned to their *own* preferences rather than those of society or of husbands (who were usually perceived as wanting a son).
Ethnic group (Filipinos)	Daughter preference	+	Arnold & Fawcett (1975). Filipino respondents in Hawaii strongly valued girls for their help with housework and child care. Other ethnic groups (Japanese and Caucasian) valued girls more for perceived psychological traits of girls and for companionship.
F. No sex preference			
Whether pregnancy was planned	No sex preference	+	Uddenberg et al. (1971) If the pregnancy was planned, the woman was less likely to have sex preference.
Length of time woman knew father of her expected child	No sex preference	+	Uddenberg et al. (1971) Women who knew the father of their child longer were less likely to have sex preference.
Social class	No sex preference	+	Uddenberg et al. (1971) Higher social class, less sex preference.
Education	No sex preference	+	Uddenberg et al. (1971) Higher education, less sex preference.
Sex-role ideology	No sex preference	+ (egal. ideology)	Markle (1974) Those with traditional or moderate sex-role ideologies were more likely to prefer a first-born boy compared with egalitarians.

women than for men (see starred "*" studies in Table 3). Husbands are less likely to say they want girls when they have girls, than are wives.

When we try to predict for a group, several other demographic factors come in—the total number of children desired and the proportion of the sample who have not had children. (See Table 3.) Both of these factors affect the degree of boy preference found in a group, depending on the measures of sex preference used.

In Part B of Table 3, we list the two studies which have noted only the extent of sex preference without breaking it down into types of sex preference. The most interesting of these variables is the "level of innovativeness" which was found (Largey, 1972a) to be associated with having definite sex preferences. Perhaps this suggests that having sex preferences is part of an "interventionist" (rather than a fatalistic) syndrome. Those willing to intervene against "nature" in other areas of life are more willing to express sex preferences which also implies a resistance against just accepting what comes. In Chapter 6, we will find some indirect evidence for this notion in the analysis of the Taiwan data.

In Part C of Table 3, we review all the determinants of son preference in the U.S. and European studies. Given the tentative nature of most previous sex preference studies, any single result may not be very convincing, but if we find the same result in several studies, we may want to take notice. The independent variables are organized according to the outline of hypotheses in Chapter 1, first listing economic factors, then social and cultural ones, and finally psychological ones. Within this framework, studies are listed chronologically.

We had six economic hypotheses about why parents might prefer sons. There is little evidence for any of these in our studies for the U.S. and Europe. Social class is not reliably related to son preference. Only one small study (Largey 1972a) with college students found evidence that boys might be considered less expensive to raise. No study even suggested that boys are economic assets.

Looking at social and cultural factors, there is some evidence that Catholics and Jews are more likely to have son preference than Protestants. (As we see in Part D of Table 3, Protestants are more likely to try for one of each sex than Catholics or Jews.) However, the Jewish samples were very small. For other social variables such as race and education, we find no pattern.

Under psychological factors associated with son preference, we included four hypotheses. The first one, that men might have more son preference than women, is supported quite strongly. In ten studies, men (or boys) did have a greater tendency to prefer a son. For two others, wives reported that their husbands had greater son preference. And for another study (Arnold and Fawcett, 1975) the husbands and wives gave different reasons for preferring boys and girls. Only one study (Markle, 1974) found higher son preference for women. This sex difference is the most consistent effect we found, looking at determinants of sex preference in the U.S. and Europe.

Our second psychological hypothesis was that women might prefer sons for security. A number of studies (for example Dinitz et al., 1954; Peterson and Peterson, 1973; Westoff and Rindfuss, 1974) did find evidence of women preferring boys over girls, especially for a firstborn. Whether this can be traced to security needs, we cannot say. There is some evidence that women want sons in order to please their husbands (who seem to prefer sons more according to the studies just discussed). This may be a stronger factor for women than the desire for security.

Two studies found that boys were considered easier to raise by those who made a sex distinction. This was our third hypothesis dealing with psychological aspects of son preference.

Finally, the Uddenberg et al. study (1971) found several other psychological factors predicting son preference for their small sample (N = 81) of Swedish women. All three are provocative, though tentative. In their data, women without brothers were more likely to prefer sons. We might speculate that women who themselves had no brothers might feel they were deprived of this learning experience and thus want a son (for themselves? for a daughter?). The finding that women wanting sons were more field dependent than women wanting daughters is interesting, combined with other evidence from Uddenberg's study. The authors felt their study refuted the Freudian notion that wanting sons was natural or healthy for women. They felt that the less mentally healthy and more conventional women among their sample wanted sons, sometimes to please the father.

Summarizing this section, the most consistent predictors of son preference (aside from the demographic factors mentioned first) were the sex of the respondent and religion (whether the respondent was Catholic or Jewish). For most of the hypotheses originally listed, there was little evidence. But in general, we might conclude that psychological (rather than economic or social) factors are now at work in U.S. and Europe. There was almost no evidence that economic factors and social factors (other than religion) were operating consistently. In part, this may be due to the weakness of the studies. Few have attempted to test hypotheses about the sources of sex preferences.

Although there was plenty of behavioral evidence (Table 1) and attitudinal evidence (Table 2) that American parents do want one child of each sex, we still do not know much about why or under what conditions. In Part D of Table 3, we list the few studies which have investigated this. Again, religion seems to be a consistent factor. Catholics and Jews are less likely to be influenced in their fertility behavior by the sexes of previous children. There may be different factors operating for these two religions groups. Jews may tend to stop at two, regardless of the sex of previous children while Catholics, during the time of these studies at least, tended to go on for more, again, regardless of sex of previous children. For Catholics, probably considerations other than the sex of children are more important in influencing their fertility behavior.

It is curious that, although Catholics and Jews may have stronger boy preference than Protestants, it is not necessarily reflected in their behavior, perhaps because other factors are more important. Looking ahead to the future when sex control may be available, Largey (1972a) studied the acceptability of sex control and found that Jews were enthusiastic while Catholics were not. Religion was the strongest variable predicting acceptability of sex control. We might speculate that Protestants might use sex control to get one child of each sex, that Jews might use it to get boys, and that Catholics would not use it even though they might prefer boys.

We found almost no research on what might lead a person to prefer a daughter (see Part E, Table 3). In 1954, Dinitz et al. suggested that an interesting research question was: "How does the person with a preference for female children differ in his role conception from those who have internalized the more traditional cultural conceptions?" (p. 130). Unfortunately, twenty years later, we have no answers to this question. In Chapter 4, we try another approach—studying cultures which differ in degrees of daughter preference. But this is only a beginning.

Only slightly more evidence has been collected on the characteristics of persons with no sex preference, a group which in some studies figures rather large. In Uddenberg et al. (1971), the women with no preference were from higher social class and had more education than women preferring sons or daughters. In Markle's study, those with either no preference for a first child or daughter preference, tended to be more egalitarian in the ideas about sex roles. This result of Markle's was consistent with one of our original hypotheses about lack of sex preference. Unfortunately, it was not possible to test the other five hypotheses about what kind of people might have lack of sex preference. It is fair to say there has been almost no scholarly interest in this group of people!

Summary

In this chapter, we first described the sex preferences of Americans and Europeans based on studies done from 1931 to 1975. We found evidence of slight boy preference especially for firstborns, desire for one of each sex, and preference for a predominance of boys over a predominance of girls if a balanced number of each was not chosen. If we tried to rank the sex preferences of Americans in terms of a scale from "-4" (very strong daughter preference) to "+4" (very strong son preference) in order to make comparisons with other populations, we might give American women a rank of "+1" (weak son preference) and American men a rank of "+2" (moderate son preference). As we showed, American men generally have stronger son prefer-

ence than women, who still would like a firstborn to be a boy and would
more often prefer a predominance of boys to a predominance of girls. For
neither men nor women is there evidence that girls are more often neglected
or that parents are desirous of having a son at all costs. Because of the paucity
of data for Europe, it is difficult to make ranks, except to say that the sex
preferences seem similar to those of Americans.

We had no evidence that preferences had changed over time. We then
considered the relationship between fertility and sex preference through three
approaches: (1) behavioral studies, (2) attitudinal studies, and (3) mathematical models and computer simulations. Our conclusion was that for most of
the forty years for which we have data for the U.S., some parents have been
acting as though they were trying to get one child of each sex. This shows up
behaviorally and attitudinally.

Finally, we reviewed the determinants of sex preferences. Although there
have been many interesting variables tried, the best predictors of sex preference remain: (1) sex of previous children, (2) sex of respondent, and (3)
religion.

We also discussed consequences of sex preferences besides fertility, specifically cases of emotional disturbances among children of the "wrong sex," the
possible effect of sex composition on marital tension and on child rearing
practices, the effect of sexes of previous children on a woman's attitude
toward pregnancy, the relationship between strength of sex preferences and
approval of sex control, and finally, the mental health consequences for
women of their sex preferences and the sex of their actual children. We
observed that most of the interest in sex preference has been in its relation to
fertility. Research on other consequences has been scattered and meager, even
in the U.S. and Europe where the bulk of sex preference research has been
done.

In the next chapter we turn to sex preference research in Latin America,
the Middle East, India/Pakistan/Bangladesh, and the Far East. Because of lack
of information, other areas of the world must be ignored.

NOTES

1. In another series of research reports based on Swedish, German and French data,
Edwards has reported that there is a slight tendency for the probability of having a boy
to vary by family. In other words, there is a weak correlation between the sexes of
children in a family. For these reports, the reader is referred to Edwards, 1958; Edwards,
1959; Edwards and Fraccaro, 1960; Edwards, 1961; Edwards, 1962; and Edwards, 1966.
The works of Renkonen (Renkonen, 1956; Renkonen, 1961; Renkonen et al., 1962; and
Renkonen, 1964) show evidence of boy-proneness and girl-proneness in several sources

of data also analyzed by Edwards, although the results are not always consistent. Families at the extremes (large families with children of only one sex) do seem to fit with the model of sex proneness, however.

2. One study of how sonless husbands and wives cope with their situation was done in Korea by Chung, Cha, and Lee (1974). A similar study in Korea was done by Ham (1971). These are the only two studies on this topic we are aware of.

Chapter 3

PREFERENCES IN OTHER AREAS OF THE WORLD

In contrast to the numerous studies extending over at least four decades for the United States, the evidence for other countries is often incomplete and incomparable. Thus most of the findings reported here should be considered illustrative and tentative.

This review of parental sex preferences in other countries will be organized by four very rough culture areas: Latin America and the Caribbean Islands, the Middle East and North Africa, India/Pakistan/Bangladesh, and the Far East. Missing are sub-Saharan Africa, the Soviet Union and most of Eastern Europe, Australia and New Zealand, and many other countries for which adequate data are not available.

This chapter will compare the sex preferences across cultures and see which of our exploratory hypotheses in Chapter 1 are supported. As we go along, we will assign a crude score according to the degree of sex preference found.

Latin America and the Caribbean Islands

A number of well-known studies[1] done on families in Latin America and the Caribbean did not mention parental sex preferences at all, even though this area is usually credited with having a strong value on masculinity (machismo). This is very weak evidence that preference for sons is not strong.

Comparable studies from India or Pakistan would certainly have mentioned parental sex preferences. Turning away from evidence by omission, there are a few studies available, first from the Caribbean area. The first three (Stycos, 1955; Hill et al., 1959; Myers and Roberts, 1968) were done in Puerto Rico and the fourth (Blake, 1961) was done in Jamaica. Stycos presented data on sex preferences of Puerto Rican mothers and fathers. He asked the fathers two questions: (1) What kind of family would you like to have, one with more girls than boys, more boys than girls, or an equal number of each? (2) When your wife is going to have a child, what do you hope for, a boy or a girl? In response to the first question, half (51%) of the men wanted more boys than girls while 40% wanted a balanced family. In response to the second question, boy preference was more obvious. Eighty percent of the men preferred a boy, 5% a girl, and 15% had no preference. Stycos comments on a possible reason for such overwhelming boy preference among men: "Men who produce females are teased and called *chancleteros* (makers of *chancletas*—cheap slippers, a revealing slang term for little girls), and occasionally such a fate is seen as a punishment" (Stycos, 1955: 51).

Mothers, in response to the first question, showed considerable more girl preference than the fathers (34% vs. 5%), with a majority of the women wanting a balanced family (48%) and 18% wanting more boys than girls. Stycos probed the reasons mothers gave for sex preferences and found the following:

The reasons for choice of either sex are similar. Some see boys as labor saving and others (a higher proportion) see girls as labor saving. Those who chose boys felt that since they are born clever *(listos)* and always capable of defending themselves *(defenderse)* against the world at large, they do not need the care and protection which must be lavished on the weak and naive daughter. In practice, this means that boys can be left to roam where they will, dressed poorly or left naked for several years. . . . These mothers who prefer girls feel that girls are less trouble than boys. In the first place, they can help the mother with the housework. Once the boy is socialized, almost by definition he causes disciplinary problems for his parents because to some extent he becomes aggressive and independent. Once the girl is effectively socialized she becomes humble and submissive [Stycos, 1955: 52].

The second Puerto Rican study (Hill et al., 1959) included only men (N=322). The sample was asked, "If you could live your life over, would you rather have more boys than girls, more girls than boys, or an equal number of each?" Forty-seven percent of the men said more boys, 11% said more girls, and the remainder, 42% said an equal number.

The third Puerto Rican study (Myers and Roberts, 1968) included only 18 women. A new approach for measuring family size and sex preferences was being tried. The women were paid a nominal fee to judge 1,176 pairs of girl-boy combinations. The researchers concluded: "The most preferred family consists of two girls and two boys; followed by one girl and one boy, and two girls and one boy. . . . One of the striking conclusions is that family balance (equal numbers of children of each sex) is very important for these women" (Myers and Roberts, 1968: 167-168). In addition, however, "there appears to be a consistent female preference by these women, although the differences are not large" (p. 169).

The Blake study (1961) provided only indirect information on parental sex preferences in Jamaica. She found that daughters were considered more reliable sources of support for family after leaving home than were sons. For the men in Blake's sample, 35% said daughters usually give more help, 31% said sons, and the rest gave other answers. Of the women, 57% said daughters give more help, 13% said sons, and the rest gave other responses. Here, again, women were more likely to favor daughters than were men, but even the men gave slightly more choices to daughters than sons. This is the only information from Blake's study on possible bases of sex preference. She did point out, however, that daughters are a source of considerable anxiety for parents who fear a daughter may "fall" (become a "loose" woman or become premaritally pregnant). The reliability of daughters must be weighed against the extra anxiety they cause parents. Based on Blake's study, it is difficult to say whether, on balance, Jamaican parents prefer daughters to sons. In short, for the Caribbean area, there is some evidence that sons are preferred by men and daughters by women.

For Latin America, meager data[2] are available only for Peru (Eliot, undated), Chile and Argentina (Inkeles and Smith, 1974), Colombia (Turner and Simmons, 1975), and Mexico City (Freedman and Coombs, 1974). The Peruvian study was a replication of a study (Eliot, 1968) done in Algeria which will be discussed in the section on the Middle East. The Peruvian study found, basically, none of the preference for sons shown in the Algerian study. For the Peruvian women, the preferred sex ratios range from 93 to 116, depending on age, whereas in the Algerian samples of women, the range goes from 106 to 312.

The next data, made available to us by Inkeles and Smith (1974), included male factory workers from Argentina, Chile, India, Pakistan, Israel, and Nigeria. The men were asked, "When a family has several children, both sons and daughters (equally), and a new child is coming, is it preferable that the new child be: (1) a boy, (2) either one, or (3) a girl?"

Of the six countries studied, Argentina shows the smallest percentage

TABLE 4: Sex Preferences of Men in Six Countries (Percentages)

	Boy	Girl	Either	Number	Percent
Argentina	33.4	3.4	63.1	841	100.0
Chile	56.1	4.5	39.4	929	100.0
India	78.1	5.0	16.9	1297	100.0
Bangladesh	90.5	1.7	7.8	999	100.0
Israel	44.1	3.6	52.2	691	100.0
Nigeria	66.9	1.8	31.3	791	100.0

Source: Harvard Project on the Sociocultural Aspects of Development. These data are
described in Inkeles and Smith (1974).

preferring a boy and the largest preferring either. Israel is second and Chile
third. With remarkable uniformity over the six countries, few males in any of
the countries preferred daughters. The range is between 1.7% (Pakistan) and
5% (India) preferring a girl.

In addition to the question above, respondents were asked why they
preferred their choice. In Argentina, respondents tended to emphasize that
sons could help their parents more on family property and in the parents' old
age and were less bother to care for. In Chile the reasons for preferring a son
or daughter were not coded comparably and cannot be used here.

Turner and Simmons (1975) collected data on the sex preferences of a
small sample of women and their adolescent daughters in Bogota, Colombia.
Using the Coombs' scale, the authors found that 46% of the mothers and 37%
of the daughters were in the daughter-preference range of the IS-scale. Thirty
percent of the mothers and 32% of the daughters were in the son-preference
range with the remainder wanting a sex balance. Hence, this study showed
slight daughter preference among women.

The last study (Freedman and Coombs, 1974) included data from Mexico
City in their comparative study of sex preferences and fertility. Unfortunately, the modest sample size (under 500) precluded most of the analysis
done in the other countries. For the parity progression ratios, there was some
evidence at the fourth parity that parents having more boys than girls were
less likely to go on for more children than other families. Perhaps, because of
the high fertility pattern in Mexico, the pattern shows up late. Other than the
fourth parity effect, the results for Mexico City were either incomplete or
inconsistent.

On a scale from "-4" (daughter preference) to "+4" (son preference), we
might put Latin American and Caribbean women at "-1" (weak daughter
preference), and Latin American and Caribbean men at "+2" (moderate son

preference). Comparable estimates for the U.S. might be "+1" (weak son preference) for U.S. women and "+2" (moderate son preference) for U.S. men. There is, apparently, a greater discrepancy between the preferences of men and women in Latin America than we found in the U.S. (though even here, there was a consistent sex difference). The data for Latin America are more meager, however.

Middle East and North Africa

Evidence is that son preference varies in this region but reaches an extreme in rural Algeria and Egypt. The seven countries in this area for which data exist are: Turkey, Lebanon, Israel, U.A.R. (Egypt), Morocco, Tunisia, and Algeria. There are many qualitative descriptions of this general area which emphasize the importance of sons. Some writers attribute the concern for sons to Islamic influence, some to Arab culture, and some to the social and economic conditions of the area. Writing about Islam, Levy (1957) described the prescribed position of males in some detail:

> Baydawi, whose word is respected by Sunnites to the present day, sets out categorically the different fashions in which men stand superior to women. Allah has preferred the one sex over the other he says, in the matter of mental ability and good counsel, and in their power for the performance of duties and for the carrying out of (divine) commands. Hence to men have been confined prophecy, religious leadership, saint-ship, pilgrim's rites, the giving of evidence in the law courts, the duties of holy war, worship in the mosque on the day of assembly (Friday), etc. They also have the privilege of electing chiefs, have a larger share of inheritance and discretion in the matter of divorce [Levy, 1957: 98].

Consequently, part of the concept of the ideal woman became tied up with producing masculine births, according to another author:

> The woman who gives birth only to daughters is far from being considered the good, model wife. Although originating in certain pre-Islamic practices, the Arabs' clear preference in favor of masculine births has a social meaning in relation to the economic organization of the family. It reflects still the cult of masculine supremacy and paternal power [Seklani, 1960: 834].

Kirk tried to summarize the important sources of son preference in Moslem societies:

> Sons are valued in Moslem societies for many purposes: for continuity of family line and land ownership; for their contribution to agricultural

labor; to strengthen family numbers in village rivalry and strife; for support in old age; for religious intervention at and after death. ... The traditional Moslem family is strongly patrilinear and patrilocal with male dominance and responsibility specifically prescribed by the Koran [Kirk, 1966: 568-570].

These illustrative statements, selected from many such descriptions,[3] provide a background for the nature of son preference in this geographical region. The few quantitative studies give some idea whether there are variations among countries in the Middle East region or whether there are differences among groups within a single country.

Turning first to Turkey which is somewhat marginal to the area because of its cultural and geographical closeness to Europe, there are three relevant studies (Berelson, 1964; Eillov, 1967; and Freedman and Coombs, 1974). Berelson provided a table based on data collected from a sample of over 5,000 married women and men which showed that those with sons were slightly less likely to want more children than those of similar parity but without sons. The results were consistent for parities one, two, and three, giving some evidence of son preference.

Eillov (1967) noted that women attending a family planning clinic in Ankara had had 117 boys to 100 girls among their previous children, compared with the sex ratio of 104 for the 1965 Census of Turkey. He concluded that women with sons were more likely to be interested in family planning. A competing explanation for these data is that the women coming were of higher economic level than the average and we might expect them to have higher sex ratios since the sex ratio tends to increase with social class (Teitelbaum and Mantel, 1971). This study cannot be considered conclusive.

Data from Ankara, Turkey, were included in the cross-cultural study of sex preference by Freedman and Coombs (1974). Because the sample was not large (N=552), the results were incomplete. But the percentage of women in the sample wanting no more children did seem to be related to the number of sons they had had for the completed parts of the table. However, on the whole we must say that the results are incomplete and inconsistent. Thus for Turkey, the evidence is poor but does not seem to point toward extreme boy preference.

The next two studies were done in Lebanon (Yaukey, 1961; Prothro, 1961). Yaukey interviewed 829 married Lebanese Christian and Moslem women from rural and urban areas. He observes,

There is little place in the community for a mature man or woman without sons. The strength and power of the family as a unit is measured in terms of the number of sons born into it. The father gauges his success as head of the family largely in terms of the number of children—and especially sons—he has produced [Yaukey, 1961: 9-11].

The same is true for the woman who gains security through sons.

Yaukey asked the question: "Suppose you had a very close friend in the same circumstances as yourself, and she asked you for advice on the convenient number of children for her. What is the number you would advise her to have, if she could? How many boys? How many girls?" This question was used after Yaukey tried other questions without success. Even then, only 59% of the women were willing to advise specific numbers of boys and girls. Nonresponse rates ranged from 74% (village, uneducated, Moslem women) to 10% (city, educated, Moslem and Christian women). The advised sex ratios Yaukey found varied with the urban-rural dichotomy and with education but not with religion (Moslem versus Christian). Educated city women advised sex ratios of 111 to 117. Uneducated city women recommended 128 to 129 while village women advised 141 to 150. The sex ratios for rural areas might have been higher had men been interviewed or had a greater proportion of the respondents answered this question, if we assume that more traditional women were less likely to respond.

Prothro, in the same year (1961), published his research findings based on interviews with 468 mothers of five year old children. Prothro mentions that a woman without children "or even one without male children, is pitied by her friends and, among Moslems in particular, threatened by divorce" (p. 52). He found that women reported being happier with pregnancy if they had not had sons yet than if they had. In the former case, their happiness was as great as if it were the first time they had been pregnant. Prothro also refers in passing to the fact that male children were more welcome at birth than female children.

Going on to Israel, one study (Inkeles and Smith, 1974) was already mentioned in the review of the research on Latin America. The Inkeles study of six countries included a sample of non-European Israeli factory workers. Forty-four percent of the men preferred a son while 52% preferred either. In Israel, the most common reason given for perferring boys was that boys were less bother to care for. The second most common reason was that sons brought in earnings. Another relatively common reason was the boys brought more benefit to the country and the society.

A second Israeli project (Goshen-Gottstein, 1966) interviewed 159 Jewish women expecting their first babies. The sample was composed of Oriental, Western, and Israeli Jews. When asked about their preferences for the sex of their baby, 42% said they had no preference, 31% preferred a daughter, and 27% preferred a son. Women in the more modern groups (European or Israeli

Jews) were more likely to express a definite preference. Women who reported having severe menstrual pain were more likely to prefer a boy as were women who reported they had at some time felt envious of the male role, results which were previously found by Newton (1955). Fifty-four percent of the women reported that their husbands preferred a male child, with 22% preferring a female child. When asked about the reasons for their preference, the preferences for a boy tended to be based on the value of the son to the group or the family, whereas daughters were valued for more personal reasons (i.e., companionship to the mother). This seems to support the findings of Fawcett et al. (1974) and Arnold and Fawcett (1975) who suggested that boys are preferred for more instrumental, long-range purposes, while girls are valued for their family contributions as children (household help, psychological traits, companionship). For some of the women in the Israeli study, an expression of daughter preference was an act of rebellion. One respondent, from Egypt, said, for instance, "I want a girl, although my husband's family thinks a boy is the Messiah and has a crown on his head. He is like an idol" (Goshen-Gottstein, 1966: 74). In this sample, sex preferences did not systematically vary by the backgrounds (Oriental, European, and Israeli) of the women.

There are several relevant studies for Egypt (Ayrount, 1963; Rizk, 1959; Rizk, 1963; Hassan, 1967). The first is qualitative, and the rest quantitative. In his book on the Egyptian peasant, Ayrount commented on the birth of a son: "If at the time of birth the father is working in the fields, and the child is a son, a friend will run to tell him the good news, for which he may claim a gift" (Ayrount, 1963: 124).

The next study (Rizk, 1959) contains a good deal of quantitative information. He studied over 6,000 ever-married women in urban, semi-urban, and rural areas of Egypt. He asked women what their ideal number of sons and daughters would be and discovered that for women who had lived with their husbands until age forty-five (his "completed family wives"), the ratio of males considered ideal to 100 females was 130 in urban and semiurban areas and 280 for rural areas (for that minority of women who would give definite answers). Here, again, as in Lebanon, there was considerable nonresponse, possibly biasing the data.

For the younger wives who responded, the ratios of males to females considered ideal was 122 for urban areas, 125 for semiurban areas, and 240 for rural areas. The urban-rural differences are greater than any age differences. The big difference in son preference is between urban settlements and rural areas for Rizk's data. There is little evidence that son preference for these women varies with the education of their husbands or with duration of marriage. All in all, Rizk looked at forty-seven separate groups of women in the course of his cross-tabulations. All the groups had mean preferred sex ratios above what nature brings (about 105). Especially in rural areas, where the ideal was a sex ratio from 200 to 280, there must be many disappointed families! Furthermore, we must keep in mind that only women were interviewed. Had men been included the sex ratios might have been still higher.

Hassan (1967) reported a more recent study, also in Egypt and also using the ideal sex ratio, which found lower preferred sex ratios. His sample was made up of 2,695 married mothers who lived in Cairo. He found: "Without exception, both the Moslems and Christians in all educational classes expressed preference for having more boys than girls" (Hassan, 1967: 18). The ratios ranged from 105 to 118, a good deal lower than Rizk found for rural areas. Religion was not an important determinant of sex preference once again. Perhaps we should modify the original suggestion that it is something about Moslem culture or religion that leads to son preference. Possibly the Moslem influence in the Middle East has been pervasive enough to affect other groups such as Christians in the area. So far for the Middle East, the only important explanatory variable found has been rural residence—not religion.

The next country to be considered is Morocco. Repetto (1972), using data from Morocco, Bangladesh, and India, tested the hypothesis that parents in countries with son preference will have fewer subsequent children if they have sons among their early parities than if they have daughters. Doing a secondary analysis, Repetto could find no evidence in these samples (which had very little use of contraception) of parents using this kind of stopping rule. If anything, parents with sons went on to have *more* children than did parents with daughters. He speculated that this might be due to the greater productivity of sons which reduced or postponed the population pressure on families with sons. In other words, the families with the first three surviving children sons could afford to go on whereas a family which began with a string of daughters could not.

Repetto did not question that there was strong son preference in these countries, but he did provide evidence that, among the sample women, son preference was not operating in the previously postulated way. Our own view is that the level of contraceptive practice was too low, the level of mortality was too high, and the ideal family sizes were still moderately high, all of which operated against the postulated effect. Couples have to be able to stop childbearing when they have enough boys; they have to be sure those boys will survive; and they have to want moderate family sizes (three or four children). If larger family sizes are desired (five or more children), chances are that there will be several children of each sex in the family. In short, it is our view that in Morocco (and the other two samples), the conditions which indicate a clear effect of son preference on fertility have not been met. Yet in the decade to come, we may see the Middle East approach these conditions.

Moving on to Tunisia (and finally, Algeria), we cite a study done by Morsa (1966) which tried to ascertain the importance of sons for a sample of 2,175 women under forty, living with husbands and living in the sample areas. Three questions relating to sons were asked and combined into an index. The first question was, "Do you think you shall go and live with your elder son when you are older?" The second was, "Suppose you had only daughters, would you have one more child, hoping it is a son?" And the third, "Do you think it is more important to have sons than to have daughters?" A response of "yes" to all three gave a score of 3 while a response of "no" to all three gave a score of 0. The study found: "The proportion of wives who stress the importance of having sons remains very high, in the younger groups as well. Only 11% state they have no sex preference, and there is no variation from one age group to another" (Morsa, 1966: 587).

The researcher related the son preference index to past or present use of contraception and to future use. Women who had high scores on the "importance of a son" scale tended not to report use of any method of contraception compared with the few women with low scores. Similar results were found for anticipated future use.

This is the first sex preference scale we have come across so far. A scale may increase the reliability and stability of the measurement. Asking more than one question may increase the variability among the sample which is desirable, especially when the goal is to study an attitude as pervasive as son preference is in many cultures. Morsa used simple "yes or no" questions which, when combined, allowed a ranking of individuals. However, this scale was not based on any theory, each question was weighed arbitrarily, and one item (the first one) might better be conceptualized as a determinant of son preference, rather than a measure of it. But, it was a start and it did relate to contraceptive practice.

The final study (Eliot, 1968) for this area has already been mentioned in connection with a Peruvian study. At the request of the Algerian Ministry of Health in 1966, a study was undertaken of women either in the childbearing period or preparing to enter it. Respondents were asked, "If you could have just the number of children you want, what would that number be? How many boys? How many girls?" The results based on this question follow. First of all, the number of children desired by the women in the four samples (cities, towns, Arab villages, and Berber villages) was high—from 4.7 to 7.6 children. The ideal sex ratios ranged from 120 for the city residents to 241 for the Berber villages. For subsamples the ratios went above 400! This figure of 241 for village women is the same as that found by Rizk for rural Egyptian women in incomplete families which would be comparable to this Algerian sample. Eliot found no consistent pattern of change in sex preference by age. Again, the urban-rural differences seem to be the most striking.

Because of underreporting of female births and deaths, it was not possible to study the incidence of female infanticide or female neglect although both are reputedly practiced in North Africa.

In the Algerian study, parents in rural areas were much less likely to be satisfied with the number of sons they had whereas about half the city respondents felt they had the right number or too many sons. Eliot summarized his results:

> The desire for sons which was most intense in the Kabylie [Berber] villages may have the effect of leading women to continue childbearing long after they have reached the total number of children they named as desirable. Hence, many women who favor the basic idea of family planning may not come soon for this help in village areas [Eliot, 1968: 6-7].

We should point out though that Eliot did not prove this by showing that women with daughters in early parities go on to have more children than women with early sons.

Summarizing the results for the Middle East and North Africa area, it is clear that there is strong son preference in rural areas of Algeria, Egypt, and Tunisia. On a four-point scale, these rural areas should probably rate a "+4". There is no information as to whether men or women have the stronger preferences here. Most of the data were based on women so if we assume men have equal or greater preference for sons, then they would also go in category "+4" which is "very strong son preference." In Morocco there was no direct evidence of the effect of son preference on fertility and no measure of son preference. For Israel there appeared to be mild son preference among non-European Israeli factory workers (perhaps rating a "+2" like the Latin American factory workers) but not among a female sample which might get a score of "0" ("no preference"). For Turkey and Lebanon there was some evidence of son preference. In Lebanon it was moderately strong for village, uneducated Moslem and Christian women (perhaps rating a "+3") but was less strong for city Moslem and Christian women (perhaps a "+2" rating would be appropriate for these women). In Turkey, the evidence was meager but perhaps a "+2" rating would be most appropriate. For urban Egyptian women, there was evidence of less strong son preference. Perhaps a rating of "+2" would fit these data best.

In short, this region shows considerable variation—from ratings of "+2" to "+4" in terms of strength of son preference. The effect of geographical region was found to be very great—with rural areas having stronger son preference than urban ones and with the North African countries having stronger son preference than the Middle Eastern ones. Although the Moslem religion may have a pervasive influence on the son preferences of people living in this area, religion as a variable (Moslem versus Christian) did not have an effect on son preference when geographical region was controlled. There was also little effect of age or duration of marriage on son preference for the studies which examined this. Similarly, there was no proven effect of son preference on fertility, although in Tunisia the women who had high scores on their "importance of sons" scale tended to report less past, present, or anticipated use of contraception. The study for Morocco showed that families starting out with more boys tend to go on for even larger families than those starting out with more girls. Whether this is related to the economic productivity of sons which reduces the population pressure on the family has not been proven. We suggest that the conditions have not been met in the Middle East which are required for a son preference effect to show up in fertility behavior.

In terms of measurement, most of the studies for this region used the ratio of desired males to females. Only one attempted to make an "importance of sons" scale (Tunisia).

In short, residents of rural areas in at least Egypt, Algeria, and Tunisia have *strong* boy preference. In the next parts of this chapter, comparisons will be made with the India/Pakistan/Bangladesh region and the Far East.

India, Pakistan, and Bangladesh

There is considerable information on sex preferences of parents (and several of children) for this area, mostly done in India. The Indian studies will be reviewed first and, for convenience, are listed and described in Table 5.

A few qualitative sources provide some context for the study of son preference in India. A poem by an unknown Indian author (presumably male) about 600 B.C. expresses some of the reasons a father might want a son:

"On the Importance of Having a Son"

In him a father pays a debt
And reaches immortality,
When he beholds the countenance
Of a son born to him alive.

Then all the joy which living things
In waters feel, in earth and fire,
The happiness that in his son
A father feels is greater far.

> At all times fathers by a son
> Much darkness, too, have passed beyond:
> In him the father's self is born,
> He wafts him to the other shore.
>
> Food is man's life and clothes afford protection.
> Gold gives him beauty, marriages bring cattle:
> His wife's a friend, his daughter causes pity:
> A son is like a light in highest heaven.
>
> [Anonymous Indian writer, 600 B.C.].

In this poem, the spiritual aspects of having a son are emphasized. Saving his father from hell (wafting him to the other shore) is mentioned by contemporary observers (Morrison, 1957; Prabhu, 1963). According to Morrison (1957: 72), "the desire for male progeny in the Hindu is very strong. A son is absolutely essential if the traditional orthodox obsequies are to be performed. The Shastras, sacred religious literature, stress the importance of male progeny." According to Prabhu (1963: 242), "the acquisition of sons was considered to be the primary aim of marriage [in ancient India]. The son rescues the souls of the deceased ancestors from the hell into which they might fall without his birth." Prabhu referred to one ancient religious work which says, "because the son protects his ancestors from the hell called *Put*, he has been called *Putra*" (Prabhu, 1963: 242). Another author described it this way: "There is little doubt that great emphasis is put on the hope of a male child, especially if it is the first child or if there are only girls in the family. This has always been true in India, pumsavana (male production) being the third of the sacred 'domestic ceremonies' " (Cormack, 1953).

Yet there are a number of other reasons Indian parents might want a son; the religious reasons discussed above are only part of the picture. According to Prabhu (1963: 242), "the Mahabharata looks at the necessity of a son in the family from another angle also; the child is looked upon as a great bond of affection in the family, the center to which the love of the parents converges."

Not to be neglected are the potentially negative aspects of having daughters:

> In many parts of India complicated rules of endogamy, exogamy and marriage residence compel daughters to marry out of the village and reside in another locality situated at a considerable distance from the parental village. Hence, if no sons are alive, the possibility of emotional and other forms of support from daughters is more limited in India than in many other agrarian societies [May and Heer, 1968: 200].

But daughters not only leave the family turning their support from the family of their parents to that of their husband: daughters are expensive to marry off in some parts of India. Several authors (Beals, 1962; Lewis, 1965; Kapadia, 1966) mention this. A group of North Indian village women living near Ludhiana described the situation in this way:

> Girls are born into a family to be given away. More than that, a dowry has to go with them. The first obligation of a wife is to produce sons for her husband's family; for her husband and herself of course, but more importantly for the good of the extended family group—to add to the earning power; to uphold family prestige by word and deed, and if necessary by physical strength [Wyon and Gordon, 1971: 83].

This source continued on the same topic:

> In addition, all married men want a son to light their funeral pyre when they die, cremation being customary. In theory, men make the family decisions; yet a woman, if she is wise, has much influence through her husband and her sons.

> One daughter is useful because she helps with the housework when she is young. After she is married and goes to live in her husband's village, she may assist in finding a wife for her brother at home through new-found friends; but to have many daughters is a burden. A number of folk sayings reflect the desire for sons: a fire is never satisfied with the amount of fuel, a woman with the number of her sons, a milkmaid with the amount of milk she gets, or a farmer with the land he owns. Most women thought that a family of two boys and a girl was about right; some said two of each [Wyon and Gordon, 1971: 83].

This discussion of son preference in northern India ended with this quotation, a translation of a Punjabi proverb: "No son begets many daughters" (Wyon and Gordon, 1971: 84).

In these quotations from the Khanna study, several other reasons for preferring sons are mentioned. Sons may add to the earning power of the family whereas few Indian daughters work for money, and if they did, they would earn less money and probably work for a shorter time. If they were married, their money would go to their husband's family. In addition, sons are more help—in the parents' old age in a society where there are few alternative sources of support. Another function of sons is to perpetuate the family line. And finally, defense of the family and its interests was mentioned.

All of these reasons for wanting sons, religious, companionship, love object, negative aspects of having daughters, earning power, help in old age, carrying on the family line, and defense are closely connected. Probably few Indians could separate them and say which was the most important reason for wanting sons. They all add up to the idea of security in a society where this is a scarce commodity for many families.

In Table 5 we list over thirty studies which collected information on parental sex preferences in the last twenty years. The types of evidence vary considerably from customs which emphasize the importance of sons, to analysis of census, survey, and clinic data, to mathematical and simulation models. The sources are listed chronologically.

The sources cited for India provide a great deal of proof that Indian men and women have strong son preference—using both attitudinal and behavioral indicators. Boys tend to be more welcomed at birth, girls are more often underreported and sometimes neglected, birth control is more likely to be used if parents have sons, and sterilization is more likely to be accepted if the man has more sons than daughters. There is some negative evidence on whether son preference leads to larger families (Repetto, 1972). It is our theory that in rural areas, contraception is not yet widespread enough and effectively used and the infant and child mortality rates are still moderately high. In addition, daughters may burden a family sufficiently that they feel they cannot go on for more children. Perhaps for these reasons, we have not seen clear evidence (except for the Freedman and Coombs, 1974 study for older women in the all-India sample) of differential reproduction by sex composition of previous children. It would be interesting to interview families with daughters who did not go on for more children to see what factors influenced their behavior. This kind of information is simply not available with the parity progression ratio approach (which simply looks at behavior).

Nevertheless, it is clear that there are strong economic and familial reasons for having sons in India along with some negative aspects of having daughters. So much for the background information.

One of the most interesting quantitative findings was that of Lahiri (1974), which found striking regional differences in son preferences of married men. His ideal sex ratios varied from 495, 379, and 322 (for Jammu and Kashmir, for Kerala, and for Gujarat) to 159, 157, and 162 (for Madras, for Maharashtra, and for Union Territories which includes Delhi). The other studies which tend to be focused on only one region might well be put in the context of these regional differences. For example, Poffenberger and Poffenberger (1973) found clear preferences for sons in their small in-depth study of 66 couples. According to Lahiri, Gujarat is one of the states having very high son preference.

Before trying to rank India on the son preference scale for comparison with the other areas, the sparse data for Pakistan and Bangladesh will be cited. For Pakistan (before its separation into two countries), El-Badry (1969) cites data on the high sex ratio and points out that the death rates of females (relative to males) are high for childhood, ages one to four. Possibly this is evidence of female neglect.

TABLE 5: Studies Collecting Evidence of Parental Sex Preferences in India (1955-1975)

Study	Sample	Approach Taken	Results
Morrison (1956)	124 married men living in Badlapur, Bombay State	Structured interview	All the respondents wanted male children but the less traditional respondents were willing to limit their families after the desired sons were produced. Three living sons seemed to be the minimal number desired by the respondents.
Morrison (1957)	126 married women living in Badlapur, Bombay State	Structured interview	As above, the number of living male offspring was significantly related to the desire for additional offspring. But the willingness to use contraceptives was not associated with the number of living male offspring for women (but was for men).
Agarwala (1961)	461 married women living in four villages near Delhi	Structured interview	Women wanted a daughter only when they had no living daughter while they often wanted more than one son. The ideal family compositions were three males and one female or two males and two females. Few women wanted more than five children unless all of these were daughters.
Morrison (1961)	166 married men who were industrial workers in Ambarnath near Bombay	Structured interview	Of the four family-size variables, only the number of living male offspring proved to be associated with attitude toward birth control. Similar results to the earlier Morrison study (1956).
Dandekar (1961 chart) (1963 ref.)	3,465 undergoing vasectomy in Maharashtra	Data collected from patient records	Found sex ratio of 140 for men who had vasectomies. As the author put it, "Male issue was the real issue to most fathers." (Dandekar, 1961: 151) 133 fathers had one son whereas 848 fathers had one daughter.
Prabhu (1963)	None	Citation of religious and literary sources	Finds considerable support for having sons.
Bhatnagar (1964)	Village survey in Madhya Pradesh	Survey	Found evidence of neglect of female children.

TABLE 5: (continued)

Study	Sample	Approach Taken	Results
Chitre et al. (1964)	A random sample of 200 men having vasectomies in a camp in Maharashtra State	Clinic records	The median number of sons of the men was three; the median number of children was five.
Lewis (1965)	Village study in Northern India	Participant observation of customs surrounding birth	Midwives are likely to be paid more if the child is a boy; there is more rejoicing if the baby is male.
Samuel (1965)	Cites Mysore Population Study (United Nations, 1961)	Survey	For 84% of rural women and 93% of rural men, one of the motives of having children was the desire to have a son. In urban areas the percentages were 71% and 73%.
Poffenberger (1967)	892 men who had vasectomies in Uttar Pradesh	Clinic records	The mean number of living children at the time of vasectomy was 4.7 with 2.9 boys and 1.8 girls. Ratio of boys to girls was 155.
Krishna-Murthy (1968)	Review of findings from many population studies done in India	Review of survey results	Several surveys found that among those not interested in contraception, wanting more sons was a prominent reason.
May & Heer (1968) Heer & Smith (1968)		Computer simulations	Indicated that, assuming Indian parents want to be 95% certain they will have one surviving son, fertility will remain high until mortality declines still further.
Poffenberger (1968)	Intensive interviews with 112 mothers and fathers in a Gujarat village	Questionnaires	Mothers were found to have more boy preference than fathers (ideal sex ratios of 179 versus 138). Respondents emphasized need for sons for security in old age. Respondents saw mostly advantages in having sons and disadvantages in having daughters.

TABLE 5: (continued)

Study	Sample	Approach Taken	Results
El-Badry (1969)	Data from censuses, surveys, and vital registration for India, Pakistan, and Ceylon (Sri Lanka)	Study of sex differential mortality	Concludes that the high sex ratios of this area are due to: (1) under-enumeration of females and, more importantly, (2) higher female mortality. The author suggested that some of this higher female mortality may be due to female neglect and the low status of women.
Khatri and Siddiqui (1969)	119 children (8 and 11 years old) from Ahmedabad	Story completion. Individual interviews	54% of the children felt hypothetical parents would prefer boy, 46% a girl. The hypothetical father was presumed to prefer a boy, the mother, a girl. No differences found by sex of the respondent.
Pohlman & Rao (1969)	1,167 Indian children living in Delhi and rural areas in the vicinity. Grades 1-11	Survey	Found strong evidence of boy preference among boys and girls. Ideal sex ratios were 124 to 182. Almost all wanted a boy first with consistency of this response over time. Reasons for wanting boys tended to be economic.
Halder & Bhattacharya (1970)	Not able to locate		
Mitra (1970)	None	Mathematical model	Estimates the excess births that will result with various "stopping rules" parents might use. Speculates that about one birth per couple could be avoided with sex control.
Pakrasi et al. (1970)	Data from National Sample Survey, 1961-1962	Parity progression ratios	"A larger proportion of couples with two female children had a third child within 3 years of the second child's birth than did couples having other sex-combinations of the first two children" (Pakrasi et al., 1970).
Pakrasi & Halder (1971)	250,000 births from the National Sample	Analysis of sex ratios	Found sex ratios for first-borns in rural areas were reported to be 127 and 123 in urban areas. Authors speculated that this might be due to

TABLE 5: (continued)

Study	Sample	Approach Taken	Results
			nonreporting of a dead first child who was female and a tendency to report a first son as older than a first daughter, even when this was not the case.
Wyon & Gordon (1971)	Longitudinal study of residents in villages in Khanna area, Punjab	Qualitative and quantitative data	Found some evidence of female neglect, of birth customs favoring boys, of verbal statements of respondents on the importance of having sons. Also, women with several living sons were more likely to practice birth control than women with only daughters.
Repetto (1972)	Intensive fertility survey, Lucknow, U.P. (1968). Also surveys of 6 Delhi and 3 U.P. villages (1961-1963)	Mean number of live births, cross-classified by sex of 1st three. Also regression analysis	No effect found. Women with more sons among first three did not have fewer overall children.
Khan (1973)	800 pregnancy histories from a survey in Patna in 1955	Examined birth intervals after a boy vs. a girl. Also considered survival status	Found generally longer birth intervals after a boy than a girl, if child survived. For first three intervals, this finding also held up when infant died within first two years. Not true for higher intervals.
Poffenberger & Poffenberger (1973)	66 married couples in village in Gujarat in 1962. Supplemented by recent information	Participant observation and intensive interviews	Men had ideal sex ratios of 138. Women's were higher at 179. Sixty-two percent of women would have six or more daughters if necessary in order to get a son compared with 35% of men. Women more concerned about having a son for support in old age than were men.
Waheed (1973)	Some illustrative Indian data used	Mathematical model	Estimated effect on family size of varying sex preference rules.

TABLE 5: (continued)

Study	Sample	Approach Taken	Results
Freedman & Coombs (1974)	Calcutta sample of 947 married women. Delhi sample of 5,242 married women. India sample of 10,246 married women.	Behavioral and attitudinal indicators from three surveys. Part of cross-cultural study.	Ideal sex ratios: Calcutta (150), Delhi (164), and India (147). Attitudinal data generally consistent with idea that having sons affects whether people want more children and the number wanted. Parity progression data available for India only. Older (30-39) women were less likely to go on for more children if they had sons. Not true for younger women (20-29).
Inkeles & Smith (1974)	Sample of male factory workers in India (and Bangladesh)	Survey data	(See Table 4 for data.) When asked the reasons for preferring a boy, respondents in India and Bangladesh emphasized economic benefits for the family. Speaking of daughters, men in both countries mentioned that daughters married out of the family, did not benefit the family as adults, and were expensive.
Lahiri (1974)	16,000 currently married men from urban areas in India. National Sample Survey, 1960-1961	Analysis of social, demographic, and economic determinants of sex preference scale (similar to ideal sex ratio)	High son preference found for all groups. *Large* regional differences within India found. Men from Jammu, Kashmir, and Kerala wanted 4 sons per 1 daughter while men from Maharashtra and Madras wanted 3 sons per 2 daughters. Son preference was highest for men with no children, those under age 16 or over 62, those with many sons, those with highest or lowest educations, and for Muslims and other non-Christian minorities.
Khatri (1974)	Same as Khatri and Siddiqui (1969)	Individual interviews with children using adoption story	Analyzing another part of the data, Khatri found more evidence of boy preference. Also found that boys were more likely to prefer boys than were girls. Reasons given for preferring boys were utilitarian and economic.
Talwar (1975)	None	Mathematical model	Examined effect of desired sex composition on birth rate, assuming different sex preferences.

Since the separation of East and West Pakistan into two countries, there have been no published studies on sex preference for Pakistan, although M. Karim is presently working on such analysis for recent survey data. For Bangladesh, we have already cited the Inkeles and Smith data (Table 4 and Table 5). Repetto (1972) included Bangladesh in his study and found no effect of sex composition on subsequent fertility for the sample of 2,500 women (rural and urban) in the 1961-1962 Demographic Survey of East Pakistan. Using regression analysis, Repetto found no effect of the number of living sons as a percentage of living children on the total live births for three different age groups of women. If anything, those with high sex ratios went on to have slightly more children, a result for which there is no ready explanation.

Two other researchers (Ben-Porath and Welch, 1972, and Welch, 1974) have included data from Bangladesh in their recent papers on sex preference, both using the same data set as Repetto (1972). The first study found that birth intervals were longest (30.1 months) for women having equal numbers of boys and girls. Those having more boys than girls had intervals of 28.9 months while those having more girls than boys had the shortest intervals, 28.1 months. Based on these data, one would have to conclude that the balanced family was most satisfying and the family with more girls than boys least satisfying. Welch (1974) elaborated the first study. He was surprised to note that birth intervals were longer after a first-born girl than after a first-born boy. He had no explanation of this result. More in line with his predictions was the finding that the chance of survival for a girl (but not a boy) depends to some extent on the sex composition of her siblings. Girls born into a family with more boys than girls have a mortality rate of 24.5%. Girls born into families with more girls than boys have a mortality rate of 26.4%. These mortality rates include deaths before age five.

This later analysis of survival chances is unique in the sex preference literature and might well be replicated in other countries known to be son preferring. It begins to answer the question of what is the cost to girls of being born into a society which prefers boys.

In comparing India, Pakistan, and Bangladesh with the three areas already discussed (the U.S., Latin America, and the Middle East), it is clear that son preference is stronger in India than in the first two areas. The problem comes with the comparison with the Middle East. The only comparable data are the ideal sex ratios (which confuse sex preference with number preference). On the basis of ideal sex ratios, Indians apparently equal (or exceed) respondents from Algeria and Egypt, countries having the highest son preference in our review for the Middle East. Lahiri's study (1974) found ideal sex ratios above 300 for samples of husbands in five states (Jammu and Kashmir, Kerala,

Gujarat, Madhya Pradesh, and Andhra Pradesh). The other Indian states are in the ranges (150 to 230) found in Egypt. One complicating factor is that we have better data on men for India. The Egyptian and Algerian data included just women or mixed men with women in the tables. Thus the higher levels for some Indian subgroups may be reflecting the fact that the samples are men. However, Poffenberger and Poffenberger (1973) and Lahiri (1974) cite data showing the women have higher son preference than men in India, probably because of the dependence of widows on sons. We cannot be sure that data from men may be exaggerating son preference.

A very tentative conclusion is that both rural India and rural Egypt and Algeria should receive ratings of "+4" (very strong son preference), while some groups in India (those in the major cities and Christians for example) should receive ratings of "+3". The data from Pakistan and Bangladesh are too incomplete to make comparisons.

Most of the economic hypotheses we began this study with seem to apply to India. Sons are more productive, provide in old age, bring in dowries (and wives who work for the family), and have a better chance of success than daughters. Similarly, the social conditions also apply. The Indian family system is patrilocal and patrilineal, sons are needed for continuity of the family, sons provide protection and perform religious rites for parents, and rural parents need them for labor. Finally, certain groups (such as Muslims within India) seem to have higher son preference than others. We did not find son preference to vary by education level or income, however, in the Indian studies. The psychological conditions we postulated in Chapter 1 seem least relevant. The Indian studies found that respondents gave instrumental or utilitarian reasons for sons, not ones based on traits of sons, realization of sex roles, pleasing the husband, and so forth. In India, apparently sons mean survival and above that, security. Thus, although our hypotheses were not explicitly tested in very many of the studies (and Lahiri's valuable study is an exception here), there was considerable evidence for the economic and social hypotheses we originally suggested.

Far East

Of the many countries in the Far East,[4] we will investigate sex preferences in only the Philippines, Thailand, and Korea, while mentioning Japan and Indonesia in passing. Taiwan will be dealt with in Chapter 6 while the People's Republic of China will be cited in the chapter on boy preference and public policy (Chapter 7). Data for other countries in the Far East are unavailable to our knowledge.

While one might assume strong son preference to be widespread in the Far

East, at least three countries (Philippines, Thailand, and Indonesia) show a different pattern, even though all three have large rural populations and one is predominantly Moslem. We will begin with the evidence for the Philippines.

All four Philippine studies are very recent (Stinner and Mader, 1975; Dela Paz, 1975; Bulatao, 1975b; and Yengoyan and Viterbo, forthcoming). The Stinner and Mader study has the largest sample (over 5,000) and most representative sample of Filipino women. The authors found that 60% of the women in Metropolitan Manila sample wanted equal numbers of sons and daughters, whereas 46%-50% of the women from provincial urban areas and from rural areas wanted a balance. Except for Manila, the tendency was for more women to prefer sons than to prefer daughters, for those not wanting a balance. However, this tendency is weak and the overall ideal sex ratio for women in the sample is only 105. Muslim women had higher ideal sex ratios (118 for rural women and 122 for urban). Only among rural Mindanao women (predominantly Muslim) was there "a strong positive relationship between the number of living sons and the proportion not wishing any additional children" (Stinner and Mader, 1975: 75). The explanation of the authors for this lack of son preference of most of the women in the sample is that Filipino women are relatively emancipated, daughters also have an obligation to support their parents, and the study evaluated only the preferences of women who might have less son preference than men. On the issue of support for parents, the authors assert that in Filipino society, responsibility for parents goes to eldest children, regardless of sex. This is a bit inconsistent with the picture given by Bulatao (1975b) who found that daughters were wanted for household, rather than financial, help. Since Bulatao has specific evidence on this point from his Value of Children study, while Stinner and Mader are only speculating, we are more inclined toward Bulatao's description. But before making any conclusions, we need more data from Filipino men who have been underrepresented up to now.

The Dela Paz (1975) paper had a conclusion similar to that of Stinner and Mader: women in the Philippines prefer a balanced number of boys and girls. For her sample of 385 urban and rural women, Dela Paz found a mean IS-scale score (the Coombs' sex preference score based on a rank ordering of 16 sex and size combinations) of 3.9 where 4.0 is the desire for a balanced number of boys and girls. She found no systematic variation by age, parity, education of the wife or urban-rural area. Small business proprietors had higher son preference scores, but the sample was small.

Bulatao (1975) reported that his Filipino sample of men and women (N=389) wanted both girls and boys, but for quite different reasons. Boys were wanted first for financial assistance and second for preserving the family name. Girls were wanted for help in the house and for personal qualities of girls. Bulatao pointed out that the reasons people report for wanting children differ from those for wanting boys and girls. Respondents said they wanted children for general happiness of themselves and the family. When they were asked about girls and boys, they thought more in terms of sex roles. Although there were differences between husbands and wives in their reasons for wanting sons and daughters, the urban-rural differences were sharper, with rural people more likely to mention financial assistance from sons and household assistance from daughters.

Yengoyan and Viterbo, focusing on the Central Philippines, made the point that cultural attitudes (here, sexual egalitarianism) and economic contingencies may conflict. They suggested, although they do not prove, that families involved in labor intensive activities, like rice farming and sugar cane harvesting, have stronger son preference, compared with families tending fish ponds or involved in deep-sea fishing. In their view, the Malayo-Polynesian culture does not make large sex distinctions. For instance, "in most Malayo-Polynesian languages, gender is not distinguished" (Yengoyan and Viterbo, forthcoming: 3). According to them child transfers among Malays do not depend on the sex of the child, whereas among the Chinese, only girls are let out for adoption. Thus, it follows that *only* when economic conditions needing labor (and when that labor has to be male) occur will son preference be found in this culture area.

In short, all four Philippine studies agreed that son preference is weak or nonexistent, especially among women—hence, their score of "0" on our scale. We suspect that men might have more son preference but predict that it would be weak relative to Korea and Taiwan. A country for which sex differences of this nature have been found is Thailand, for which we have three studies (Knodel and Pitaktepsombati, 1973; Prachuabmoh, Knodel and Alers, 1974; and Knodel and Prachuabmoh, 1975), the last of which includes men and women. Using data from the first and second rounds of the Longitudinal Study of Social, Economic, and Demographic Change and from a family planning Follow-up Survey, the authors found a weak but consistent attitudinal bias for boys but little effect on fertility behavior, except for the urban Chinese sample. For this latter group, there was a tendency for son preference to affect desire for additional children and family planning practice. Comparing Thai attitudes with those of other groups we have described, we note that the ideal sex ratios reported by Knodel and Prachuabmoh (1975) ranged from 110 for ethnic Thai women and 136 for ethnic Thai men, while the Chinese Thais had ideal sex ratios of 125 and 150 respectively. The sex difference is slightly greater than the ethnic difference.

The conclusions which can be drawn from the different Thai studies are the following: (1) men have more son preference than women; (2) Chinese have more son preference than ethnic Thais; (3) families want at least one son and one daughter; (4) men may want sons more, but in general they want fewer children; (5) there is some desire for a balanced number of children, but when an odd number is desired, a predominance of sons is preferred; (6) wanting one child is rare, but such respondents usually want a boy. Among the reasons why son preference seems to be weak among ethnic Thais, especially in its effects on behavior are: the relative lack of concern with lineage, the general position of the sexes in social and economic spheres, the lack of ancestor worship, the lack of reliance on male heirs for old-age insurance, the lack of a dowry system, the tradition that daughters living away from home send their parents money, and the helpfulness and companionship of girls in the household.

Because the data are longitudinal, based on a recent national sample, seem to be of high quality, and include both men and women, we can be fairly confident of the results for Thailand. In addition, several earlier sources (Hawley and Prachuabmoh, 1966; Boserup, 1970) mention the low level of son preference in Thailand.

A country with a similarly low level of son preference is Indonesia, although the data are not as complete here. In a book which collected articles on thirteen villages in Indonesia (Koentjaraningrat, 1967), there were almost no direct references to son preference. In one tribe, for example, the Mure-marew, women are described as valuable because of their economic productivity and because of the marriage-exchange system. Another study (Gille and Pardoko, 1966) dealt more directly with sex preference. The Public Health Institute in Surabaya, Indonesia did a survey of 1,000 households selected randomly from a complete list of more than 2,500. In 1961, married men and women were interviewed in this poor and densely populated area in East Java. The finding was:

A strong preference for boys, similar to that noted in many studies in other Asian countries, was not found in the study. The same number of boys and girls was wanted by 55% of the married women and by 45% of the men. A preference for more boys was expressed by 24% of the women but nearly as many (21%) wanted more girls than boys. Of the men, 32% wanted to have more boys, but 24% desired more girls [Gille and Pardoko, 1966: 515-516].

In this study the respondents were from rural areas and were mostly Moslems, although not necessarily observant Moslems. Thus it is all the more notable that more boy preference was not found. The same result was obtained by Terry Hull of the Australian National University. When his valuable study of Indonesian population dynamics is published, we will have a better source on Indonesian sex preferences.

The only other evidence on Indonesia comes from Freedman and Coombs (1974). Using data from Jakarta and rural East Java, there was no evidence that son preference was strong or was affecting fertility. Thus we conclude that both Indonesia and Thailand have little or no son preference. For Thailand, the conclusion needs to be modified to include the stronger son preferences of the Chinese and of men. In neither country did we find consequences for fertility of sex preferences.

Before concluding our observations with material from Korea, we will consider Japan briefly. Taiwan will be dealt with in Chapter 6 and China in Chapter 7.

Unfortunately, the data from Japan are inadequate. Impressionistic material on the importance of sons is found in Raucat (1927) and Dore (1967) found that eldest sons were very important sources of anticipated support for parents in a Tokyo ward in 1951, although Dore predicts that daughters will have an increasingly important role in looking after parents. Dore reasoned that this change could be expected in the future, because daughters and mothers would get along better in general than mothers and daughters-in-law, because women often feel closer to their family of origin than do men, and because the tradition of male dominance would mean that men can more easily adapt to the wife's family than the reverse. We do not know whether this change has come about, but it may be significant in helping Japanese parents adapt to very small families and few or no sons.

A discussion of the Japanese kinship system (Pelzel, 1970) sheds some light on the need for sons in Japan. Comparing the Japanese and Chinese kinship systems, he concluded, "the two systems are in essence radically different" (Pelzel, 1970: 227). One important feature of the Japanese system is that the ideal is the stem family rather than the joint family as in China. The stem family is quite common in Japan—more common than the joint family is in China. Only one son is needed to carry on the family successfully. Even if there are more sons in the family, only one will assume the position as head of the family and its assets. The other sons will either start new families nearby or move to the cities in research of employment. Farms tend to be small and the opportunities in the cities have been increasing in recent times. Even though the new Japanese Civil Code requires equal inheritance, "other siblings regularly sign away their rights to the brother chosen by the parents to succeed" (Pelzel, 1970: 230). Thus, "nonsucceeding sons, like daughters, have no right to any of the other assets of the house" (232).

From this and other descriptions of the Japanese kinship system, there is little question that it is characterized by male supremacy and son preference, but it is important to note that this does not necessarily lead to high fertility, because only one son is needed and even this son can be adopted into the family:

In the absence of a qualified direct-line descendant, a close or a distant kinsman, or with great frequency even a male with no genetic link whatsoever to the house, may be adopted as the successor to the head. If there are daughters but no son, it is usual for the adopted successor to be brought in simultaneously as the husband of the eldest daughter. Whatever the successor's origin, once adopted he takes the family name, and in all formal and legal respects he becomes the authorized head of the household and house he has entered and is incorporated into its genealogy. These practices are by no means limited to farm families or to those with extensive properties: the mystique of the durable house is itself sufficient to require such arrangements [Pelzel, 1970: 232].

This culturally-approved pattern of adopting a male heir cited also by Dore (1967), which reduces some of the pressure to have sons, is not available for parents in Taiwan, India, or Korea, to cite three son prefer-ring societies. In Taiwan there is a pattern of adopting girls (often to be servants). In the Taiwan study to be discussed in Chapters 5 and 6, we found that about 90% of the children adopted into the families of our 8,000 respondents were girls. The adoption of boys is quite rare in Tai-wan and Korea.

The accounts of Japanese kinship emphasize that the male heir, whether he is the eldest son, another son, or some unrelated male, has many important tasks in the family—managing the property, maintaining family traditions, representing the family in community organizations, and supporting depen-dents, both young and old. But because only one son is needed and because adoption is acceptable, the desire for sons has apparently not kept Japan from reducing its fertility.

The only other data on Japan is from Koya (1963) who examined whether families with abortions or sterilizations tended to have more sons than one might normally expect in the population. Data are available for 1,382 families in the Keihin and Takai regions of Japan where the wives had had their first induced abortion approved by the local eugenics committee during the period August 1, 1949 to July 31, 1950. These women had had a total of 793 sons and 708 daughters with a sex ratio of 112 (Koya, 1963: 71). This is slightly above the 106 one might have expected but nowhere near the high sex ratios found in India for men having vasectomies. In a sample of women who were sterilized, the women had had 611 boys and 529 girls for a sex ratio of 115 (Koya, 1963: 93). This again is slightly higher than one might expect but not remarkably so. In still another study of sterilized persons, (Koya, 1963: 114) the number of boys was 1,337 and the number of girls was 1,325 giving a sex ratio of 101. In this last study, even though the overall sex ratio was lower than normal, there were more families with one male than one female, with two males than two females, and with three males than three females. The author concluded on the basis of these results "that families with male children resort to sterilization more readily than do those having only female children." But this conclusion is not justified, given the fact that one would expect more males in the population even if there were no son preference.

It is unfortunate that we do not have more complete information on Japanese sex preferences since Japan is an example of a country with boy preference but low fertility. It would be interesting to know how Japanese parents have adjusted to having just one, or even no, boys.

Finally, we will report on boy preference in Korea where a very large amount of research has been done recently. Korea ranks with the U.S. and India in the amount of research done on boy preference. We will summarize the results of the most comprehensive and interesting of the Korean studies.[5] Problems of public policy in Korea are dealt with in Chapter 7.

We will consider first behavioral and attitudinal evidence of boy preference, then reasons for the persistence of boy preference, and finally its individual determinants. Many of the hypotheses suggested in Chapter 1 will be relevant to the Korean case.

There is no shortage of different types of behavior in Korea in the past and present which indicate boy preference. In the past "son praying" (i.e., rituals designed to bring sons) was very common. A very drastic version of son praying was navel cautery, described in Chung, Cha, and Lee (1974: 90-91):

> According to this custom blue salts and musk powder were mixed into wheat flour dough, which then was placed over the navel of a woman from whom a son was desired and cauterized with salt moxa. Usually two or three hundred cauteries were prescribed for sonless women. Sometimes cautery was carried to an extreme by zealous husbands who believed that the more salt burned, so much the better. Instead of burning the moxa on the navel, the husband brought a red-hot iron rod against the navel of his wife and held it there while the wife screamed in unbearable pain. Evidence shows that this seeding of sons through cautery over the wife's navel was practiced fairly widely as late as the first two or three decades of the present century.

Still practiced are nativity customs distinguishing between a welcome boy and a less welcome girl, naming girls with boys' names in hope that this will bring a boy next time, giving girls names which indicate disappointment, consulting soothsayers about the sex of the next child, eating certain foods, using certain sex practices, and stealing objects from households with sons. It is likely that these practices are dying out in urban areas, however. Yun (1974) lists thirty-two beliefs mentioned by Korean soldiers about how to obtain the desired sex of child. There are also many common proverbs about sons and daughters such as the following one which has a perversely feminist flavor: "If you have to marry someone you dislike, give him many daughters" (Chung, Cha, and Lee, 1974: 96).

Sex preference in Korea affects fertility behavior. Many studies have found that sex composition of children affects contraceptive usage, for example. Boy-skewed families are more likely to use birth control, to use it earlier, and to want no more children. The more the sons (but not the more the daughters), the higher the likelihood of a woman using contraception. These effects are stronger for people with moderate family sizes (three to four children) than those with more or fewer and for those who approve of family planning and want moderate sized families. Furthermore, comparing the *actual* number of families with different sex and size combinations with the *theoretical* number, one finds fewer all-girl or predominantly-girl families, controlling for family size. Thus, among those with three children, there are fewer three daughter families or two daughter and one son families than one would expect and more three son families. The three son families presumably were more content and began practicing contraception. Three daughter families went on for more and left the category.

The attitudinal evidence is also consistent and strong. Ideal sex ratios vary from 144 to 180 for Korean women, depending on the study cited. The ratios are lower for students (125 to 150) but still above the biological sex ratio of 107 for Korea. For those wanting odd numbers of children, almost all would prefer a predominance of boys. Some researchers in Korea question the validity of the ideal sex ratio measure because it requires people to state the number of girls desired. According to one researcher (Cha, 1975: 8), "the concept of [desired] number of daughters is only poorly developed in the mind of Korean people." Because of discontent with old measures, many new measurement approaches have been tried in Korea. These are discussed in Kong and Cha (1974), Chung, Cha, and Lee (1974), and Cha (1975).

Many Korean women assert in surveys that they would continue child-bearing until they got a son. Fifty-three percent of women in a national sample (Chung et al., 1972) said they would continue—29% of Seoul women and 73% of rural women. Furthermore, many women say they would allow their husbands to take a concubine if they were sonless: from 41-68% of rural women and 25-27% of Seoul women, depending on the study. Although we could cite additional evidence of Korean boy preference, the above findings should be sufficient.

We should say a few words about measurement problems. More work is being done on this problem in Korea than anywhere else. Yet, researchers like Ham (1971) and Chung, Cha, and Lee (1974) still find it difficult to get people to articulate their reasons for wanting sons. There are several explanations for this. One is that in Korea son preference is not simply a personal preference, but rather is an "institutionalized value" (Kwon and Lee, 1975: 11). The customs, laws, and family system all incorporate the idea of boy preference. Thus individuals have not needed to work out a personal rationale for their boy preference. Chung, Cha, and Lee (1974: 21) suggest that the need for sons is related to the need for security which is "less well verbalized and in this sense is unconscious." Ham makes a similar point (1971: 6): "The inability of most Koreans to articulate the thoughts and emotions buried near the subconscious realm of the mind was of course the greatest obstacle in our study [of sonless couples]." This latter study ran into a special problem. According to Ham (1971: 4) his couples "found it a height of rudeness to be reminded of the fact. It was as if our interviewers cruelly poked a knife into their painful wound. The interviewers often found it difficult to elicit cooperative response from sonless couples." An additional problem was of finding meaningful individual differences for such a widespread and slowly changing value.

Even with these problems, Korean researchers have persisted in trying to understand the reasons and conditions behind boy preference. Kwon and Lee (1975: 11) tried to put boy preference into its proper context:

> This persistently strong son preference can only be explained by the cultural and social system of traditional Korea. Korean society was basically family oriented and the Korean family was established into [a] patriarchal, patrilineal and patrilocal system during the past several hundred years. Strong normative emphasis upon the succession of the family name by male line, dependency on sons in old age and absolute authority of men over women are a few examples of the cultural elements fostering and supporting absolute preference of sons to daughters in traditional Korea. Bearing no son to the family was considered a sin for a couple, and [a] man could desert his wife in such circumstances. . . . In spite of drastic transformation of Korean society, no satisfactory institutions have so far evolved, to take over the major functions of the son in the traditional family.

When specifically asked about the reasons for boy preference, Korean women emphasize the need for support in old age, first, and desire for continuity of the family, second. For men, the order of the reasons is reversed. Other reasons such as the need for sons for ancestor worship or for physical labor are mentioned by few men or women.

Both Ham (1971) and Chung, Cha, and Lee (1974) feel that the desire for emotional security is the primary motive behind wanting sons. Ham cites poignant examples of slights and insults inflicted on sonless men and women: children may call such an adult by a given name (or first name), which is action showing flagrant disrespect in Korea. Workmen may give shoddier service to such a couple, knowing that there is no son to protect the couple's interests. Women probably feel more pain at being sonless than do men, since they are blamed for being barren or producing only daughters and since their main duty in life is often thought to be the production of sons. Chung, Cha, and Lee (1974: 192) mention some of the coping mechanisms used by a sonless woman: "She is attracted to magical or impractical means of obtaining sons; she displaces the responsibility of being sonless away from herself to others; she minimizes the value of a son; she exaggerates the value of a daughter; and she seeks out values in her daughters that are normally reserved for sons." Some of the women in their small sample of sonless wives practiced contraception or had abortions for fear of producing another girl, behaviors which would be opposite to the predictions of most demographers who would probably expect such women to be eager to get pregnant in hopes of having a son.

Indicative of the importance of emotional security, as opposed to financial security as a reason for wanting sons, is the finding of Ham (1971: 7):

Emotional security in this context is much more complex than economic. When our interviewees were given a choice between a well-providing affluent son-in-law who is sincerely willing to support them generously and an indigent son who is not financially able to provide a decent living, they still chose the latter. They were certain that they preferred to live with an impoverished son any time even if the son was not particularly happy to live with them.

At the societal level, many of our original economic hypotheses apply to Korea. Sons are economically more advantageous since daughters leave the family at marriage, daughters often have fewer educational and occupational advantages, and sons tend to support their parents in old age (and are legally entitled to larger shares of inheritance in order to fulfill this responsibility). However, dowries are not as important in Korea as in India. There is some evidence that parents want at least one daughter to help with women's work and because it is seen as "natural" to have one daughter.

Similarly, many of the social hypotheses apply. The Korean family system is patrilocal and patrilineal. A son is needed to continue the family line and to preside over ancestor worship ceremonies. Sons provide some protection against the community and bring respect to the parents. Rural areas are more son preferring in Korea and there the Confucian influence seems to be stronger. This is seen by some Koreans as ironic, since Confucianism began as the religion of the elite.

Psychological aspects of son preference are harder to pin down. We already discussed the significance of sons for emotional security. Women were more concerned about security in old age than were men. On the individual level,

based on the empirical literature, a person having high boy preference is likely
to: have a boy-skewed family, have a larger family, want more children, be
married longer, be female, be from a rural area rather than from Seoul, have
less education, be of lower economic status, be less mastery-oriented and less
individualistic, have more traditional attitudes toward family, social, political,
and economic institutions, perceive less pressure to adopt family planning and
to innovate, perceive more pressure from authority figures, and be less
oriented to modernity. However, we should point out that at the present
time, boy preference attitudes are more difficult to predict in Korea than
fertility ideals or behavior. This may be because less change is occurring in sex
preferences than in family size preferences (Kwon and Lee, 1975). Presumably if the current rate of social change continues in Korea and improve-
ments are made in measurement instruments, prediction will become more
accurate very soon.

In ranking Korea in terms of boy preference, we note that we found no
evidence of serious female neglect or excess mortality among girls in Korea,
based on our reading of the literature and a brief visit there in the summer of
1975. Differential neglect may exist but is probably not a widespread phenomenon. Furthermore, the ideal sex ratios are only moderately high. They do
not go above 200 or 300 as in some Indian states or in North Africa. This is
partly an artifact of the measure since most Koreans want moderately-sized
families (three or four children) and the ideal sex ratios cannot as easily go as
high as where larger families are desired. Thus, assuming that wanting at least
one girl is fairly universal, the ideal sex ratio can go only to 2 to 1 or 3 to 1
for those wanting moderate-sized families but could go to 4 to 1 for those
opting for larger families. Nevertheless, for these reasons, we have given Korea
a rank of "+3" (strong son preference) rather than "+4". We disagree with
Kong and Cha (1974: 2) who asserted: "Boy preference in the Korean
family . . . is undoubtedly one of the strongest in the world." In our view it is
less strong than in parts of India and North Africa.

Overview of Parental Sex Preferences in Latin America, the Middle East, India, and the Far East

We have summarized in Table 6 our impressionistic rankings of parental
sex preferences for the different samples for which comparable data were
found. We have included material from Chapters 4 and 6 as well so the table
will be more complete. This means that the reader will have to wait for
substantiation of the rankings for the daughter-preferring societies (Chapter
4), daughter preference of U.S. adopting parents (Chapter 4), and among
Taiwanese (Chapter 6). The work of Coombs and Freedman (1974) has been
helpful in checking these rankings. The ideal sex ratio data were the most

TABLE 6: Summary of Rank Orderings of Parental Sex Preferences for Societies and Subgroups Discussed in Chapters 2, 3, 4, & 6

"−3" (strong daughter preference)	Mundugumor men (New Guinea) Iscobakebu men (Peru)
"−2" (moderate daughter preference)	Tiwi men (North of Australia) Tolowa Indian men (Northern California)
"−1" (weak daughter preference)	Latin American and Caribbean women Garo men and women (Assam) Adopting parents in the U.S.
"0" (desire for equal numbers of sons and daughters among many and of those having a sex preference, girls are as likely to be desired as are boys)	Indonesian women Israeli women Filipino women (non-Muslim)
"+1" (weak son preference)	Indonesian men U.S. women Ethnic Thai women Northern Europeans
"+2" (moderate son preference)	U.S. men Latin American and Caribbean men Thai men (Chinese and ethnic) Israeli men (factory workers) Urban Lebanese and Egyptian women
"+3" (strong son preference)	Rural Lebanese women Urban Indians Indian Christians Korean men and women, with stronger son preference in rural areas Taiwanese men and women
"+4" (very strong son preference)	Women in rural Egypt, Algeria, and Tunisia Men in the Indian states of Jammu and Kashmir, Kerala, Gujarat, Madhya Pradesh, and Andhra Pradesh Women in Gujarat

useful for making comparisons, even though this is not an ideal measure. The chart reflects the most current information available and ignores historical populations.

In our view, sex preferences can be seen as the outcome of a number of social and economic conditions, none of which seems to be sufficient to explain the phenomenon. Boy preference is often stronger in rural areas than in urban areas, but there are many rural groups which do not prefer sons. The Mundugumor, the Tiwi, and the Tolowa Indians to be discussed in the next chapter are examples. Similarly, rural women in Latin America, the Caribbean, Indonesia, and the Philippines do not prefer sons.

Looking at sex differences, we note that in general women are more likely to prefer girls or prefer boys more weakly than are men. But there are clear exceptions even here. The strongest daughter preference noted in Chapter 4 is found among Mundugumor, Tiwi, Tolowa, and Iscobakebu men. And in several countries such as India and Korea, rural women are more concerned about having sons than men are, perhaps because they fear widowhood. There is a slight tendency in Table 6 for men to be at the extremes in either son preference or daughter preference. Perhaps men are more sensitive to the economic aspects of sons or daughters. Certainly the motives for their strong daughter preferences are economic as will be shown in Chapter 4.

Religion sometimes makes a difference as in the U.S., but other factors may override its influence. Moslem populations tend to be son preferring, but Moslems in Indonesia do not prefer sons and there is little difference in son preference between Moslems and Christians in the Middle East. There urban/ rural differences are stronger.

In some countries, higher education was related to lower son preference, but this did not always hold. In countries like Korea, India, and Taiwan son preference is found in all education groups. We may see an educational differential developing soon in these countries, however. Along the same line, we cannot simply say that the more developed countries do not prefer sons and the less developed countries do. A weak son preference is found in the U.S. and other developed countries, and some less developed countries like Indonesia and the Philippines do not have son preference. The data of Freedman and Coombs illustrate this point. We can say that the variation in sex preferences seems to be greater among the less developed countries.

In general, son preferring societies are patrilineal and patrilocal, whereas the daughter preferring ones are matrilineal and matrilocal (or neolocal). The patrilocal family system puts women at a clear disadvantage since women come into the family situation as strangers. Some of the son preferring societies had strong dowry systems, like India, but some did not, like Korea and Taiwan.

Closely tied with the family system is the social security system. Son preferring groups tend to rely on sons for support in old age, whereas daughter preferring ones consider daughters a source of wealth or source of support. This generalization does seem to be consistent with the data we have.

In addition, women's economic productivity relative to men's is probably important. Although we will present evidence on this only for the daughter preferring societies, at least there women's economic contributions seem crucial to their relatively high status. Unfortunately, we did not systematically collect data on women's productivity for other groups we presented. This, of course, would have been difficult since we were relying on the studies of others who seldom mentioned women's economic productivity.

Thus, in our view sex preferences are created by a convergence of factors at the societal level—the degree of urbanization of the society, the sex roles assigned to men and women including economic roles, the religion, the dowry system, the degree of education of the population and whether the country is highly developed economically (if it is, we would predict only weak son preference; if it is not, we would hesitate to make any predictions), whether the family system is matrilineal or patrilineal and patrilocal, and the nature of the social security system. No single factor is enough to explain this complex phenomenon. Until the data become more comparable, it is even difficult to say which factors are the most important.

Even when both boys and girls are wanted by parents, even in equal numbers, they are wanted for different reasons. The preliminary results from the Value of Children study (Fawcett et al., 1974), which included data from Korea, Taiwan, Japan, Hawaii, the Philippines and Thailand, indicate that girls are wanted for the help they give in the home and for personality characteristics which make them good companions, particularly for the mother. Boys are wanted for continuity of the family name, for economic reasons, and for companionship with the father. Thus, sex preferences are a reflection of sex role definitions common in the society. So the question becomes: What are the origins of sex role definitions?

NOTES

1. A. Aguirre (1966); C.A. Miro and F. Rath (1965); J.V.D. Saunders (1958); J.M. Stycos (1964); J.M. Stycos (1962); J.M. Stycos and K. Back (1964); J.M. Stycos (1968); J.M. Stycos (1971); F.B. Waisanen and J.T. Durlak (1966).

2. Brief mentions of sex preferences appear in these studies: P.M. Kazen and H.L. Browning (undated); U.M. Cowgill and G.E. Hutchinson (1963); and N.F. McGinn (1966). The latter two found boy preference and the former mentions that some Mexican immigrants (into Texas) considered a complete family to have at least two children of each sex so that each child could have a playmate of the same sex. In addition, C.H. Wood (1975) is beginning some research on sex preferences and fertility in Brazil (personal communication).

3. H. Granqvist (1950); H. Ammar (1954); D.F. Beck (1957); R. Levy (1957); D. Kirk (1966); and K.A. Hakim (1967) among others.

4. We will use the term "Far East" even though it could easily be seen as ethnocentric. From the point of view of people living in this area, they are not "far" from any place. It is just from the viewpoint of Americans and Europeans that the area is the "Far East." Yet the term is commonly used and understood and we find it convenient.

5. We are fortunate that there are two good reviews of the boy preference literature (Kong and Cha, 1974; Chung, Cha, and Lee, 1974). This second work is an amazingly rich collection of many studies on boy preference using the historical approach, the case study approach, the anthropological approach, and the survey approach. Samples range from sonless couples to students of all ages to elites. This work is the most outstanding in the sex preference literature and will fortunately soon be available as part of the Rose Monograph Series. Another more modest but very interesting monograph is that of Ham (1971) who studied 192 sonless individuals, using an in-depth interviewing technique.

Chapter 4

DAUGHTER PREFERENCE

So overwhelming is the evidence that parents in many countries would rather have a predominance of boys than girls, that the question arises of whether there exist any daughter-preferring societies or whether there are special circumstances in which daughters are preferred. In this chapter we will describe five daughter-preferring societies[1] in an effort to see what conditions support this deviant preference. Then we will consider sex preferences in adoption in the U.S. and Europe. There is considerable evidence that girls are often preferred for adoption, a curious fact in light of the evidence in Chapter 2 of preferences for first-born boys or a predominance of boys.

Five Daughter-Preferring Societies

Several early sources (Sumner, 1906 and Aptekar, 1931) mentioned briefly the existence of daughter-preferring societies, citing Sumatra, Tahiti, Polynesia, New Guinea, the Zuni, the Pima, and the people of the Banks Islands. But in this analysis, we will focus on the following five societies, which are spread around the globe and are culturally independent: the Mundugumor of New Guinea (Mead, 1935), the Tiwi of North Australia (Hart and Pilling, 1960 and Goodale, 1971), the Garo of Assam (Burling, 1963), the Iscobakebu of Peru (Braun, 1975), and the Tolowa Indians of Northwestern California (Gould, 1966).

In the early thirties, Mead went to New Guinea to study the conditioning of the temperaments of the two sexes. One of the three contrasting societies in New Guinea was the river-dwelling Mundugumor, a cannibalistic group. In this society, Mead found that the behavior of both men and women was actively masculine by Western definitions and without any of the "softening and mellowing characteristics that we are accustomed to believe are inalienably womanly" (Mead, 1950: 162).[2] There are several features of this society which combined to make daughters preferred strongly by the men and less strongly by the women. In the first place, women were economically very productive:

> For the manufactures of the impoverished swamp-dwellers, the Mundugumor trade tobacco, areca-nut, and coconuts, which grow abundantly upon their rich land. This rids them of the necessity of doing any manufacturing themselves and frees the men for head-hunting and theatrical spectacles, and the women for gardening, tobacco-curing, and fishing [Mead, 1950: 168].

> Cheerfully and without overexertion, the strong, well-fed women conduct the work of the tribe. They even climb the coconut-trees—a task from which almost all primitive New Guinea exempts grown women. Upon this basis of women's work, the men can be as active or as lazy, as quarrelsome or as peaceful, as they like [Mead, 1950: 180].

In the second place,

> All property, with the exception of land, which is plentiful and not highly valued, passes down the rope [a form of kinship organization]; even weapons descend from father to daughter. A man and his son do not belong to the same rope, or respect the same totemic bird or animal. A man leaves no property to his son, except a share in the patrilineally descended land; every other valuable goes to his daughter [Mead, 1950: 172].

Thus descent goes through daughters rather than sons. This then is another reason for preferring daughters.

And finally, the marriage system uses women as a medium of exchange: "Every man is supposed to obtain a wife by giving his sister in return for some other man's sister" (Mead, 1950: 174). The result of this system is that men are constantly fighting among themselves for wives. The Mundugumor social organization is based on the notion that members of the same sex (especially men) cannot get along well and that ties between members of the same sex must go through members of the opposite sex.

The upshot of this economic and family system is that daughters are preferred strongly by men and less by women: "Children are used as hostages because if there is treachery between the allies and the hostages are killed, after all it will be only a child, and in most instances a male child—who is less valued than a female child—who pays the penalty" (Mead, 1950: 167-168). Girls are pampered, dressed up with shell ornaments and earrings, and made to feel they are desirable. Boys go around in a naked, unadorned state. Fathers carry around their daughters, but not their sons, to be admired by other men.

Since this is a male-dominated society, the preferences of the fathers for daughters have more social significance than the preferences of mothers for sons. Thus we have called it daughter-preferring. In practice, there is conflict between men and women over whether to save an infant:

> Before the child is born there is much discussion as to whether it shall be saved or not, the argument being partly based upon the sex of the child, the father preferring to keep a girl, the mother a boy. The argument is weighted against the mother, however, because her father and brothers also prefer a girl. Boys in the kin-group lead to trouble if there are not enough girls to purchase wives for them. . . . A girl-child, therefore, has a better chance of survival than a boy; she is an advantage to her father, to her brothers, and also to the entire kin-group on both sides [Mead, 1950: 185].

In the following quotation, Mead suggests that male infanticide is practiced but does not say how common it is: "if a man deserts his wife during her pregnancy, his chances of having a son survive are much higher, for he will not be there to command her to kill it" (Mead, 1950: 185-186).

In short, three conditions are operating in this small society which contribute to daughter preference. Women are the main economic producers, descent passes through daughters, and women are a valuable medium of exchange in the marriage market. Since men are more powerful than women, their strong daughter preferences dominate the weaker son preferences of the women.

The next society, the Tiwi, has a complicated matrilineal system. From accounts by Hart, Pilling, and Goodale, the Tiwi also valued daughters (but not sons) as wealth. They live on two islands off Australia where the food supply is good. The description of their daughter preference applies primarily to the period 1928-1929 although Pilling corroborated many of the details as did Goodale whose research took place in the 1950s and 1960s.

As the editors of the Hart and Pilling (1960) ethnology put it: "This is a case study of a system of influence and power which is based on a strange currency. The currency is women. Newborn females, nubile marriageable females, toothless old hags—all are valuable in Tiwi terms. Because men compete for prestige and influence through their control over women, women have the value of a scarce commodity" (Hart and Pilling, 1960: v).

As the authors put it: "Put bluntly, in Tiwi culture daughters were an asset to their father, and he invested these assets in his own welfare. He therefore bestowed his newly born daughter on a friend or an ally, or on somebody he wanted as a friend or an ally" (Hart and Pilling, 1960: 15). In short, "only by getting wives could he [an ambitious young Tiwi male] have daughters, and only in having daughters could he build alliances and obtain influence, power, and more wives" (Hart and Pilling, 1960: 24).

It was also desirable for a woman to have a daughter: "By giving birth to a girl she [a young Tiwi woman] gains status in the eyes of her son-in-law and her husband. By giving birth to either sex the wife has begun to insure that she and her husband will be looked after in their old age" (Goodale, 1971: 149). As in the Mudugumor, the men of Tiwi society had more reason to prefer daughters than did the women who often had close relationships with their sons. But women without daughters were not held in respect so probably most women acquired a preference for daughters themselves: "Widows without daughters and bachelors without sisters rated very low in the scale of desirable assets sought either by elders or by contemporaries" (Hart and Pilling, 1960: 55).

Thus in traditional Tiwi society, daughters were welcomed and sons were not. The following quotations illustrate some of the attitudes of men toward their sons and toward younger men in general:

[There was a] general hostility of all old men to all young unmarried men that ran through all aspects of Tiwi culture [Hart and Pilling, 1960: 36].

This group [boys below age 20] comprised the male children—boys and youths—and such males were of no importance whatever in the Tiwi scheme of things. They lived in the households of older men and were ignored by the male elders [Hart and Pilling, 1960: 54].

A father bestowed his daughters where he wished and at puberty they joined their husbands. Where his sons found wives was no concern of the father, and hence where they established their households was of no interest to him either. The father would wish, however, that they would establish their households as far away from his as possible since then he would not have to worry about them interfering with his young wives. On the other hand, it was thought to be 'unfatherly' actually to throw sons out [Hart and Pilling, 1960: 32].

Step-sons were liabilities which new husbands had to take over in order to get rights in the real assets—the step-daughters [Hart and Pilling, 1960: 61].

However, there was no evidence presented of male infanticide or neglect of male children among the Tiwi (as there was among the Mundugumor).

Related to being the medium of exchange in the marriage system, women were important economic producers: "If a man had a lot of wives there was no need for him to help his wives in the bush collecting. His many wives could provide him and his nonproducing dependents with a balanced diet of meat and vegetables without his lifting a finger" (Goodale, 1971: 154). As is the case in many hunting and gathering societies, the women's contribution was central: "the women not only could but did provide the major daily supply of a variety of foods to members of their camp. . . . Men's hunting required considerable skill and strength, but the birds, bats, fish, crocodiles, dugongs, and turtles they contributed to the household were luxury items rather than staples" (Goodale, 1971: 169). Hart and Pilling agree with this analysis.

This was a society in which men (particularly, old men) dominated. In general, women were not powerful but were valuable, both as economic producers and as currency in the exchange system.

Tiwi society has recently changed drastically and the description just given is based on the traditional system. Goodale notes that Western culture and influence have reduced the position of women, especially old women, who did acquire some power in the traditional social organization:

In recent years, however, much of the power of older women appears to have been lost. Many of the older women are not being remarried after the death of their latest husband, and they seem to have lost a certain amount of 'face' by remaining widows. The large polygamous families have almost disappeared, and so the relative power among co-wives has also diminished. Husbands are considered by the government and mission to be the boss of the domestic group, and should some woman . . . step in to 'interfere' in a family debate, the officials usually back up the husband's word. It seems rather paradoxical that Western culture, the great 'protector' of women's rights today, has contributed to the loss of many of the Tiwi woman's traditional rights . . . she has lost much of her power to direct the lives of others [Goodale, 1971: 229].

Going on to the third daughter-preferring society, we will examine the system which produces daughter preference among Garo villagers in Assam,

India. Less information is available on the sex preferences of Garo parents compared with the Mundugumor or the Tiwi but what there is, seems to point toward daughter preference. The Garo have a matrilineal system. The following quotation describes the system of inheritance:

> In practice the system works with remarkable smoothness. Enough boys and girls are found to fulfill the requirement of heirship while the others do not feel handicapped by their omission. The first step in arranging a marriage of heirs is the choice by the parents of one of their daughters as heiress. Because they need a girl to perform these duties, Garo parents welcome a daughter more than a son, though if they have many children, they say that they like best to have some of each. However, if a couple should have no daughters, they can adopt a close relative who will come into their home and assume the duties of an actual daughter [Burling, 1963: 78].

Thus, security in old age for Garo parents is assured by choosing (or adopting) a daughter to stay at home and become an heiress and then finding her an appropriate husband. This young couple then gradually takes over the responsibilities of the household and eventually inherits the property and house itself, upon the death of one or both the parents. Daughters who do not stay at home have to find husbands for themselves. These daughters and their new husbands then establish new households. Men always leave their parents' house at marriage, giving up the advantages of familiarity and kin ties which men have in the patrilocal family system.

Women in Garo society are economically productive:

> Much of the daily work is assigned to women. One of their regular jobs is pounding rice, which they must do throughout the year whenever the family supply of husked rice runs low. . . . Women also collect wood for the cooking and heating fires. . . . Fields must be continually cultivated to prevent the weeds from overwhelming the crops and women share this job with the men. All baskets are made by men. . . . Men sometimes fish with round nets, which they throw into the water in the hope of entagling small fish. . . . All men know how to butcher. . . . At a few festivals men prepare the food. . . . Daily cooking is done indoors in smaller pots by the women [from the captions of pictures 13-19, Burling, 1963].

In addition, Garo women do much of the marketing. In short, Garo women perform many of the essential economic tasks. It is clear that the Garo have a highly interdependent division of labor between men and women:

From the time he marries, a man's routine work is entirely centered around the home he shares with his wife ... by the time they have been married for a few years, a man and wife have each become the most important person in the other's life.... If husband and wife meant nothing else to each other, their economic interdependence would keep many of them together. If the work of a household is to be kept up, there must be at least one man and one woman to share it, since many tasks are the exclusive province of one or the other of the sexes. Because their work is complementary, both men and women regard it as catastrophic to be for long without a partner [Burling, 1963: 92].

Thus, among the Garo we have several factors contributing to a mild daughter-preference: the matrilineal family system, the dependence of parents for security in old age on a daughter and her husband, and the economic necessity of women's labor. Unfortunately, we do not have more details about whether daughters are treated better than sons or whether men and women have different preferences.

We have even less information on our fourth group, the Iscobakebu of Peru, a very small native-American population. "Discovered" near the Peru-Brazil border in 1959 by two North American missionaries, the group numbered only twenty-five:

Decimated by incessant raids of enemy groups and trigger-happy Brazilian fortiersmen, the last twenty-five suvivors did not even include any males under the age of ten, for the Iscobakebu had had to resort to male infanticide in order to increase group mobility when flight was necessary. That female babies were spared reflected their importance as 'trade goods' for predatory enemies, and the strong inclination of Iscobakebu men for child brides [Braun, 1975: 8].

Although the evidence is fragmentary, again we come across the pattern of women being wealth (here, for trading and as wives). This was also the case among the Mudugumor and among the Tiwi. It is equally characteristic among the fifth group, the Tolowa Indians of Northwestern California.

Describing Tolowa culture "as it existed during the first few decades after intensive white contract began" in the 1850s, Gould notes, "daughters were greatly desired by a man, for they added to his labor force for a time and could be expected to attract a brideprice" (Gould, 1966: 87). As a matter of fact, "the quest for wealth among the Tolowa hinged primarily on the acquisition and disposal of women" (Gould, 1966: 68). As among the Tiwi, "the more women a man had working for him within his household the more food he could expect to store away for future use" (Gould, 1966: 71). The more food he had, the more treasures (such as shell beads and red-headed woodpecker scalps) he could obtain when others ran out of food. Further-more, the more food he had, the more royally he could entertain others, adding to his own prestige. Hence, the following comment was exchanged among men: "He has lots of daughters, he's going to get rich" (Gould, 1966: 75).

Men could have more than one wife: "The more wives a man could afford to marry (that is, if he had enough wealth to pay the brideprice) the more women he had working for him—not only the wives themselves but their daughters as well" (Gould, 1966: 75). Furthermore, a man not having enough for a brideprice could "exchange an unmarried sister of his for the woman he intended to marry" (Gould, 1966: 77). In order to do this, such a man would have to be the eldest surviving male in the household: "Not many men could meet these rather particular requirements, but when one did the oppor-tunities which this situation offered were readily seized" (Gould, 1966: 77). Finally, a poor man faced with a heavy debt could promise an infant daughter as payment. When she was old enough to work, she joined her husband's household. Thus daughters were valued.

Again, as with the Mundugumor, the Tiwi, and the Garo, the basis of their value in the marriage system seems to be the economic productivity of the women. In Tolowa society there was a clear division of labor by sex:

> While the men engaged in the strenuous food-getting activities, it was the women who bore the brunt of the tedious, day-to-day labor of preparing and storing away the food. These tasks did not require much vigorous activity, but they did require constant attention. . . . Catching and collecting those foods were relatively easy, but preparing them for storage was a constant and tedious task—a task performed only by women" [Gould, 1966: 70-71].

Based on Gould's description, Tolowa males were more powerful than females. Men acquired women to gain wealth for themselves. We do not know whether the women also preferred daughters—certainly the men did. Nor do we know if boys and girls were treated differently. Furthermore, the evidence we have is based mostly on the memories of elderly Tolowa, artifacts, a few remaining practices and newspaper articles, since Tolowa culture changed greatly after contact with whites.

Daughters in these five societies were valued for among the following reasons: they were wealth; they were hard workers; they supported their parents when they were old; they carried on the family line; they brought the parents a brideprice; they could be exchanged for other valued goods; and they reproduced more daughters. Some of these are similar to the reasons sons are preferred in other cultures, particularly those reasons related to economic productivity, lineage and support for parents. But the other reasons such as use of women as a medium of exchange and as reproducers of more daughters are unique to women.

If we try to classify the strength of daughter preference among these five societies, we should point out that in the three for which we have more information (the Mundugumor, the Tiwi, and the Tolowa), there was reason to believe that men had stronger daughter preference than women. The strongest daughter preference was among the Mundugumor men, who might rate "-3" (strong daughter preference) in our scheme. Male infanticide was practiced by the Mundugumor and young boys and girls received markedly different treatment. The Iscobakebu of Peru also were reported as practicing male infanticide, so perhaps that group ought to be in the same category. On the other hand, the Tiwi men and the Tolowa men seemed similar in their degree of daughter preference (and in the motivations behind it). Because there was no evidence of male infanticide or differential treatment of girls and boys, perhaps a rating of "-2" might apply better. The Garo probably had less strong preference than the other groups and might rate a "-1" (weak daughter preference). It is harder to classify the women in these societies because we have less information for them. No difference between women's and men's preferences were noted among the Iscobakebu or among the Garo. Tiwi women were probably weakly daughter preferring ("-1"). Mundugumor women preferred sons, and we have no information for Tolowa women.

These five societies serve the purpose of showing that the common patrilineal and patrilocal system and the widespread desires for sons are not universal as many people assume. However, even in these daughter-preferring societies, women are not dominant. The work done by men is considered more honorific and men hold relatively more power in religious and political activities. Yet, for girls it is probably much more advantageous to be "valued goods" than "lost goods" as in patriarchal cultures like traditional China.

Daughter Preference in Adoption

Although this is not universally true, there tends to be a preference for daughters when parents are adopting children, especially when the child is from a completely different family. When the adoption is from one's own kinship group, boys seem to be preferred particularly if the goal is to obtain an heir to continue the family line. Here we will present evidence mainly from the United States that girls are preferred in extra-familial adoptions. We will then speculate as to possible reasons for this preference, citing evidence that girls adapt more successfully to adopted families than do boys.

The study with the earliest data is apparently Leahy (1933). This researcher notes that in Minnesota during the 1920s about 84 males were adopted for every 100 females. Pointing out that the sex ratio of illegitimate children during this period was 104, the conclusion is drawn that there is "a preference on the part of adoptive parents for girls" (Leahy, 1933: 557). This evidence is not very conclusive, however, since the researcher did not know for sure that the sex ratio of children up for adoption is 104.

Another study (Jaffee and Fanshel, 1970) had a different problem: it had only retrospective sex preferences from adoptive parents. However, as with the previous study, it suggests girl preference. One hundred families who adopted children under three during 1931-1940 through four social agencies in New York City were interviewed twenty to thirty years later. When asked about what sex preferences they had had when they adopted, 21% of the couples reported having preferred a boy, 31% a girl, 28% no preference, and 14% reported conflict between husband and wife. This study noted that Catholic Home Bureau adopters were more prone to specify a preference for girls. Furthermore, those wanting girls had stronger preferences than those wanting boys. Finally, the researchers noted that childless families were more likely to want a boy and those with children already were more likely to want a girl.

Another small study was that of Brenner (1951) who reported on 50 Jewish families who adopted between 1941-1945. Of these families, 39 expressed a sex preference at the time of first application. Of those who had a preference, 72% wanted a girl. A higher percentage of families wanting a girl, 85%, was reported by Michaels (1963) although no information was given on his sample. A third study also found evidence of daughter preference. Lawder et al. (1969) did a follow-up study of 200 adoptive couples who adopted 250 children from the Children's Aid Society of Pennsylvania between 1950 and 1957. Sex preferences of the mothers were: 46% no preference, 19% boy, 34% girl, and 1% no information. Comparable percentages for the fathers were: 48% no preference, 23% boy, 28% girl, and 2% no information. In each case, there were more preferences for girls than boys but the effect was stronger for women.

Up to now our studies included only white couples. A small sample (n=51) of black couples studied by Woods and Lancaster (1962) found the same results. Again, there were more people wanting a girl: 40% a girl, 14% a boy, 14% no preference, and 25% no information. The authors of this study speculated that girl babies were preferred because of the traditionally favored position of women among blacks.

The most convincing data for the U.S. was reported by Lockridge in 1947. Analyzing 20,994 requests for children to adopt, spanning the records of the State Charities Aid Association's Child Adoptions for nearly fifty years of adoption, Lockridge reported the following: There were 11,665 requests for girls, 6,383 requests for boys, 2,599 requests for either, 314 requests for both, and 33 requests for which information was not obtained. The number of children placed was quite different: 3,230 girls and 3,306 boys were actually placed.

There is only one contradictory study which is discussed in Kirk (1964a). Researchers at McGill University studied adoptive parents in Ohio, Ontario, and Quebec in 1956. Looking at 670 childless couples who expressed a sex preference at the first application, 46% asked for a girl and the rest a boy. This anomalous finding might be explained by the fact that these were childless couples (who tend to prefer boys according to Jaffee and Fanshel, 1970), or the fact that many of these couples adopted two children and wanted one of each. Furthermore, as Kirk notes, the percentage of those wanting a girl is still considerably higher than sex preference studies not involving adoption have found. Such studies are summarized in Chapter 2. Thus, Kirk still takes this study as indicating a remarkable degree of girl preference.

Before speculating about the causes of the daughter preference in adoption, we might just note that one study in Germany (Gordon, 1930) and one in England (Kornitzer, 1968) also found evidence of girl preference in adoption. Kornitzer observes that there is such a scarcity of children to adopt in England that potential adoptive parents are taking whatever they can get. Because of publicity about the higher demand for girls for adoption, more clients are expressing preference for boys or no preference in hopes of getting a child more quickly (or at all). The same phenomenon may be true in the U.S. Certainly the knowledge is widespread in the U.S. that it is difficult to adopt these days. Whether American parents are aware that girls are in greater demand we cannot say.

The only sociologist to speculate at length about why girls tend to be preferred for adoption is Kirk (1964a). He gives a brief summary of the explanations found in the adoption literature. (1) It is less difficult to bring up a girl than a boy. (2) A girl is seen as a symbol of affection. From a "cuddly" little girl she becomes "companionable" as she grows up, and throughout life, even though married, stays closer to her parents than does a son. (3) A daughter costs less to raise. (4) A daughter is more of a help in the parental household. (5) The wife usually suffers most by the childlessness and her normal preference is for a girl. (6) People who fear that taking a child born to others is risky find it easier to take a girl for adoption than a boy.

Kirk eliminates the first four reasons with the following logic: these explanations would be as true for biological parents as for adoptive parents and it is known that biological parents want boys more frequently than girls.

Hence, these explanations cannot explain the unique girl preference of adoptive parents. As regards the fifth explanation, as we showed in Chapter 2, women are more likely to prefer girls than are men, even though the majority of women (especially those without children) still prefer boys. So *some* of the girl preference may be a deferment to the wife's preference. There is evidence (Kirk, 1964a) that childless wives report more distress than childless husbands.

The last hypothesis is also plausible. In American society, girls are often thought to be more obedient, neater, quieter, less disruptive, and less aggressive than boys. When bringing in a child from an unknown family, parents might feel that a girl would adjust better to family and school. Indeed, several studies show that girls adapt to adoption better than boys. Both Green and Godfrey (1963) and Ketchum (1962) found that more adopted boys than adopted girls had problems which brought them to the attention of health clinics. The same was found in a British study (Addis et al., 1954). A more sophisticated study was that of Hoopes et al. (1969). One hundred adopted children were followed up. According to the authors:

> Prior research has indicated that girls show certain early developmental advantages over boys in terms of social adjustment. These observations were born out in this study. Contingency coefficients showing the significant relationship between girls and higher scores and ratings occurred in the following areas of child functioning: (1) social adjustment (c=.33), (2) total adjustment (c=.25) on the California Test of Personality, (3) school work in relation to class (c=.23), (4) school work in relation to own ability (c=.30) and (5) attitude toward own school work (c=.24). Thus, prior findings of better social and school functioning by girls as compared with boys were confirmed [Hoopes et al., 1969: 72-73].

Perhaps a more conclusive study was that of Kadushin and Seidl (1971). These researchers examined placements which did not result in legal adoption between 1960 and 1967. Such adoptions were labelled failures. Of 2,945 children who were placed in their sample, only 2.8% were returned to the agencies. Boys were overrepresented among the placement failures: 62% were boys and 38% girls. However, because of the very small number of such children, these results did not achieve statistical significance. The authors' explanation of their results was that boys are generally more problematic than girls and impose a greater adjustive burden on adoptive parents. The authors did note, however, that research in England had come up with the opposite results (i.e., girls were more likely to be returned), and perhaps they were only describing an American phenomenon.

So, in short, there is some evidence that girls make a better adjustment to adoption. Perhaps parents are aware of this possibility. Even if they are not, common sex role notions might lead parents to believe girls would be more adaptable.

Another explanation developed by Kirk (1964a) is that adoptive parents, especially husbands, are not enthusiastic about incorporating a nonrelative into the family line. Since girls in American society usually change their names at marriage, this problem does not come up with girls. Kirk speculates that people from more socially cohesive groups, such as Catholics and Jews, will be more likely to want girls for adoption. Kirk cites some evidence for this (1964a). According to Kirk, a man from such a social group is in a bind. He is socially pressured to have a biological male offspring. If he and his wife cannot have children, he cannot fulfill people's expectations (including his own). If his wife pressures him to adopt, and there is evidence that men are more reluctant to adopt than women, they may compromise on adopting a girl. Then the couple can enjoy the pleasures of childrearing but will not have an outsider carrying on the family line and name.

Although we did not cite any research on adoption of Oriental children by Americans, additional factors may be at work here, particularly related to the physical appearance of the children. There seems to be a notion among many Americans that Oriental women are beautiful but at the same time compliant. This idea might make girls preferred for adoption. Also some adoptive parents may reason that it is likely that an Oriental child will be shorter than an average American child. It is certainly easier to be a short girl than a short boy in American society. Finally, some people might believe that an Oriental girl would have an easier time marrying in the U.S. A couple which is thinking of the future might prefer a girl for these reasons.

In this chapter, we have presented data from five girl-preferring societies and from several studies on adoption. In both cases, we sought to discover the conditions under which the near-universal preferences for boys are violated.

NOTES

1. We are grateful for Colin Loftin (Brown University) for calling the Garo to our attention, Betsy Gould (East-West Population Institute) for alerting us to the Iscoba-kebu, and to Richard Gould (University of Hawaii) for introducing us to the Tolowa Indians.

2. The references from Mead (1935) are from the 1950 edition which was reprinted many times up to 1963. In 1963 a new edition came out.

Chapter 5

THE TAIWAN STUDY: DATA AND METHODOLOGY

In this chapter and the next we present some of our own material on parental sex preference. The data for this Taiwan study come from a large fertility survey done during 1969-1971 in two townships, Hsinchuang and Kungliao. In Hsinchuang, all the ever-married women who lived in the more rural *li* (sections of the township) were to be interviewed. In one-fifth of the households currently married males, if present, were to be interviewed. A total of 5,000 residents of Hsinchuang were actually interviewed, 4,137 of whom were women and 863 were men. In Kungliao, a more rural township, all of the ever-married women and a one-fifth sample of their husbands were to be interviewed. In the end, 2,677 women and 501 men were actually interviewed successfully in Kungliao. This makes a total of 8,178 respondents from both townships.

One year later, 6,685 of these same respondents were interviewed again with a shorter interview form. For questions asked on both interviews, it is possible to compute reliabilities. This has rarely been possible in family planning surveys. Some of the reliabilities will be presented in this chapter.

The study was contracted by the Agency for International Development (A.I.D.). The principal investigator was Dr. David M. Heer of the Harvard School of Public Health. The director of the field work was Dr. Hsin-ying Wu of the Institute of Public Health, College of Medicine, National Taiwan University.

The interviewing took place during 1969-1970 for the first interview and 1970-1971 for the reinterview. The interviewers were mostly high school graduates from the areas being studied. Interviews were done in the local dialect of Chinese. Dr. Wu and his staff trained the interviewers.

The questionnaire was drawn up in Boston during the summer of 1968. John B. Williamson, Tilly Teixeria, David M. Heer, and myself wrote and revised the questionnaire on the basis of interviews done in Boston with low-income respondents. The next pretest was done in McCreary County, Kentucky by John B. Williamson, Dr. Heer, and myself. I interviewed sixty very poor women in the area and John B. Williamson and David Heer interviewed forty-eight of their husbands. In the fall of 1968, we analyzed the pretest and revised the questionnaire again. In the summer of 1969, the questionnaire was translated into Chinese by Perry Link, a Harvard graduate student, and another pretest was done. This pretest was in Shuingkeng, an area south and east of Taipei City. One hundred and thirty persons were interviewed.

In the choice of the two areas for the study, several considerations were kept in mind. There had to be competent interviewers in the area who could speak the local dialect. There had to be enough people in the areas to add up to the approximately 8,000 we wanted in the final sample. And, most importantly, one area had to be relatively low in infant and child mortality while the other had to be relatively high. This was because the major focus of this study was on perceptions and experience of infant and child mortality by parents and their possible effects on fertility attitudes and behavior. In addition, the areas had to be accessible from Taipei and the local Health Department had to be cooperative. Both areas had to be rural to increase the comparability. And finally, the area where the pretest had been run was eliminated. The first choice and one finally selected for the high mortality area was Kungliao, a township about forty-five kilometers to the east of Taipei, on the railroad from Taipei to the east coast city of Ilan. The first choice for the low mortality area was Wu-ku. Since the interviewers recruited from this area were not sufficiently competent, a decision was made to use the urban township immediately to the south of Wu-ku which was Hsinchuang. This township is only ten kilometers from Taipei, with frequent buses to Taipei. Since there were too many ever-married women in Hsinchuang who qualified for our sample and since Hsinchuang was quite urban, only the most rural areas of Hsinchuang were selected.

Each township might be described briefly. Hsinchuang is a rapidly growing area, almost a suburb of Taipei. Its roads are crowded with cars, trucks, jeeps, buses, ox carts, motorcycles, and bicycles. It is the home of Fu-jen University, a modern Catholic institution. Economically, it is becoming increasingly industrialized. There are car assembly plants, clothing factories, lumber mills, a 7-Up plant, small chemical plants, a soap factory, and other small businesses in the urban area of the township. The rural parts of Hsinchuang have rice farms and vegetable gardens. The area does some truck farming for Taipei City. In the hilly regions, there is some lumbering.

In contrast, Kungliao is a very lush, hilly area with bad roads and beautiful scenery. The hills are terraced with rice paddies. Part of the township is on the East China Sea and many of the men are fishermen. There are few businesses other than farming and fishing and only a modest tourist trade. In addition, there is some coal mined in Kungliao.

There are many differences between the two areas. Here we will list only a few. At the time of the study, the total fertility rate in Hsinchuang was around 4,400 per 1,000 females. In Kungliao, it was around 6,000. The crude birth rate was currently about the same in the two areas but the age distribution in Hsinchuang was more favorable to fertility. Hsinchuang was an area with rapid in-migration; Kungliao was not. From 1964 to 1969, the population of Hsinchuang rose 47.1% whereas it rose only 7.1% in Kungliao. The health services in Kungliao were inadequate compared to Hsinchuang. In general, Kungliao was a poorer area than Hsinchuang. Both the lack of health services and the poverty (and perhaps the higher fertility) are reflected in the higher infant and child death rates in Kungliao. The death rates for infants and children were on the average twice as high in Kungliao as in Hsinchuang. Both areas had family planning programs but the one in Hsinchuang was more successful in terms of new loop and pill acceptors. But both areas have experienced declines in fertility in recent years.

As one might expect, there are fewer illiterates in Hsinchuang than Kungliao and more women employed in nonagricultural activities. In short, although the intention was to select two townships similar except for mortality, this was not possible and there are other systematic differences between the two townships. The differences between our two *samples* are less however, since the more urban and more modern areas of Hsinchuang were eliminated from the survey. Descriptive data on the samples appear in Table 7.

Returning to a discussion of the data, the response rates for the surveys in the two townships were only moderately good. About 78% of the interviews of eligible women were completed and a lower percentage of the interviews of eligible men. It was not possible to compute the percentage of eligible men who were successfully interviewed because of the sampling procedure. The interview of women took about fifty minutes while the shorter form for men took about thirty-five minutes to administer. The female questionnaire dealt with marital and pregnancy history, perceptions of child survival, family size attitudes, background variables, son preference attitudes, attitudes about support in old age, and family planning attitudes and practice. The husbands'

TABLE 7: Descriptive Information on Taiwanese Respondents

	Sex	Kungliao	Hsinchuang
1. Respondent's age	F	41 yrs.	37 yrs.
	M	45 yrs.	38 yrs.
2. Age at first marriage	F	18 yrs.	20 yrs.
	M	24 yrs.	25 yrs.
3. Total number of years married	F	21 yrs.	15 yrs.
	M	21 yrs.	13 yrs.
4. Number of persons eating at the respondent's house	F	8	7
	M	8	7
5. Number of breadwinners in the family	F	1.7	1.8
	M	1.7	1.7
6. Number of persons per breadwinner in the family	F	5.2	4.5
	M	5.3	4.6
7. Number of live births	F	5.2	4.0
8. Number of pregnancies	F	5.6	4.4
9. Number of additional children expected	F	.6	.7
	M	.1	.7
10. Number of children currently living with respondent	F	3.5	3.0
11. Number of years of schooling of respondent	F	1.5 yrs.	4.2 yrs.
	M	3.6 yrs.	7.4 yrs.
12. Number of fen of land owned by family	F	1.4 fen	1.7 fen
	M	2.5 fen	1.6 fen
13. Number of modern objects owned out of a maximum of 14	F	4.5	8.6
	M	5.3	9.1
14. Number of rooms in respondent's house	F	4.5	4.4
	M	4.5	4.3
15. Husband's income (in units of 100 New Taiwan dollars with 40 NT dollars to every U.S. dollar	F	$137	$286
	M	$148	$373

questionnaire dealt with the same topics, excluding the pregnancy history questions and with the addition of a few questions on the dowry system. One year later, 81.7% of the original respondents were reinterviewed. The reinterview response rates were slightly better for men than women.

The cost of the pretests in the United States and Taiwan was about $60,000, while the cost of the final surveys and analysis was about $120,000. This money paid for about 15,000 interviews in all plus coding, keypunching, and computer costs.

A more detailed report on the procedures for this study appears in the final report to A.I.D. written by the project director, David M. Heer and submitted to A.I.D. on August 31, 1972.

The main dependent variables to be used in the analysis appear below. Most of our analysis will include only the first interview. Some variables are available for men only, some for women only. Unless otherwise specified, they are available for both men and women. The questionnaires for the two townships were identical.

Dependent Variables.

(1) *Proportion of Sons Among All Children Advised for a Daughter/Son.* This is a scale made up from two questions. The first was: "If you had a daughter/son who was going to get married soon and she/he asked you how many children it would be good to have altogether, what, in your opinion, would be the best number of *girls?*" The second question asked about the best number of *boys.* Male respondents were asked about a hypothetical son; female respondents were asked about a hypothetical daughter. A ratio of the number of sons advised to the sum of sons and daughters advised was created.

(2) *Proportion of Sons Desired if Life Could Be Lived Over Again.* This scale was similar to the one above except that the question was about how many children the respondent would like to have if life could be lived over. Again, a ratio was created of the number of sons desired to the sum of sons and daughters desired.

(3) *Son Preference Based on Response to Pictured Five-Child Family.* This item was based on the respondents' reactions to two pictured families. A respondent was assigned a *zero* if she/he recommended the family pictured go on for another child if the family had one boy and four girls but not if the family had one girl and four boys. This combination of choices was taken as an indication of son preference. The respondent was assigned a *one* if the responses were the same to the two pictures. In other words, the respondent either recommended that the family have another child in both cases or in neither case. The respondent was assigned a *two* if she/he recommends not going on if the family pictured had one boy and four girls but going on if one girl and four boys. This was taken as an indication of daughter preference. This single item was chosen to be a separate dependent variable because it was thought that this five-child family would solicit few responses of "go on for more children" for both pictures. A family of five children is larger than the ideal of most of the Taiwan respondents. The goal was to eliminate pro-high-fertility respondents from the middle category of the scale. Such respondents tend to confuse the meaning of the scale.

(4) *Five-item Son Preference Scale.* This scale included four other items besides the one above. All of the first four were similar. They were based on different-sized pictured families. A score of *zero* was given if there was son preference shown by the pattern of response; a score of *two* was given if there was evidence of daughter preference; and a score of *one* was given when there was any other response (such as recommending the families have more children regardless of sex or that the families stop having children regardless of sex). The fifth item was based on the question: "If a couple already had one daughter and one son and wanted three more children, how many of these three children would you want to be boys and how many girls?" (The interviewer then checked the number of boys desired.) A respondent who specified three boys was assigned a *zero;* a respondent specifying two boys was assigned a *one;* and a respondent specifying one boy, no boys, or "it doesn't matter," was assigned a *two.* These five items were summed in such a way that respondents with N.A.'s were not penalized in their total score. The final scale was a percentage of the total possible score achieved, ranging from 0 to 100%.

VALIDITY AND RELIABILITY OF THE DATA

Several measures were taken in this study to increase the validity of the responses. The training and supervising of interviewers was carefully done. Outside checks on the interviewing regularly took place. Other quality control measures came in later with the coding, keypunching, and cleaning of the data. Nevertheless, numerous errors may have accumulated.

One unknown is whether the nonresponders differ systematically from the responders. As was mentioned earlier, response rates were only moderately good (about 77% for eligible women and a lower percentage for eligible men in the first interview). This is considerably lower than the 97% response rates in the Taichung studies. One explanation for this lower response rate is that a greater age range was covered. All ever-married women were eligible so some of these were quite elderly. In the Taichung study only women twenty to thirty-nine were interviewed. Furthermore, when all the adult women in a township are eligible, rumors about the interview spread and people can prepare their excuse for why they do not want to be interviewed. (Incidentally, there may be some lack of independence in this sample as people talked among themselves about the questionnaire and how they answered. We have no idea how much this occurred but it is reasonable to expect that some discussion went on.) And finally, interviewing had to be done during the day because of the bad roads and inaccessibility of the homes of respondents. This made it difficult to find men at home.

Probably some of the nonresponders from Kungliao, at least, were men who were in the cities. In Hsinchuang on the other hand, where women have a greater opportunity to work outside the home, we probably missed some working women. We know that over 100 men were interviewed in Hsinchuang whose wives were not interviewed. These men had unusually modern attitudes about fertility. Presumably their wives had outside jobs. Whether, in general, more traditional people tended to have higher refusal rates we do not know.

In this analysis, we have not made inferences beyond our samples. However, because there have been many other studies in Taiwan, it is often possible to compare our results with those of other researchers as we will do in the next chapter.

As to the reliability of the data, we present in Table 8 information on this. About 82% of the respondents were interviewed a year later, using many of the questions in the first interview. Respondents were asked at the second interview about events which had occurred since the first interview. For example, in the first interview, women were asked how many times they had been pregnant. In the second interview, women were asked whether they had been pregnant since the first interview and altogether how many times they had been pregnant. By subtracting any pregnancies during the intervening year from this second interview total, we should have exactly the same number as in the first interview. For variables measured on an interval scale, the first and second interview responses were correlated with the Pearson product-moment correlation coefficients. For ordinal or nominal variables, contingency tables were used. In general it is clear that the behavioral information, especially on family size, has higher reliability than the attitudinal information. Most of the items in our analysis are attitudinal as opposed to demographic so we know that this limits the strength of the relationships we can hope to find.

We have information on how reliable two of our dependent variables are. The reliabilities from the first interview to the second, for those persons who could be located for both interviews, can be expressed as correlations as we have done in Table 8.

These reliabilities are not strong for the items making up these two dependent variables. However, this is partly because at least a year intervened between the first and second interview. Some of the difference may be due to attitude change during the one year period. The second dependent variable tends to be a little more reliable than the first. This may be because it tends to elicit more of a rationalization for the number of children the person already has, which would have remained approximately the same during the year.

The third and fourth dependent variables can also be examined for reliability by looking at contingency tables. The reliabilities for one question making up the third dependent variable (Son Preference Based on Response

TABLE 8: Correlations Between Responses on the First and Second Interviews for Items Making Up Two of the Different Variables on Son Preference for the Taiwan Data

Dependent Variable	Correlation Coefficients
1. Proportion of Sons Among All Children Advised for a Daughter/Son:	
a) Number of Children Advised	.52
b) Number of Girls Advised	.45
c) Number of Boys Advised	.46
2. Proportion of Sons Desired if Life Could Be Lived Over	
a) Number of Children Desired	.55
b) Number of Girls Desired	.48
c) Number of Boys Desired	.50

TABLE 9: Cross-Tabulation of Responses on the First and Second Interviews for the First Item Making Up the Third Dependent Variable on Son Preference for the Taiwan Data. Question: Should This Family (with 4 Girls and 1 Boy) Have Another Child?

SECOND INTERVIEW

First Interview	No, Should Not Have Another	Uncertain, Depends	Yes, Should Have Another	N.A.	Total
No, Should Not Have Another	3,338 (81.0%)	77 (1.9%)	694 (16.8%)	10 (.2%)	4,120 (99.9%)
Uncertain, Depends	87 (64.4%)	11 (8.1%)	36 (26.7%)	1 (.7%)	135 (99.9%)
Yes, Should Have Another	1,141 (52.4%)	40 (1.8%)	990 (45.5%)	6 (.3%)	2,177 (100.0%)
N.A.	5 (55.6%)	0 (0.0%)	4 (44.4%)	0 (0.0%)	9 (100.0%)
Total	4,571 (71.0%)	128 (2.0%)	1,724 (26.8%)	17 (.3%)	6,441 (100.1%)

to Pictured Five-Child Family) appear in Table 9. Similar results were found for another item appearing in the fourth dependent variable (Five-item Son Preference Scale). We do not have the reliabilities over the one year period for the other items in the fourth dependent variable since not all the questions were asked a second time. Nevertheless, Table 9 can be considered illustrative.

Several things should be noted about Table 9. First, the category with the most responses both times is the one, "No, Should Not Have Another." A category which is at an extreme and which has a large number of respondents in it is bound to be reliable. Eighty-one percent of those giving this response the first time, stick to it on the second interview. The comparable percentages for the second and third categories are 8% and 46%. The intermediate category, "Uncertain, Depends" has few people both times and respondents can move to two other categories, one on either side. Second, there is a general tendency for more people to say "No, Should Not Have Another" on the second interview than on the first interview. Sixty-four percent gave this response on the first interview while 71% gave it on the second interview. On a number of the questions, there is a tendency for respondents to move in the more "modern" direction on the second interview. This may be due to social change during the intervening year, to a greater sensitivity on the part of the respondents as to what the interviewer wants, or to discussions among respondents after the first interview during which some respondents became aware of the more "up-to-date" responses. We cannot distinguish among these three possibilities on the attitude questions.

Because it is too cumbersome to include the complete cross-tab to indicate reliabilities for all of the twelve independent variables used in the analysis, several summarizing measures will be given for each independent variable for which reliability information is available. We will give the percent of persons who responded identically the two times, the percent of people who answered identically for the category with the fewest responses, the number of categories and the sample size. The fewer the categories, the higher the reliability since there are fewer categories to move to the second time. Similarly, if there is one category that has most of the cases (say, 80% or so), then this operates to effectively reduce the number of viable categories, hence increasing the reliability. Giving the percentage of people remaining in the smallest category possibly overestimates the degree of unreliability, since it is the most unreliable category. In Table 10, the reliabilities for the twelve independent variables are presented.

A word about significance tests: Since we do not have a probability sample, strictly speaking we should not use significance tests which are a way of estimating whether the results found could be due to sampling error. Furthermore, with samples as large as ours, the differences are very often "statistically significant." Thus, we have not presented significance tests in Chapter 6.

In the next chapter, we will describe the sex preferences of our Taiwanese respondents, discuss briefly effects on fertility, review our unsuccessful attempt to predict the four measures of sex preference, using many independent variables including the twelve in Table 10, and pursue the reasons behind sex preference in Taiwan, using both quantitative and qualitative data.

TABLE 10: Test/Retest Reliability Information for the Twelve Independent Variables Used in the Taiwan Analysis

Independent Variables	N	% of Persons Who Responded Identically Both Times	% of Persons Who Responded Identically Both Times for Smallest Categ.	No. of Categ.
1. Expectation of Support from Children in Old Age	N.A.	N.A.	N.A.	N.A.
2. Respondent's Education	6,440	86.5%	30.6%	8
3. Urban Experience	N.A.	N.A.	N.A.	N.A.
4. Extent of Mass Media Exposure. Only Newspaper Readership available.	6,431	79.3%	22.4%	4
5. Importance of Sons for Security in Old Age. Items Available: a) Whether R. intends to rely on sons in old age	4,445	89.7%	63.6%	2
b) Most important source of support in old age	4,472	67.5%	4.8%	8
c) Number of sons necessary for support in old age	6,038	43.7%	0.0%	8
6. Importance of Male Heir	N.A.	N.A.	N.A.	N.A.

TABLE 10: (continued)

Independent Variables	N	% of Persons Who Responded Identically Both Times	% of Persons Who Responded Identically Both Times for Smallest Categ.	No. of Categ.
7. Modern Objects Owned	N.A.	N.A.	N.A.	N.A.
8. Township	N.A.	N.A.	N.A.	N.A.
9. Occupation of Husband. Only available for 8 categories of occupation which are not exactly the same as our scale.	5,776	82.6%	41.2%	8
10. Wife's Labor Force Status. Item available: Female employment history (i.e., whether wife has ever had an outside job)	5,324	82.1%	72.1%	3
11. Husband's Income	N.A.	N.A.	N.A.	N.A.
12. Number of Living Daughters of Wife*	N.A.	N.A.	N.A.	N.A.

*We do not have information for "number of living daughters" but we do know that the correlation between number of live births reported in the two interviews is .97 based on 3,785 female respondents who answered the live birth questions on both interviews. Presumably, the reliability of the "number of living daughters" would be similar.

Chapter 6

AN ANALYSIS OF SEX PREFERENCES
OF TAIWANESE PARENTS

Taiwan has been a laboratory for students of modernization, especially demographers. In this chapter we investigate sex preferences of Taiwanese parents, presenting data from a large study which made a special effort to understand the bases of son preference. For example, we tried to answer the question of whether expensive weddings for daughters are part of the reason behind son preference and collected information from men who had had a son or daughter married recently. Although it is difficult to say which factors are the most important reasons for the persistence of son preference, at least we will be able to eliminate insignificant reasons for son preference.

Evidence of Son Preference: Attitude Data

Only in the last few years has serious attention been given to problems of measuring sex preference (Williamson, 1974; Westoff and Rindfuss, 1974; Coombs et al., 1975). In our study we experimented with several new ways of measuring sex preference. One set of questions used pictures with different size and sex compositions and asked the respondent if such families should go on for more children. The other set asked the respondent how many children she (or he) would recommend to a daughter (or son). Women were asked about a daughter; men were asked about a son. Then hypothetical situations were proposed such as a death of one of the sons, and the respondent was asked if she (he) would want to revise upward the original recommendation. If a revision was made for a son who died but not a daughter, son preference was inferred. We also included measures used in other studies such as the ideal number of boys and girls the respondent would have if life could be lived over again. No matter which measures we used, son preference was striking.

Starting with the simpler measures, the mean number of boys and girls desired if life could be lived over were:

| | Sex of Resp. | Township | | | |
		Kungliao		Hsinchuang	
Ideal number of *sons*	F	2.5	(2.5)	2.2	(2.2)
if life could be lived over	M	2.4	(2.4)	2.0	(2.1)
Ideal number of *daughters*	F	2.1	(2.0)	1.6	(1.6)
if life could be lived over	M	2.0	(2.0)	1.6	(1.5)

In parentheses we have given the ideals recommended to a daughter (or son). It is clear that these two questions give the same results. The differences between townships are greater than the sex differences, with the higher ideals being found in Kungliao, the more isolated, poorer township. In order to make comparisons with previous data, we also present the ideal sex ratios for these two questions:

| | Sex of Resp. | Township | | | |
		Kungliao		Hsinchuang	
Ideal ratio of sons to	F	122	(123)	136	(135)
daughters if life could	M	121	(120)	131	(136)
be lived over					

The ideal sex ratios (120-136) are above the biological one but are far below those found in India and North Africa. The interesting result here is that the ideal sex ratios are higher in Hsinchuang than in Kungliao. This is an unexpected finding. If son preference is seen as part of a traditional orientation, as we found in Korea, then Kungliao residents who are less educated, less connected to the media, and poorer, ought to have higher ideal sex ratios. Although we do not have longitudinal data, what may be happening is that Hsinchuang residents have reduced their ideal family sizes by reducing the ideal number of daughters more than the ideal number of sons. A family planning evaluator who noted the lower ideal family sizes in Hsinchuang might interpret this as a sign of progress. However, if Hsinchuang respondents are serious about wanting two or more sons, then it matters little that they want fewer daughters. As Keyfitz (1971, 1972) and others have shown, stopping after having at least two boys cannot change the population sex ratio without sex control. Such families will get slightly less than four children on the average. Hence, Hsinchuang residents may not end up with much smaller family sizes if they act on their son ideals.

Another interpretation of this result is that Hsinchuang respondents are less fatalistic and hence more willing to express a preference which is contrary to "nature," which brings sons and daughters in nearly equal numbers. Kungliao respondents may not want the additional girls but may just assume that they are inevitable.

Whatever the explanation of this result, it is certainly worth further investigation. It suggests (but does not prove) that the process of change in ideal family size may be initially at the expense of daughters.

We can compare our ideal sex ratios with those of Sun (1968) and Freedman and Takeshita (1969) in their studies from the 1960s. They both found that women wanted 3.8 children with 2.2 boys and 1.6 girls with an ideal sex ratio of 138. Finnigan and Sun (1972) cited data from a 1970 Taiwan-wide survey where women wanted 3.9 children with 2.3 sons and 1.6 daughters with an ideal sex ratio of 144.

These ideal sex ratios, which are a little higher than ours, have apparently been quite constant in Taiwan until very recently. According to Sun (1975) a 1973 "KAP" (knowledge, attitude, and practice of family planning) study found that Taiwanese women now preferred 3.2 children with 1.9 sons and 1.3 daughters. Sun noted (1975: 2): "The drop in the preferred number of children was contributed more by the drop in the preferred number of daughters than by the drop in the preferred number of sons." These most recent preferences yield an ideal sex ratio of 146.

A program designed to try to reduce further the preferred number of children in Taiwan was described by Finnigan and Sun (1972). However, people who wanted more sons were the very ones not to enroll in the educational incentive program. A plan is needed to reach these families as well.

Another result which is of *comparative* interest was based on the question, "If a couple already had one daughter and one son and wanted three more children, how many of these three children would you want to be boys and how many girls?" This question was inspired by the one Inkeles used in his six-nation study and for which the data are in Table 4. Although the questions are not identical, a rough comparison is possible. Eighty percent of the Taiwan respondents wanted subsequent children to be predominantly boys (i.e., two or three boys). Four percent would want a subsequent predominance of girls. These results are similar to those for the Indian factory workers, 78% of whom wanted a subsequent boy and 5%, a girl.

For this question, the difference between the two Taiwanese townships was mainly that more people from Hsinchuang, the more developed township, said that "it doesn't matter" about the sexes of subsequent children. Again, as in the Inkeles' data, if there was movement away from boy preference, it was toward "no preference" rather than toward "daughter preference." There is no question that positive daughter preference is very rare in Taiwan. Sun (1975: 20) found this to be true for the most recent data available, the 1973 KAP data:

> The son preference [as measured by the Coombs' scale] is somewhat stronger among older women, those [who] already have or expect a greater number of children, those with lower education, live in [a] rural township, with low income and occupation, and with little exposure to mass media, but the relevant comparisons are between moderate and strong son preference, and not between boy and girl preference. In none of the subgroups examined is there more than 5 percent with a girl bias.

The question arises of how motivated Taiwanese are to have any daughters. Are they simply saying they want one or two daughters just because chances are they will get one or two and they might as well get used to the idea? Our two sets of hypothetical questions give us some information on this.

Turning to the picture set first which solicited respondents' reactions to stick figures of families with different numbers of boys and girls, we have four relevant comparisons, (1) - (4). We asked about families with four boys and one girl and the reverse:

(1)	Sex of Resp.	Township Kungliao	Hsinchuang
Percentage recommending that family with four girls and one boy should have another child	F M	48% (1,287) 36% (178)	27% (1,128) 18% (153)
Percentage recommending that family with four boys and one girl should have another child	F M	14% (382) 9% (44)	4% (178) 3% (29)

These differences range between 3 and 7 times more respondents recommending the pictured families try for a second son than a second daughter. Women were more likely to recommend that both families go on for more. Kungliao people were more likely than Hsinchuang people to recommend both families go on. But greater son preference was shown by Hsinchuang residents who recommended going on for the first family 6 to 7 times as often as for the second family. In Kungliao, the differences were of the order of 3 to 4 times.

Similarly, many more respondents would recommend replacing a single son who died than a single daughter when each was from a five-child family:

(2)	Sex of Resp.	Township	
		Kungliao	Hsinchuang
Percentage recommending	F	70% (1,874)	55% (2,265)
that a single son who died	M	73% (366)	46% (398)
should be replaced			
Percentage recommending	F	43% (1,148)	23% (957)
that a single daughter who	M	36% (183	17% (150)
died should be replaced			

As with the previous comparison (1), the numbers in parentheses are the numbers of people responding that the pictured family should have another child. The patterns by sex and by township are similar in (2) and in (1). A majority would recommend replacing a son, but a minority would recommend replacing a daughter.

We also asked about two four-child families: one with four girls and one with four boys. Since the ideal family size is about four, this question asks whether the ideal should be exceeded if there is not at least one of each sex:

(3)	Sex of Resp.	Township	
		Kungliao	Hsinchuang
Percentage recommending	F	76% (2,036)	59% (2,438)
that a family with four	M	73% (364)	56% (484)
daughters have another child			
Percentage recommending	F	48% (1,272)	26% (1,096)
that a family with four	M	37% (184)	22% (186)
sons have another child			

Again, we see the differences by sex and township. Respondents from Hsinchuang are less interested in obtaining a daughter than residents of Kungliao. The last families we asked about had two girls and one boy or two boys and one girl:

(4)	Sex of Resp.	Township	
		Kungliao	Hsinchuang
Percentage recommending that a family with two girls and one boy have another child	F	53% (1,424)	34% (1,409)
	M	48% (239)	25% (219)
Percentage recommending that a family with two boys and one girl have another child	F	26% (691)	11% (456)
	M	19% (95)	9% (74)

There is considerable satisfaction with the two boy and one girl family in both townships. But in Hsinchuang, two-thirds to three-quarters would also be satisfied with the one boy and two girl family. Having only one boy is not completely abhorrent to half the people in Kungliao and is even more acceptable to the people of Hsinchuang.

The results here are consistent: there is a very strong desire in having at least one son even if it means continuing after four daughters or replacing a son who died. The desire for at least one daughter is not great. Less than a quarter of Hsinchuang men and women would attempt to replace a single daughter (from a five-child family) who died. More people from Kungliao (36%-43%) would do so, however. Similar percentages would recommend going on if the family had had four boys and no girl to begin with.

In a similar vein, respondents were given the hypothetical situation that their daughter had had the recommended number of children, but all were of one sex. Again, respondents made a sharp distinction between the two situations:

	Sex of Resp.	Township	
		Kungliao	Hsinchuang
Percentage recommending that a daughter/son try to have a boy if all children were girls	F	64% (1,721)	61% (2,536)
	M	67% (334)	55% (473)

Percentage recommending	F	29% (788)	25% (1,029)
that a daughter/son try to	M	24% (118)	17% (150)
have a girl if all children			
were boys			

In these questions the respondents had the option of recommending adoption of a child of the needed sex. Twice as many respondents recommended adopting a girl (9%) as a boy (4%). This situation could be considered unfortunate since adoption would be a pragmatic way of satisfying sex preference. Perhaps parents are reluctant to adopt a male heir because they would doubt his loyalty. Adopting a boy was unacceptable to sonless couples in Korea for this reason (Ham, 1971). Adopting a girl might not be as risky, since if she did not turn out well, she would have at least contributed some housework and then could marry out. If she did turn out well, she might become an inexpensive wife for one of the sons. As we noted in Chapter 4, girls are often preferred for adoption in other countries, and Taiwan is apparently not an exception. Another consideration might be the supply of boys available for adoption. In a son-preferring society like Taiwan, few families would be willing to put up one of their sons for adoption, as one of our sources pointed out (Gallin, 1966: 166):

A family willing to give up a son for adoption is usually under the pressure of financial necessity and has more than one son. The necessity must be serious, since a family "selling" its son for adoption gives up all claim to him. The adopting family gives the boy's family money for him, and the villagers say, "When a son is adopted out, it is like cutting off one's finger."

According to Gallin who studied a village he called Hsin-Hsing, a childless couple may adopt a girl because they believe that "having a child in the house will make it possible for the woman to conceive, or more accurately, that the adopted girl is supposed to invite a baby boy" (1966, 162).

In short, adoption of a boy is not a very popular solution to the problem of sonlessness in Taiwan. More Taiwanese are willing to consider adopting a girl, but, as our data have shown, the desire for at least one girl is not very strong.

In all three groups of questions, ideal sex ratios, responses to pictured families, and advice to daughter/son, we found strong evidence of preference for at least one son and weak desire for at least one daughter. A large majority of respondents would not recommend replacing a single daughter from a five-child family. All of our data showed strong differences by township. The sex differences were weaker but also consistent, with women more likely to recommend more children.

Sex Preferences and Fertility Behavior

Previous studies in Taiwan have found the following: (1) women with one or two sons are more likely to continue the use of contraception after an I.U.D. has been inserted and then removed or expelled (Cernada, 1970); (2) acceptors in the Taichung family planning program had more living sons than women in the general population (Freedman and Takeshita, 1969); (3) women with more sons are more likely to have used various types of family limitation in the past (Freedman and Takeshita, 1969); (4) pregnancy rates are higher for women without sons (Freedman and Takeshita, 1969); and (5) women with three or more sons are more likely to have an abortion after their I.U.D. has been removed or expelled, compared with women with fewer sons (Cernada, 1970).

Our analysis of sex preferences and fertility used the technique of Multiple Classification Analysis (MCA), which is a form of dummy variable multiple regression. For a description of this technique, see Andrews, Morgan, and Sonquist (1967). David M. Heer did this analysis which appears in the final report of the project (1972) and has been published in a collection edited by Kantner. We will only summarize the results here without presenting the actual MCA tables. We will review the behavioral evidence first, comparing the importance of actual numbers of sons (versus daughters) and a son preference attitude scale in predicting fertility (runs 1 and 2) and the use of contraception (runs 3 and 4).

The first MCA looked at "Number of Subsequent Births Among Currently Married Women of *3rd* Parity and with 3rd Birth at least 1 Year Prior to the Interview" as predicted by a number of social and demographic variables, including numbers of sons and the son preference scale. This scale included the items in our five-item scale, discussed in Chapter 5, plus three other questions (two on advice to a daughter/son and one on whether wealth should be measured by money or number of sons). The most important predictor, after age, was the number and sex of survivors of the first three live births. When there had been no child deaths, the respondents had fewer subsequent births when two or three of the first three births were male than if they were female. However, "when there have been one or more child deaths, the pattern of fewer subsequent children with more male survivors does not hold" (Heer, 1972: Ch. 6, p. 3).

If we were to infer attitudes from behavior, we would conclude that respondents were most satisfied with the family of two sons and one daughter, then three sons, then one son and two daughters, then three daughters, then one son and one daughter, and so forth through the various combinations of numbers and sex of children. The least satisfactory family had no surviving children.

In this MCA the son preference scale, which was split into three categories (high, moderate, and low son preference), was only very weakly related to subsequent fertility, whereas the actual number of sons was a good predictor.

The second MCA was a slight variation on the first, with the dependent variable being "Number of Subsequent Births Among Currently-Married Women of 2nd Parity or Higher and with 2nd Birth at least One Year Prior to the Interview." Again, after age, the sex and survival status of the first two live births was the most strongly-related variable, after holding constant other variables like education of the respondent, labor-force status of the wife, husband's occupation, township, birth control knowledge, mean length of lactation for all live births, perception of child survival, and educational aspirations. (These were the same control variables used in the first MCA also.)

In this run, in addition to being concerned with births after the 2nd rather than 3rd parity, the independent variable, "Number of Sons and their Survival," is broken down so that we know the sex of the child who died, if a child death occurred. As we expected, families with two sons, both of whom survived, had fewer subsequent children than families with two daughters, both of whom survived, controlling for the variables listed above. In addition, there was a slight tendency for families with two sons, both surviving, to have fewer subsequent births than families with a daughter and a son, both surviving. Again, the inconsistencies came in when there were child deaths. For example, among families with one son and one daughter born with the son surviving, there was a greater tendency to go on for more children than among families with one son and one daughter with the daughter surviving. We would have predicted the opposite. Furthermore, when a family has two sons born and one survived, there was a greater tendency for the family to go on than when the family had two daughters and one survived. We have no ready explanation for these two results. David M. Heer (1972) suggests the following:

> An interpretation which is congruent with some of the . . . findings . . . is that the death of an only son produces great trauma and a consequent unwillingness to have further children. On the other hand, the death of a daughter or of a son who is not the only son may inspire fear that the remaining son might die and thus might motivate the couple to have additional children as insurance against future loss of sons [Ch. 6, p. 10].

It is clear that we need further study of the effects of child deaths on the childbearing motivations of parents. As far as we know, there have been no in-depth studies of this topic.

In this second MCA, the eight-item son preference scale had only a weak curvilinear effect on fertility with persons in the "moderate son preference" category having the highest subsequent fertility.

The third MCA tried to predict the "Current Use of Contraception Among Currently-Married Women Born in 1925 or Later." The control variables were the same as in previous runs. Again, the son variables were the strongest predictors of the dependent variable with the daughter variables definitely less strong. In addition, "when either one, two or three sons have been born, respondents reporting that one or more of these sons were dead reported less practice of contraception after adjustment for other variables than those with no sons dead" (Heer, 1972: Ch. 6, p. 8). For daughters, this relationship was very weak. The demographic son variables again outranked the poorly-showing son preference scale, which showed a weak curvilinear relationship with contraceptive use.

And finally, the last MCA tried to predict current *or* past use of contraception. As before, the number of sons and their survival did noticeably better in predicting contraceptive use than did comparable daughter variables. The same pattern in the third MCA, for the son preference scale, held here as well.

Thus, for all four MCA's, the variables relating to actual number of sons (and their survival) were good predictors; the son preference scale was not. For three out of four MCA's the people with "moderate son preference" had higher subsequent fertility or more use of contraception with no evidence of the predicted linear effect (i.e., higher son preference, higher fertility, and lower use of contraception). We concluded that our effort to measure son preference was not successful because higher fertility ideals and son preferences were confused. The recent effort of the Coombs (1975) makes some progress on this problem. We might have had clearer results if we had used only the one-item measure instead of the five-item scale.

Additional MCA's attempted to predict attitudes such as the desire for additional children, number of children advised for a daughter, number of children desired if life could be lived over, and attitude toward birth control. The logic of why the number of sons (or degree of son preference) should be strongly related to these variables is a little less clear here. And indeed, the son variables did less well here than in the four behavioral MCA's just discussed with the exception of the first attitude MCA, predicting a desire for additional children. Here, the number of sons and their survival did extremely well in predicting the dependent variable, which is an important finding. In the attitudinal MCA's, again, the son preference scale was a poor predictor.

In short, we can conclude two things from this discussion. First, the number of sons is an important variable (in our Taiwan study at least) because virtually all of our respondents have son preference but do not necessarily succeed in having a sufficient number of sons during the course of their childbearing. The number of sons is more important than the number of daughters in determining when to stop childbearing. Second, the attitudinal preference for sons scale did not show up as an important variable in predicting fertility behaviors and attitudes. We have speculated that this was due to several factors: the unreliability of the measure, the lack of variability among our respondents (i.e., almost all had moderate to high son preference and almost none had daughter preference), and the confusing of high fertility desires and son preference. If we had studied a population where son preference was more variable and we had come up with a more reliable way of measuring son preference, possibly we would have had more success in predicting fertility attitudes and behaviors.

Individual Determinants of Son Preference

After developing the four son preference scales described in Chapter 5, we tried to see which of some forty social and economic variables were related to son preference. Limiting ourselves to the data for 6,800 women who were interviewed in the first round of interviews in 1969-1970, we computed zero-order correlations and ran multiple regressions in order to see how strong the relationships were and what percentage of the variance in son preference could be explained. The social and economic variables were chosen on the basis of the hypotheses about son preference presented in Chapter 1.

Unfortunately the correlations between the social and economic variables and the four son preference scales were uniformly low (.00 to .20), and only a very small percentage of the variance (6% to 20%) could be explained by twelve main independent variables in combination. The most variance was accounted for in the one-item scale which asked respondents about whether a family with four boys and one girl or four girls and one boy should go on. Those women who thought the second, but not the first, family should go on for more children, thus indicating son preference, tended not to be in the paid labor force, thought sons were important for security in old age, and felt it was important to have a male heir. These were the three variables which were most strongly related to the one-item son preference measure. As we will show in the next section, the desire for sons for security in old age and for continuity of the family appear to be at the crux of son preference in Taiwan.

Bases of Son Preference in Taiwan

Using the theory of child bearing motivation suggested by Chung, Cha, and Lee (1974), we will consider here: (1) the motivation for sons, which is seen

TABLE 11: Usefulness of Sons in Husband's Occupation According to Taiwanese Women and Men

	Sex of Resp.	Township			
		Kungliao		Hsinchuang	
A. Young Son					
A young son would be of no help	F	75%	(2,015)	77%	(3,177)
	M	69%	(346)	92%	(797)
A little help	F	19%	(516)	17%	(718)
	M	17%	(83)	5%	(45)
Much help	F	2%	(62)	2%	(85)
	M	14%	(71)	2%	(13)
N.A.	F	3%	(84)	4%	(157)
	M	0%	(1)	1%	(8)
Total	F	100%	(2,677)	100%	(4,137)
	M	100%	(501)	100%	(863)
A. Grown-up Son					
A grown-up son would be of no help	F	41%	(1,105)	54%	(2,224)
	M	46%	(231)	75%	(644)
A little help	F	14%	(389)	17%	(717)
	M	12%	(61)	12%	(102)
Much help	F	27%	(718)	14%	(599)
	M	26%	(133)	9%	(78)
N.A.	F	17%	(465)	14%	(597)
	M	15%	(76)	4%	(39)
Total	F	100%	(2,677)	100%	(4,137)
	M	100%	(501)	100%	(863)

as the sum of the approach tendency for sons and the avoidance tendency for sons; (2) the motivation for daughters, which is also seen as the sum of approach and avoidance tendencies.

Many positive motivations for sons have been suggested in our discussion throughout this book: sons may provide labor when young and when older; sons may bring in money at marriage if there is a dowry system; sons are more likely to receive an education and later be more successful than daughters; sons provide continuity of the family; sons may provide financial and emotional security in old age and may provide a place for elderly parents to live. We will look at qualitative and quantitative evidence for these positive reasons for having sons.

DECLINING SIGNIFICANCE OF LABOR OF SONS

For most of our respondents, the value of sons as labor is not crucial. First of all, only 25% reported that their families owned land. Presumably sons would be more useful if the family had its own land. Furthermore, Taiwan does not have a large class of landless people working the land of others. However, sons might still be useful to the family if sons helped in a family activity besides farming. We asked respondents about this.

There was good agreement that a young son provided little or no help to his father. (See Table 11.) The value of a grown-up son was more in dispute. People had a harder time answering this second question, as indicated by the higher nonresponse rates (4% to 17%). At best, however, a quarter or fewer of the respondents thought a grown-up son would offer "much help." Sex differences in response were inconsistent. Kungliao residents thought a grown-up son would be of more help, compared with those of Hsinchuang. It should be recalled that Hsinchuang residents showed higher son preference. For them, at least, son's labor does not seem to be the explanation for son preference. In Kungliao, it may be a small part of the explanation.

THE LACK OF A DOWRY SYSTEM

Taiwan does not have a dowry system so this cannot be part of the explanation of son preference. Gifts flow in both directions and often the boy's family pays more. In our survey we asked male respondents whether they had had a son or daughter married within the last three years. Data were collected on sixty marriages of daughters and fifty-four marriages of sons. In both townships, parents paid four to five times as much money for weddings of sons than those of daughters. The average amount spent for *daughters* was 2,900 New Taiwan dollars ($72 in U.S. currency) in Kungliao and 4,400 ($110) in Hsinchuang. The comparable figures for *sons* were 15,700 ($392) and 16,100 ($402). Gallin (1966: 208) found the same pattern in Hsin-Hsing: "Usually in a marriage, all gifts considered, it costs the boy's side more than the girl's."

Possibly this pattern originated in the historical shortage of women in Taiwan, a frontier country. The influx of men coming with Chiang Kai-shek in the late 1940s and 1950s created a more recent sex imbalance. In any case, it cannot be claimed that Taiwanese prefer sons because of the marriage system. If anything, the system would encourage daughter preference.

SIMILAR EDUCATIONAL ASPIRATIONS FOR GIRLS AND BOYS

Another argument might be made that only boys need to receive formal education and, having received it, are more likely to be successful, hence son preference. In our survey, parents were asked about the *lowest* level of years of schooling a boy and a girl now needs to be successful. In general, most parents thought that ten to twelve years were the lowest number. They thought girls needed only slightly less—about one year less. In response to

TABLE 12: Importance of a Male Heir to Taiwanese Women and Men

	Sex of Resp.	Township			
		Kungliao		Hsinchuang	
In this day and age, having a male	F	0%	(2)	0%	(11)
heir is not at all important to a	M	0%	(0)	1%	(9)
family					
Not very important	F	1%	(19)	7%	(277)
	M	3%	(13)	14%	(125)
Uncertain, depends on the	F	1%	(15)	3%	(106)
circumstances	M	0%	(2)	2%	(22)
Quite important	F	3%	(69)	20%	(820)
	M	93%	(465)	32%	(272)
Extremely important	F	96%	(2,557)	70%	(2,904)
	M	4%	(21)	50%	(435)
N.A.	F	1%	(15)	1%	(19)
	M	0%	(0)	0%	(0)
Total	F	100%	(2,677)	100%	(4,137)
	M	100%	(501)	100%	(863)

another set of questions, respondents were a little more likely to encourage boys to stay in school compared to girls. But overall, the educational aspirations were not grossly discrepant at least at the *lower* levels. Data cited by Finnigan (1972) for aspirations of married women under thirty (with three or fewer children) in Hua Tan township showed larger differences at the higher levels: 71% of the women expected their sons to go on to college or other educational institution beyond high school while 54% expected their daughters to do so.

PERSISTENCE OF THE DESIRE FOR A MALE HEIR AND FOR CONTINUITY OF THE FAMILY NAME

Almost all of our respondents felt that it was quite important or extremely important for the family to have a male heir. This was true for both men and women. (See Table 12.) Fawcett et al. (1974) also found that this was the primary reason for wanting sons given by parents in Taiwan. Sixty-nine percent of their urban middle class sample, 80% of their urban lower class sample, and 65% of their rural sample mentioned this reason for wanting boys. These percentages tended to be higher for Taiwan than for the other countries in the Far East which were studied. Gallin (1966: 188) stressed the same point in his study of Hsin-Hsing:

A son is of greater importance and value than a daughter, simply because it is the male who remains with the family and insures its continuity; his sister's marriage inevitably takes her away from her natal family and ties her future to that of her husband and his kinship group.

The continuity of the family seems to be an especially important goal for men, as M. Wolf (1968: 45) pointed out:

A man with a son becomes a link in the long chain of descent. His struggle with the land for enough to eat takes on new meaning: he will one day be the head of a household, the senior representative of the family, no longer an adult child living under the authority of his father. And if the birth of their first male child is a matter of rejoicing for the child's parents, the birth of their first grandchild is even more of an eventful day.... More than anything else, they [the grandchildren] stand as evidence that these people have done their duty to their own parents and grandparents.

Women's motivations are a little different, according to Wolf (1968: 42-43):

To them [her husband and his family], her infant son is the next link in a long chain of descendents carrying their name and their future. To her, he is the source of the first bit of security she has felt since she entered the family. ... the whole quality of her future life depends on the strength of the ties she develops with her son.

In short, Wolf (1968: 45) asserted:

until a woman bears a male child she is only a provisional member of her husband's household, merely a daughter-in-law; with the birth of a son, she becomes the mother of one of its descendents, a position of prestige and respect.

ECONOMIC REASONS FOR PREFERRING SONS
INCLUDING OLD AGE SECURITY

For many Taiwanese still, sons are wealth. As an old man put it in Hsin-Hsing (Gallin, 1966: 130): "People here don't ask how much money you have. They ask how many sons you have." Curious about how many people would agree with the old man's statement, we included a question in our survey based upon it: "Some people appraise a man's blessings by how many sons he has and others by how much money he has. Which do you think is correct?" About 40% of our respondents agreed with the old man. Only about 10% felt that the amount of money alone could be used to assess wealth. The remainder felt that both money and sons had to be taken into account.

TABLE 13: Reasons of Taiwanese Women and Men for Preferring Boys or Girls

	Sex of Resp.	Township			
		Kungliao		Hsinchuang	
Boys provide more economic	F	64%	(1,699)	36%	(1,508)
support than girls	M	48%	(238)	38%	(329)
Girls provide more economic	F	0%	(3)	0%	(13)
support than boys	M	1%	(6)	1%	(4)
Boys are more emotionally	F	11%	(302)	15%	(626)
rewarding than girls	M	7%	(37)	13%	(109)
Girls are more emotionally	F	0%	(7)	2%	(65)
rewarding than boys	M	0%	(1)	0%	(3)
More boys are needed to insure	F	0%	(1)	1%	(19)
against possible deaths of sons	M	0%	(1)	2%	(13)
Tradition and custom	F	13%	(346)	20%	(809)
require boys	M	13%	(66)	20%	(171)
Other reasons	F	2%	(66)	4%	(177)
	M	10%	(52)	10%	(84)
N.A.	F	10%	(253)	22%	(920)
	M	20%	(100)	17%	(150)
Total	F	100%	(2,677)	100%	(4,137)
	M	100%	(501)	100%	(863)

In Table 13, we present data from a question asking *why* the respondent preferred sons or daughters. Economic reasons for wanting sons stand out, especially in Kungliao and particularly for Kungliao women. Even in Hsinchuang, economic reasons were favored by over a third while "tradition and "custom" and emotional reasons were also subscribed to by quite a few respondents. It must have been somewhat difficult for some respondents to articulate their reasons for sons, judging by the high nonresponse rates (10% to 22%) for this question.

We asked specifically about a number of sources of support (listed in Table 14) to see how important sons were, relative to other possible sources. It is clear that sons are the most frequently chosen source. In another question, we asked which would be the most important source. In Kungliao, 86% of the women and 71% of the men selected sons; comparable percentages in Hsin-

TABLE 14: Anticipated Sources of Support in Old Age for Taiwanese Women and Men Aged 45 or Younger

| Anticipated Source | Sex of Resp. | % Anticipating Each Source of Support | | | |
		Kungliao		Hsinchuang	
Government pension	F	9%	(151)	10%	(324)
	M	9%	(25)	15%	(112)
Savings	F	59%	(1,004)	71%	(2,213)
	M	72%	(200)	67%	(489)
Rent	F	10%	(171)	14%	(433)
	M	1%	(2)	9%	(68)
Nongovernment pension	F	3%	(58)	5%	(146)
	M	0%	(1)	9%	(64)
Sons	F	97%	(1,661)	85%	(2,652)
	M	92%	(256)	73%	(531)
Daughters	F	40%	(687)	25%	(791)
	M	15%	(4)	16%	(115)
Relatives and friends	F	9%	(154)	2%	(75)
	M	3%	(8)	1%	(8)

NOTE: Respondents could choose more than one source of support. The sample sizes were: Kungliao women (1,714); Kungliao men (279); Hsinchuang women (3,113); and Hsinchuang men (726).

chuang were 57% and 42%. Men were more reluctant to rely on either sons or daughters. They mention impersonal sources (pensions, savings) more often. Perhaps they are more likely to have these sources because of their greater participation in the paid labor force. The second source of income anticipated is savings. About two-thirds of our respondents hope to rely on savings (usually in addition to sons).

It is true that these are *anticipated* sources. Perhaps by the time these respondents are older, there will be new sources available. We also asked about *actual* sources of support for those respondents who were not self-supporting. Thus we do have data on actual behavior as well. First of all, women were more likely to be dependent on someone other than a spouse than were men. Also, residents of Kungliao were more likely to be supported by others than were residents of Hsinchuang. About 80% of those reporting that they were supported by others reported that source of support as sons. Daughters (and son-in-laws) were the next most common source, with about 12% reporting this source. So it is clear that sons are still very important for economic security in Taiwan. Almost all respondents expected to live with their sons and be supported by them. We asked about whether they would

TABLE 15: Number of Sons Necessary for Support in Old Age

	Sex of Resp.	Township	
		Kungliao	Hsinchuang
Mean number of sons necessary	F	2.3	1.8
	M	2.4	1.5
Range of sons necessary	F	6.0	7.0
	M	4.0	6.0
Standard deviations	F	1.0	.8
	M	.8	.7
Sample sizes	F	2,645	4,064
	M	360	847

still want to live with sons if some kind of conflict developed. About half would still want to live with their children. About 30 to 40% would live separately in that case.

The final question we asked in this set on security in old age was: "If a couple in your village has to rely on their sons in their later years, how many sons would you say are necessary to support them?" The results appear in Table 15. Clearly, more than one son is considered necessary in both townships.

After all this discussion of positive advantages of having sons, is it then true, the more the better? This does not follow. Freedman et al. (1964: 19) presented data from Taichung surveys which showed that one can have too much of a good thing: "Those with larger numbers of sons do not regard themselves as especially fortunate. In fact, the great majority of those with more than three sons are willing to say that they would have preferred fewer." After three sons, avoidance of sons sets in although we cannot be sure of which costs are felt most keenly.

So much for approach and avoidance of sons. What about daughters? There are also reasons for approach and avoidance of daughters. We will discuss the positive aspects of having girls (girls perform housework, may bring in incomes and provide companionship for parents when they are young) and the negative aspects (they are expensive).

THE USEFULNESS OF GIRLS FOR HOUSEHOLD WORK

Three studies done in Taiwan (Gallin, 1966; Wolf, 1968; and Fawcett et al., 1974) have pointed out the value of daughters for doing housework. In Hsin-Hsing, for example, "girl children are considered necessary in any household, and the ideal family consists of four or five children, of which two are girls. There are countless chores around the house for which daughters are needed" (Gallin, 1966: 188). These chores begin early, according to Wolf (1968: 45-46): "by the time they are five, most little girls are doing a few chores regularly and certainly are minding their slightly younger siblings."

Fawcett et al. (1974) found that rural families were more likely to mention the value of girls for their help in housework than were urban respondents, which helps put the findings of Gallin and Wolf, both of whom studied rural areas, in context. Urban respondents mentioned either that girls provided companionship (especially for the mother), or that girls were valued for certain positive personality traits. Although some urban lower class respondents mentioned valuing girls for their housework, almost no urban middle class respondents did so.

INCREASINGLY GIRLS ARE BRINGING IN INCOMES

Gallin (1966: 188) mentioned in passing "today unmarried girls often contribute financially to the family income." We found in our study that a third to a half of the men who reported that they had had daughters married also mentioned that the daughters had contributed some of the money for the wedding expenses. This may be increasingly important in Taiwan as it is now in Hong Kong where, according to work by J. Salaff, the incomes of unmarried women are very important for many families and have contributed to their rise in status.

GIRLS ARE VALUED AS COMPANIONS

As we just noted, Fawcett et al. (1974) found that girls were valued by urban residents for their personalities and as companions for the mother. Wolf (1968: 42-43) also mentioned that fathers may enjoy daughters since there is very little responsibility attached to them:

> As long as she does not become wantonly immoral while a member of her father's household, she is a luxury he can enjoy. Fathers who are acting against their natural propensities in the treatment of their sons, find considerable satisfaction in a relaxed informal exchange with their daughters.

ON BALANCE GIRLS ARE ILL-AFFORDED LUXURIES

We have mentioned a few of the reasons why parents might desire girls. However, as we demonstrated in the first part of this chapter, there is only weak motivation for having daughters, especially in Hsinchuang. M. Wolf (1968: 40) tried to sum up the village attitude:

> As soon as a daughter is old enough to be useful in the house or in the fields, she is also old enough to marry and leave the family (at no small

expense to her parents) to give her labor and her sons to another family. The general village attitude is summed up in the words of an old lady who told me why she disposed of her daughters: "Why should I want so many daughters? It is useless to raise your own daughters. I'd just have to give them away when they were grown, so when someone asked for them as infants I gave them away. Think of all the rice I saved."

Summary

In this chapter we showed the extent of son preference among our Taiwan respondents using attitude questions. We concluded that almost no families would be content without at least one son, but many would be content without one daughter. We then showed that the actual number of sons (and their survival status) tended to be a very good predictor of subsequent fertility, contraceptive use, and desired number of children. Our son preference attitude scale, by contrast, did not predict well. When we tried to predict individual differences in sex preference, we were not successful. Apparently our attitude scales were too unreliable, confused high fertility desires and son preference, and contained too little variability. One measure, containing only one item, was found to be predicted by whether the woman was currently in the labor force and whether she thought it was unimportant to have sons for security in old age and as heirs. Such women were low in son preference.

We then turned to the bases of son preference, using the approach and avoidance model suggested by Chung, Cha, and Lee (1974). Eliminating labor, the dowry system, and educational aspirations as primary reasons for son preference, we concluded that the desire for a male heir and the need for sons for economic and emotional security were the most important factors. Basically, Taiwanese parents currently have little alternative to being supported by sons. Furthermore, they believe that being supported by sons (supplemented by savings) is the proper way to live.

We finally considered the positive and negative aspects of having daughters. At present, the balance still seems to be tipped against daughters. However, if daughters become more economically productive before marriage (and perhaps postpone their marriages longer), they may not be considered such luxuries.

Chapter 7

BOY PREFERENCE AND PUBLIC POLICY: THE CASES OF SOUTH KOREA AND CHINA

Recently social scientists have been called upon to broaden their research to include questions dealing with public policy. This chapter will examine two countries where policy makers have become aware that boy preference is an obstacle to population control. Each of the two countries, the Republic of Korea and the People's Republic of China, has been pursuing, sometimes through nongovernmental organizations, policies designed to reduce boy preference. These two countries were chosen because of their contrasting approaches and because they are among the first of the developing countries characterized by son preference to encounter this obstacle of boy preference. Both countries have relatively successful family planning programs and strong governmental commitment to population control.

Looking at the Republic of Korea first, Korean scholars and family planning activists are almost unanimous in their agreement that boy preference is an obstacle to population control. This judgment is based on a review of the extensive literature on boy preference in Korea[1] and on recent (summer, 1975) interviews with twenty such individuals in Korea.[2]

Only one researcher in our small sample asserted that the difference between the ideal number of sons and daughters Korean parents wanted was decreasing dramatically. He felt that in a very short time, people would want equal numbers of boys and girls or have no sex preference. Several researchers and policy makers pointed out that there were other obstacles besides boy preference to further reductions in the birth rate which should not be ignored. For example, the post-Korean War baby boom children are now reaching the childbearing ages. This demographic phenomenon is expected to slow down the success of the family planning program, regardless of whether boy preference diminishes.

The disagreement among the Koreans interviewed came when we raised the question about policies to counteract boy preference. We asked about what policies were currently being employed and what policies should be considered in the future. However, before discussing these, we might give a brief background on historically important influences on the status of women in Korea: Christianity, American influence, the Korean War, and general economic development and urbanization. All of these have provided some challenge to the very long tradition of male supremacy.

According to Young Bok Koh (1971) and Kyung Sook Bae (1973), both of whom have written on women and the law in Korea, Christian missionaries and their ideas have been influential in promoting greater sexual equality in Korea. Christian missionaries considered Confucianism to be a form of idolatry. They opposed ancestor worship and the subjugation of women within the family. Monogamy (rather than the double standard which allowed men to take concubines) was extolled along with the possibility of remarriage for widows. The first schools for women were opened by missionaries, who encouraged a more liberal and democratic form of education. Deemphasizing rote learning, the mission schools encouraged students to explore their self-identity. Women who became Christians left their homes for church services and were exposed to new ideas. Today, many of the schools founded by missionaries remain influential. There are also organizations like the YWCA that have played a modest part in popularizing notions of greater freedom for women.

The strong American influence dating from 1950 may have contributed to a greater concern with sexual equality than might otherwise have been the case. For example, Korean women have been given fellowships to study in the United States and have been encouraged to continue their careers afterward. The Korean War itself (1950-1953) may have expanded the roles of women since women were needed to perform the jobs of men who were away or who had been killed.

The notable degree of economic development in Korea since the War has opened up more opportunities for women, especially in the cities. Even in rural areas women's roles may have expanded as women and children are left behind to manage the land. Without any specific governmental plan or goal to increase the status of women, urbanization and development have probably increased the freedom of women in Korea.

With respect to policies themselves, the Korean Government has not had an explicit policy to reduce boy preference (or, to put it another way, to increase the status of women). It has passed laws insuring equal pay for equal work and making other forms of sex discrimination illegal. Women participate in some military training and have been entering state educational institutions in greater numbers. Otherwise, the approach seems to have been one of laissez-faire. There has been no explicit attempt to mobilize women politically or economically, although more women have entered the paid labor force. After World War II some reforms of the family system were made which would allow a woman to be head of a household if there was no son. But, since 1960, there have been no substantial changes in the Family Law. The present Government did not come to power with an explicit ideology or commitment to increase sexual equality, to reform the family system, or to reduce the Confucian influence within the society. Rather, the commitments were to economic development (including population control) and to defense.

As we noted in Chapter 3, son preference in Korea seems to be rooted in the desire of parents for economic and psychological security, especially in old age. Another aspect is the desire for continuity of the family and the desire to be revered after death by one's sons. In Korea, there has been no systematic governmental attempt to reduce these needs, other than through general economic development, which makes families better off and in less need of support from sons. There has been no attack on religious practices, including ancestor worship. There is still no widespread system of social security, and collectivization has not been encouraged. Individuals must still rely on kin for their economic and psychological security. Since daughters marry out of the family and leave their parental household (and their family register), the kin to be relied upon are still sons for many families in Korea. Thus, it is probably fair to say that the Korean government has not had an explicit policy to undermine the bases of son preference.

However, in the family planning program there has been an effort to reduce boy preference. In Korea, the information, education and communication (IEC) part of the family planning program is the responsibility of a private agency, supported by the government and international agencies. This agency is the Planned Parenthood Federation of Korea (PPFK). The motto of PPFK from about 1962 to 1970 was: "Have the Proper Number of Children and Bring Them Up Well." In 1970 to 1974, the motto became: "Daughter or Son Without Distinction—Stop at Two and Bring Them Up Well." This was recently changed to: "Stop at Two and Bring Them Up Well." This most recent motto is designed to deemphasize sex preference. According to several staff at PPFK, the 1970-1974 motto was thought to suggest, unwittingly, sex preference. Posters also evolved during this time from having children of each sex to posters with just two daughters to posters having two children of ambiguous sex. According to the Secretary General of PPFK, Mr. Lee Joo Hyun and Dr. Yun Sung Hee, Planning Consultant to PPFK, there was considerable criticism of the posters with just two daughters. The criticism came from university professors, Confucianists, and National Assemblymen. The present posters with ambiguous sex of the two children cannot be thought to be discriminatory.

Some of the educational materials of PPFK mention specifically the advantages of daughters (and the disadvantages of sons) in order to challenge the traditional value that daughters are useless to the family. PPFK plans to organize in the largest cities "Only One Daughter" Clubs, according to the Secretary General of PPFK. The members would be couples who chose to use a permanent method of birth control after just one child, a daughter. Already there are "Two Child Family" clubs whose members speak at public education meetings, trying to convince others to do likewise. The "Only One Daughter" clubs would be smaller and fewer in number, but might still have some shock and publicity value. The goal is to help Korean parents to think the unthinkable (i.e., stopping childbearing permanently after only one daughter). PPFK has also tried education programs combatting boy preference with the men in the military reserve units. Planned for the future are special meetings with soothsayers and fortune tellers who often convince people that if they try just one more time, they will have a boy. The idea of these meetings would be to convince the fortune tellers that they are giving bad advice. In addition, PPFK has cooperated with women's groups in trying to change the Family Law which will be discussed below.

In short, when we consider present policies against boy preference in Korea, we must discuss general trends, outside influences, and private organizations primarily, since the government has not been explicitly committed to greater sexual equality. We next turn to the question of future policies. Since many people have only recently become concerned about the persistence of boy preference and its relation to population, it is natural that most of the debate centers on future policies of the government and private organizations.

In our interviews, the most popular viewpoint was that the government ought to continue the current development policies and that these would have an indirect effect on boy preference. Policies cited were: continued emphasis on economic development, expansion of public education, including population education, and continuation of the "Stop at Two" campaign. Many respondents felt that boy preference would gradually decline as the population became more urbanized, educated, and richer. An accompaniment of this view was that direct intervention in the family was not desirable because it might lead to social disorganization and neglect of older people. Some respondents implied that the government did not have sufficient popular support to successfully change the family system, even if it wanted to.

The next most popular viewpoint was that the Family Law needed to be changed. We will discuss this here and finally mention several other policies suggested by individuals interviewed in Korea.

Legal experts, such as Dr. Tai Young Lee and Dr. Byung Ho Park, were particularly adamant that the place to begin combatting male supremacy was with changes in the Family Law. Dr. Lee emphasized that the debate engendered by the proposed amendments to the Family Law helps to remove family practices from the unconscious to the more conscious level. The debate about the Family Law raises questions about the fairness of the patriarchal family system and of Confucianist teachings.

Concern with the family laws increased from 1973 to the spring of 1975 at which time ten proposed changes in the family system were introduced into the Korean National Assembly. The ten proposed revisions, which are supported by the Pan-Women's Committee to Promote Revision of the Family Law, are: (1) Succession should no longer be automatically through the eldest son but should depend on the circumstances of the family. (2) The legal definition of blood relationships should be the same for the maternal and paternal sides of the family. Currently blood relatives "include anyone within 8 degrees of kinship in the father's line or 4 degrees of kinship in the mother's line" (translation by Kim Jae-Ho). (3) People of the same clan and branch name should no longer be prohibited from marrying. (4) Common ownership of property by husband and wife should be acknowledged. Previously, if the ownership of any property was unclear, it became the husband's. (5) In the event of divorce, the wife should be entitled to "a portion of the property accumulated during marriage through the common effort of the husband and wife" (translation by Kim Jae-Ho). (6) The procedures for divorce by mutual agreement should be made more explicit. "To insure the protection of the wife and any young children, therefore, certification of a statement of the intentions of both parties at a family court should be required" (translation by Kim Jae-Ho). (7) Parental authority should be exercised in common, including child custody in the event of divorce. As the law stands now, the husband has primary parental authority and is entitled to child custody if there is a divorce. (8) Laws regarding relations between stepmothers and stepchildren should be revised. As the law stands now, a husband can enter an illegitimate child into the family register and it becomes "legally recognized as of the same status as the relation between the legal wife and her own natural children," even if the wife has not consented to the arrangement. The reciprocal situation has not been legal, however (i.e., the entering of illegitimate children of the wife without the consent of the husband). The charge is made that the present law encourages the practice of concubinage. (9) Sons and daughters should have equal rights of inheritance. "Daughters currently receive one half the share of sons in inheritance unless they are married or are listed in a different family register, in which case they receive one-fourth of a son's share" (translation by Kim Jae-Ho). Presently wives are entitled to a share only one half of a son's portion. (10) There should be some restrictions on wills, providing that at least "one half of the inheritance should be reserved for the survivors of the deceased to ensure their future livelihood, regardless of the provisions of any will" (translation by Kim Jae-Ho). Presently, the head of the household can write a secret will with no protection for the members of the family. The logic of this proposed revision is that the inheritance belongs to the whole family since it was accumulated with the cooperation of the family. Thus, it should not be possible for the head (or other person) to dispose of it completely freely.

Amendments 1 and 9 (succession and inheritance) were considered by the people interviewed to be the most socially significant ones. Some people went as far as to say that the Korean family system depends on these two provisions. Therefore, most of the controversy centers on them. According to Kim Yoon Duk, a woman who is a member of the National Assembly and one of the strongest supporters of the revisions in the Family Law, these two provisions are unlikely to pass this fall (1975). Other knowledgeable respondents agreed. Mrs. Kim felt, however, that the other eight would probably pass, perhaps with some changes. This would be the first major revision in the Family Law since 1960 when the new Civil Code took effect (Chung, Cha, and Lee, 1974). If these two most important provisions do not pass in the fall (1975), then it may be a long time before they are reconsidered. In any case, the significance of the introduction of these proposed revisions is that the structure of the Korean family is now open to debate and discussion, more than previously.

One could argue that these provisions do not go far enough. They do not question the concept of "head of household"—just the rigidity with which the headship is presently conferred. The amendments do not challenge the system of giving the children the father's family name. Nor do they specify what the fair share of the wife should be or specify the guidelines for deciding child custody. Finally, there is no discussion of the problems of enforcement and administration of the provisions. The assumption appears to be that the present court system, administrative structure, and registration system are adequate to handle these new provisions. Perhaps in the version of the proposals discussed by the National Assembly, some of these problems will be worked out.

Although the proposed changes in the Family Law could be defended as an extension of human rights, in Korea, the argument that boy preference (due to the family system) is an obstacle to reducing the population growth rate is more effective, according to Mrs. Kim Yoon Duk. The government is already committed to reducing the population growth rate since the density of population is already quite high and the country's resource base is weak. Thus Mrs. Kim and Dr. Lee Tai Young both mentioned that they use the population-growth argument. The idea that equality for women is a basic human right does not seem to have much acceptance in Korea yet.

In addition to the view that social and economic changes combined with higher education will reduce boy preference and the view that the Family Law must be changed, several scholars made other suggestions. Dr. Cha Jae-Ho, a psychologist at Seoul National University, was impressed with the recent finding of one of his graduate students (Chang, 1975), who studied about sixty urban middle class couples, that people with liberal sex role ideologies tend to have low sex preference. He, therefore, advocated school education programs which try to counteract traditional sex roles. He suggested that changes in textbooks and elimination of single-sex courses from schools might be a place to begin. He also felt that the current demand by industry for young women's labor was significant since young women were often conscientious about sending money home to their parents. He felt that this pattern might have some effect on reducing boy preference in the long run.

Dr. Yun Sung Hee of PPFK mentioned the desirability of a campaign to inform parents of their chances of having a son and that one son is sufficient for their needs, while emphasing *rational* rather than *emotional* appeals for family limitation. In his view, son preference now tends to be one of the more important emotional reasons for continued childbearing. Dr. Yun also felt that sex preselection clinics, when technically feasible, might have appeal to Korean parents and cited the opening of such a clinic in Singapore (Sung, 1975). Finally, he noted that the growing Women's Movement in Korea might eventually have some effect on reducing boy preference.

Dr. Ahn Kye Choon, a sociologist at Yonsei University, pointed to a general education population course at Yonsei which, according to before and after tests, had some effect on reducing the male preference of the men students in the course (Ahn and Kim, 1975).

Dr. Chang H.S., former Minister of Health and Social Affairs and now Congressman to the National Assembly, felt that an expanded social security system might be the answer. He cited the beginning of a social welfare system next year and the present social security program covering about 400,000 of the poorest of Korea's population as eventually having an impact on boy preference. He, along with most others, also emphasized the importance of changing the Family Law.

Dr. Lee Hae Young felt that a general rise in the standard of living might be the most significant factor reducing boy preference, since then parents would not have to rely on their sons as much. He also saw significant change from the older to the younger generations with the younger being less concerned about sons. Yet rural areas still remain the source of son preference. He noted, however, that Korea was fortunate to have a rather balanced urbanization pattern with several other large cities in addition to Seoul. Currently more than 50% of the population of Korea is living in urban areas. This urbanization pattern, he felt, may help mitigate son preference. He did not consider the increase in female labor force participation to be too significant since most women quit working when they married (or were fired, if they did not quit).

Dr. Lee Tai Young, one of the first female lawyers in Korea who now heads the Legal Aid Center for Family Relations, emphasized the importance of women obtaining decision-making positions in the society so that policies more favorable to women could be passed, pointing out that less than 5% of the members of the National Assembly are women, and some of these were traditionally educated and do not favor changing the Family Laws.

Perhaps as interesting as those suggestions which were made are those that were not made. No one suggested a direct and comprehensive campaign against Confucianism. No one suggested incentives, for example, for men who have vasectomies after only one son. No one considered the organization of "mutual criticism" (to use the Chinese term) of the older generation who may be pressuring young couples to have sons. No one suggested mobilization programs to encourage married women to work. Typically, suggestions that the status of women needed to be raised were not accompanied by specific suggestions of just how this might be accomplished other than as the gradual outcome of development, urbanization, and increasing education. For example, we did not hear suggestions from professors that there was a need for more women professors nor from government officials that more women should be given high positions in Government. Finally, there was no spontaneous mention of developing alternative child care arrangements which might free women from household responsibilities and allow more social participation.

On balance, there is certainly concern in the Republic of Korea that boy preference may be an obstacle to development through its effect on the population program and that some kinds of policies may soon be called for. At this point, however, many people seem to be hoping that boy preference will gradually decline as a result of other social and economic changes and that deliberate tampering with the traditional family will not be necessary. The laissez-faire approach is consistent with the country's economic policies (although not with political and defense policies) of the country. In the meantime, there is some support for changing the Family Law, among our respondents. A similar finding with a more systematic elite sample is reported in Chung et al. (1974). If, however, the important amendments (succession and inheritance) do not pass in the National Assembly, then it cannot be said the Korean government has a new priority to reduce boy preference.[3]

Comparison with China's policies is useful at this point. Unfortunately, we were not able to visit the People's Republic of China and must rely on written sources mainly from recent visitors. Our knowledge is certainly less complete about the efforts of China to reduce boy preference; yet a few generalizations might be attempted.

That Mao Tse-tung himself had been concerned with the continued existence of boy preference in China is indicated by the following discussion Mao had with the late Edgar Snow in 1970 about the slow progress of family planning in many rural areas:

> In the countryside, a woman still wanted to have a boy child. If the first and second were girls, she would make another try, if the third one came and was still a girl, the mother would try again. Pretty soon there would be nine of them, the mother already 45 or so and she would finally decide to leave it at that [Katagiri and Terao, 1972: 2].

According to the same source, "Mao said that it would take time to change such attitudes—as clearly as it will for so much of the rural population of the world" (Katagiri and Terao, 1972: 2).

The campaign against sons intensified in 1975, according to a September 8, 1975 article in the *New York Times:*

> Provincial broadcasts indicate that meetings are being held to study the instructions [issued by the Communist Party Central Committee in the name of Mao Tse-tung] and to carry them out, but none have been made public. The broadcasts make it clear that the age-old desire for sons is a prime target.

> As in agricultural societies elsewhere, the desire for sons is linked to the parents' search for security in their old age. To combat this the authorities are stressing that daughters can provide such security too. In the past it was customary for a woman to leave her parents and move in with her husband's family to take care of his parents. Now the authorities, stressing equality of the sexes, are saying that when a man and a woman marry, the woman can live with the man's family or the man with the woman's.

There is no question that China was a boy preferring society in the past. Taeuber, speaking of the recent past in China, put it this way:

Imperatives of subsistence and the hazards to life dictated small, co-living households and few surviving sons. Reproductive and familial behavior were alike pragmatic. Lower order sons might be adopted within the larger family, while daughters might be placed for adoption outside the family. In difficult conditions, boys had priority over girls, while those already maturing had priority over the newly born [Taeuber and Orleans, 1966: 47].

The question is whether boy preference is still widespread at present and what policies have been employed to reduce sexual inequality. We will discuss mainly past and present policies since we have little information on what policies are contemplated for the future.

In our discussion of China, we will try to show that, relative to Korea, postrevolutionary China has had a stronger commitment to sexual equality and has made a concerted effort to undermine the social, economic, and psychological bases of male supremacy. On the other hand, China has deliberately slowed down the growth of cities. This may make it more difficult to bring about sexual equality.

One place to begin a discussion of China's policies on the status of women is with the views of Mao Tse-tung. As early as 1919, Mao wrote many impassioned articles on the situation of Chinese women and their role in the family. A particular suicide of a young woman, Miss Chao, on her wedding day, was the subject of at least nine articles by Mao. Mao himself resisted an arranged marriage and freely contracted his first marriage based on love. The woman he married was well educated and the daughter of a philosopher known for his strong opposition to the traditional family (Witke, 1973a).

In his writings, Mao attacked the double standard of morality and asserted that women were not "some sub-human species for which special restrictions and a retributive morality had to be contrived" (Witke, 1973a: 14). Since the revolution, Mao has often been quoted as saying, "Times have changed and men and women are the same. Whatever men comrades can do, women comrades can also do." In 1965, before the Cultural Revolution, Mao realized China had a long way to go to realize its ideals. He was quoted as saying to Andre Malraux: "The Chinese woman doesn't yet exist among the masses; but she is beginning to want to exist" (Maloney, 1972: 10). Mao himself has consistently supported greater sexual equality.

Before the 1949 revolution but after taking over territory in China, the Communist Party tried to put its egalitarian ideology into effect by changing marriage and divorce laws and by mobilizing women into production (Davin, 1973). Less than a year after the success of the revolution throughout the country, the new government promulgated the Marriage Law of 1950. A month later, the Land Reform Law was passed.

For a translation of the brief Marriage Law, see Meijer (1971) who gives an excellent history of the development and application of the Marriage Law. The Law was thoroughly and explicitly egalitarian. It stated, for example: "Husband and wife are companions living together and shall enjoy equal status in the home. Husband and wife are in duty bound to love, respect, assist and look after each other, to live in harmony, to engage in productive work, to care for the children and to strive jointly for the welfare of the family and for the building up of the new society" (Meijer, 1971: 301).

The Law received wide publicity at the time and ever since. In the early 1950s, local cadres did not enforce it with vigor or with sensitivity. Many cadres were more concerned with land reform. Occasionally, the land reform policies conflicted with the Marriage Law as when a poor peasant (male) received an allotment of land which was then claimed by his wife who wanted a divorce.

Because the Law was still not being properly understood or enforced in the mid-1950s, the Chinese leaders began an education program which reached down to the small groups to which most Chinese belonged. These small groups could exert face-to-face pressure on individuals to change their attitudes toward the ideal described in the Marriage Law. People, especially women, were encouraged to "speak bitterness"—describing how bad things were before the revolution. For a description of how these small groups work, see Whyte (1974). The Marriage Law was directed to the whole population, not just to those who had broken the law or who wanted a divorce. All the people were encouraged to study the Law which was brief and idealistic.

Besides the use of small groups practicing mutual criticism, the leaders used public trials as an educational device. The judge was expected to analyze the causes of the family dispute using a socialist analysis. Then he (or she) criticized the participants' ideas and actions and made a decision. Important court cases received widespread publicity.

Newspapers featured case studies illustrating both desirable and undesirable behavior. Women heroines (often martyrs) were given widespread attention. Ordinary people were encouraged to write "dear comrade editor" letters to seek advice on family problems. For instance, a woman trying to balance housework, children, and outside work was given support and advice. The case of a woman trying to decide whether to marry a serious-minded party worker or a more attractive but less revolutionary man was discussed at length. Probably some letters were written by newspaper staff or political workers to illustrate some important dilemma.

Yet the Chinese approach has been much broader than the changes in the family laws, the mutual criticism groups, and the media approaches would suggest. Women have been strongly encouraged to work outside the home. Women's work teams have been organized, married women are given work points independently of their families, women are given training in traditionally male jobs, goals to increase the number of days women work per year have been set, and child care facilities have been established in neighborhoods and work places. Women are encouraged to marry late and have small families so they will have time to receive education and job training. Apparently, primary and secondary education is identical in content for boys and for girls.

Representation of women in higher leadership positions is still poor, but there is governmental awareness of this. Any progress toward greater female participation is heralded in the news. Still, women in the very top of the government are likely to be either wives of top men or figureheads.

During the "Great Leap Forward," attempts were made to socialize child care, dining facilities, and laundry services. The goal was to increase the productivity of women and to increase loyalty to units larger than the family. Many of these efforts were not successful. Later the Cultural Revolution attacked the traditional family as a "haven of self-interest." Women were again encouraged to go beyond the family. The spotlight of criticism was put on jobs, schools, and organizations which had excluded women. Sex distinctions were declared to be irrelevant. There were to be no special "women's viewpoints" or "women's interests."

Analysts of the Cultural Revolution now believe that its intention was to shorten the lag between changes in objective conditions (which had occurred) and in subjective viewpoints (which were slow to change). "The message of the Cultural Revolution was precisely that ideological formulations *inappropriate* to the new society have enormous staying power, despite radical transformation of the material base of the society" (Young, 1973b: 5). Again, as with previous campaigns the traditional family was challenged.

Very recently, the target of the Chinese leaders has been Confucius and Lin Piao:

> A second major theme of Confucian tradition is male superiority, summed up in the Confucian maxim, "It is a virtue if a woman has no ability." For centuries, women were told to observe the "three obediences"—to obey their fathers and elder brothers when young, their husbands when married, and their sons when widowed. Women were also taught the "four virtues"—knowing their place and complying with the moral code, not talking too much and boring people, adorning themselves to please men, and doing all housework willingly. Although the Chinese Communist Party has always actively promoted women's equality, attitudes of male superiority are still present among some of the Chinese people. The campaign to criticize Lin Piao and Confucius is part of the continuing effort to eliminate these old ideas [Pincus, 1975: 34-35].

Since the revolution, the Communist regime has also attempted to undermine ancestor worship which might be considered one of the bases of son preference: "The solidarity created by the common ritual of ancestor worship was weakened by the campaigns against 'superstition' " (Meijer, 1971: 103). In addition:

> They [party workers] foster employment of women so they may make income contribution to the family, urge that daughters should help their own parents (not just the husband's), and are taking steps to erode traditional values in which the son only could carry on the family name and line. A son-in-law may be encouraged to marry into a girl's family where there are no sons [Chen, 1974: 27].

Even if these efforts have not yet been effective, they are significant attempts to reduce son preferences.

Another important basis of son preference is the need for support in old age. The Communist government has not challenged the idea that elderly parents should live with their children (and usually in newspapers and other public information sources the assumption seems to be that they will live with their sons). In fact, the government has fought the "bourgeois idea" that one has no responsibility to old people. At the same time, it has tried to create a climate of collective responsibility. More specifically,

> In the urban industrial sectors, a generous retirement pension (up to 70 percent of the wage at retirement time) has been provided for the majority, but not all, of retired workers and employees. In the rural areas, the commune provides "five guarantees" (food, clothing, shelter, medical care, and burial) for childless old people. All of this has resulted in a highly equitable income distribution pattern, and helps reduce the need for sons as old age security [Chen, 1974: 14].

However, for many elderly parents in rural areas, sons are probably still important.

How successful have all these efforts been in bringing about sexual equality? Most recent observers who had been in China previously report that there has been remarkable improvement in the status of women. However, the description in this report is typical:

> Feudal-patriarchal ideology has not yet died out. Many peasants still feel they must have male children, an attitude which was generated in the old society where a son was valued because he continued the family line and added a new laborer to the family. Raising a boy was a

worthwhile investment, while raising a girl amounted to "pouring water out of the door," since she consumed grain while growing up and then left to become the property of her husband's family. The bride price her family got at the time of her marriage represented payment for the cost of her upbringing. Today, a holdover from this still exists in some parts of the countryside. Parents of the bride often ask for money or various articles from the husband-to-be. This limits free choice in marriage [Hinton, 1975: 31-32].

One countervailing trend to these efforts to reduce male preference should be noted. By intent, China is remaining predominantly rural. Perhaps as much as 85% of the population still live in rural areas. In addition, city youth are sent to rural areas to teach and learn. In our view, it is more difficult to raise the status of women in a predominantly rural country (and one with little mechanization), given the disadvantages women, especially mothers, have in producing equal amounts of physical labor compared with men. Whether China can overcome this problem remains to be seen.

In this chapter we have discussed two case studies. Leaders in both the Republic of Korea and the People's Republic of China realize that the traditional boy preference is undesirable. The Chinese Communists began even before 1949 to try to increase the status of women. In 1950, the Marriage Law was announced, and since then the population has been exhorted through the media and through small groups to give up traditional family patterns and become members of new socialist families. Women have been mobilized into the labor force and child facilities have been gradually built up. Although there has been vacillation in the demand for female labor since 1949, there is no question that China has had a serious commitment to sexual equality since the Communist takeover. Success has apparently been more marked in the city but only a small proportion of the people live in the cities.

By contrast, Korea has not had such an explicit policy. Perhaps in reaction to China and North Korea, South Korea has not tampered with the traditional family. Furthermore, some of the impetus for sexual equality has been from external sources (Christianity and American influences). Only now, with concern about boy preference slowing down the population program, is there serious consideration with changing the Family Law which still favors the male. Even so, the two most important revisions, dealing with succession and inheritance, may not pass the National Assembly.

The approach in Korea up to now has been to encourage economic development, expansion of education, and rapid urbanization with the view that these changes will reduce traditional attitudes in due course. (Only very recently, the government has had misgivings about the pace of urbanization and plans to put a tax on urban residents) Yet, there *is* evidence (Chung et al.,

1974) that the middle class urban resident has only weak boy preference. About half of the population of Korea now lives in urban areas. Since the source of boy preference in Korea seems to be the countryside, this change alone *may* cause a steady decline in boy preference.

The only formal campaigns in Korea to counteract boy preference have been those led by voluntary women's organizations and by Planned Parenthood. There has been no deliberate attack on Confucian ideas or on ancestor worship. The government has not made a big effort to organize child care facilities and as yet, there are few people covered by social security, pensions, or insurance programs. However, increased prosperity has probably reduced the dependence of parents on their sons.

Hopefully, data from Korea and China will be more complete by the next decade. Then we may be able to see which strategy, the direct one of China, or the indirect one of Korea, was more effective in bringing about greater sexual equality.

NOTES

1. There are two especially good reviews of previous studies on boy preference in Korea: a) Kong Chung-Ja and Cha Jae-Ho, "Boy preference in Korea: a review of empirical studies related to boy preference," Korean Institute for Research in the Behavioral Sciences, 1, 8 (January 1974): 1-30; b) Chung Bom Mo, Cha Jae-Ho, and Lee Sung Jin, Boy Preference and Family Planning in Korea. Korean Institute for Research in the Behavioral Sciences, 1974, Seoul, Korea.

2. Persons interviewed in Korea July, 1975 were: Dr. Ahn Kye Choon (Professor of Sociology, Center for Population and Family Planning, Yonsei University), Dr. Chung Bom Mo (Dean, College of Education, Seoul National University), Dr. Hahn Dae-Woo (Chief, Division of Family Planning, Center for Population and Family Planning, Yonsei University), Dr. Hong Jong Kwan (Director, Korean Institute for Family Planning), Ms. Kim Jae Hee (Director, Information and Publications Division, Planned Parenthood Federation of Korea), Dr. Kim Mo Im, Secretary General, Center for Population and Family Planning, Yonsei University), Ms. Kim Yoon Dun (member of the National Assembly), Dr. Koh Kap Suk (Chief, Evaluation Division, Korean Institute for Family Planning), Ms. Kong Chung-Ja, Research Associate, Center for Population and Family Planning, Yonsei University), Dr. Lee Hae Young (Director, Population and Development Studies Center, Seoul National University), Professor Lee Hyo-Chai (Department of Sociology, Ewha Woman's University), Dr. Cho Hyoung (Department of Sociology, Ewha Woman's University), Mr. Lee Joo Hyun (Secretary General, Planned Parenthood Federation of Korea), Dr. Lee Tai Young (Director, Legal Aid Center of Family Relations), Dr. Park Byung Ho (College of Law, Seoul National University), Dr. Yoon Soon Young (Anthropology, Ewha Woman's University), Professor Yoon S.D. (College of Law, Ewha Woman's University), and Dr. Yun Sung Hee (Planning Consultant, Planned Parenthood Federation of Korea). Ms. Hong Sawon (Ph.D. candidate, Department of Sociology, U. of Hawaii), and Ms. Kim Jung-Im (M.A. candidate, U. of Hawaii) helped arrange the interviews and were interpretors during the interviews conducted in Korean. Ms. Hong helped draw up the original list of persons to be interviewed and made

this brief study possible. Note on names: In this chapter we have followed the Korean convention of putting surnames first.

3. One year and one month after the interviews reported here were conducted, the debate was still going on in South Korea. The laws which discriminate against women in household headship and in inheritance had not yet been changed. A recent article (brought to my attention by Dr. J.M. Bolton) by Philip Bowring, "Population Control: Turning the Screw," Far Eastern Economic Review (August 27, 1976, p. 27) discusses a forthcoming package of population measures in Korea. According to him, the measures are expected to include changes in the law to raise the status of women. Bowring comments on this particular proposal: "Koreans are used to simultaneous application by the Government of economic carrots and sticks, but the last item on the list could well provoke opposition from traditionalists. It would be aimed at overcoming the very strong preference for boys which exists in Korea and which results in parents having more children than they would otherwise have in an effort to produce at least one male heir. Under existing law, women cannot be heads of households, and daughters come last in terms of inheritance. Women are also strongly discriminated against in terms of jobs and wages. Thus, it is felt that legal changes in favor of women would not only be desirable in themselves, but would reduce the boy preference. "However," as Bowring continues, "not all Koreans are convinced. They argue that the main reason for boy preference is economic, particularly in rural areas where sons are needed to till the fields and keep the parents in their old age. Even in city areas, the trend towards nuclear families and the absence of a satisfactory pension system creates pressures in favor of boys." Bowring concludes, "However, it is difficult to argue that legal and institutional changes would not be a major step forward."

Chapter 8

MODERNIZATION AND SON PREFERENCE

Parental sex preferences are important both because they are sometimes an obstacle to population control programs and because they are a rough indicator of the extent of sexual inequality in society. Being interested in both aspects, we have used the comparative approach to study sex preferences, which increases the range of variation of human patterns. We found societies characterized by strong daughter preference and by very strong son preference. The data used, both qualitative and quantitative, came from the findings of anthropology, psychology, demography, and sociology, including the Taiwan study.

We have been limited by lack of comparable data for some geographical areas and no data at all for others. Countries in sub-Saharan Africa, Europe, and Central America are among those lacking data.

The focus has been on contemporary conditions, partly because of the dearth of historical data. Only one Korean study (Chung, Cha, and Lee, 1974) attempted to trace the history of boy preference in that country. Furthermore, most research on this topic is very recent. In the U.S. empirical research on this topic has been carried out for more than forty years but elsewhere, most of the research has taken place in the last fifteen years.

In addition to describing the sex preferences of parents around the world, we also attempted to discover what effects they had on fertility, what social and economic conditions were associated with which preferences, and what public policies had been tried (or might be tried) to reduce son preference in particular, which predominates in the most populous developing countries like India and China.

Because parents would not have sex preferences unless the social and economic and familial roles of boys and girls were distinctly different, this really became a cross-cultural study of sex roles. We found that boys and girls are often wanted in different numbers and almost always for different reasons, as Fawcett et al. (1974) have shown.

We found wide variation in parental sex preference. The daughter-preferring societies were all very small in population, and several, such as the Tiwi, the Tolowa, and the Iscobakebu, are no longer practicing their traditional customs. These daughter-preferring societies were mostly matrilineally organized and women were economically productive. Women were considered wealth or were necessary for security in old age. We also found evidence of daughter preference among women in more populous areas in Latin America and the Caribbean. Finally, many parents who want to adopt prefer girls, perhaps on the logic that if you cannot have a biological male heir, one might as well have an easier, more adaptable girl to enjoy.

Although women in the daughter-preferring societies were politically weak, their position was better than in some of the son-preferring societies. Women in the daughter-preferring societies did not run the risk of being killed or neglected as infants or of being treated as boy-producing machines as adults as is sometimes the case in the strongly son-preferring groups.

In addition to noting the importance of the lineage system for parental sex preferences, this review found evidence that rural people had stronger son perferences than urban people (although not all rural people prefer sons), that men often preferred sons more strongly than women (for example in the U.S. and Latin America), and that in some areas, son preference varied by religion, education, and variables indicating the degree of modernity. Preference for boys was not absent in the developed countries nor was it present in all the less developed countries. We found that in Thailand, Indonesia, and the Philippines there was little evidence of son preference (especially among women) even though these areas have been influenced by "Oriental" and "Moslem" cultures to some extent. (We should add that Moslems in the Philippines did have higher son preference.) We speculated that the lack of son preference in these areas might be due to the economic productivity of women, the lack of a strong patrilineal family system, and the expectation that daughters also have responsibility to parents, even after marriage. In our discussions of India, Taiwan, and Korea, we emphasized the importance of sons for parents' security in old age, especially for widows. In our discussions of China and Japan we found hints that new sources of security in old age (communes, state responsibility, and daughters) may have reduced the need for sons in those countries. We summarized our findings in Table 6 which gives rough rankings of groups in terms of sex preference.

Future Research Problems

In our view, future researchers in this field should place greater emphasis on understanding the historical roots of parental sex preferences. The Korean study of Chung, Cha, and Lee (1974) serves as a model in its comprehensiveness and its attention to history. Unfortunately, it is unique in the literature. This Korean study also attempts to build up a theory of child bearing motivations (including the need for sons), a task which will be of increasing importance in the future as we need to integrate past work and decide on the direction of future studies.

In our opinion, we also need to know more about how people develop preferences for different numbers of boys and girls. Up to now, only a few studies of children's sex preferences have been done with little attention given to the sources of these preferences.

Another research need is to extend the analysis beyond the individual. Most empirical studies of parental sex preferences have interviewed individuals and reported on their attitudes or behavior. However, it is obvious that most individuals do not act alone, especially when it comes to having children! Thus, husbands and wives must somehow resolve their different fertility ideals and sex preferences, and parents-in-law may increase the desire for sons in their daughter-in-law. We need to develop the theory and methodology for studying sociologically significant groups—not just individuals.

A final topic needing research is whether different techniques of sex control are likely to have any appeal, especially in the populous son-preferring countries. Whether or not one feels sex control would be beneficial, we should at least know about its acceptability so that possible effects can be anticipated. A small amount of research has been done on this in the developed countries (for example, Westoff and Rindfuss, 1974), but since sex preferences tend to be weak there, the results cannot be generalized to areas like India, North Africa, Taiwan, or Korea.

Modernization and Parental Sex Preferences

In many of the populous developing countries, the patriarchal, patrilineal, and patrilocal family system, with a strict division of labor by sex, has long been considered "natural." Such a family system took care of old people, provided a social place for individuals, and specified norms for the behavior of individuals occupying different age and sex roles. Presently this system is being challenged both from new ideas and from new social and economic conditions. When the technology of public health and medicine substantially reduced the death rate, the need to reduce the birth rate became salient to many. After noticing that it was a need for sons rather than a need for children per se which was leading to large families, a few countries like China, Korea, and Taiwan became more concerned about the traditional organization of the family.

At the same time new ideas about sexual equality have begun to spread. Thus, in most countries, it has become established that girls should also go to school (even if for the reason that educated men prefer educated women).

A related ideology, that of individualism, appears also to be gaining ground. It, too, is a challenge to the traditional family since it encourages individuals to question whether what is good for the group is also good for them. Thus, when a Taiwanese woman at the university decides she is not going to marry a man who wants to live with his parents, she is asserting her own individual interests. Individualism also questions the idea of dependency on others, whether it is dependency on sons or on husbands.

Major social and economic changes are also beginning to affect the traditional family. New industries are opening up which use the abilities of young women and provide them with a small, but independent source of money. The development of new sources of livelihood has freed some from reliance on kin for jobs. The movement to urban areas also frees some individuals from traditional controls such as the family. In general, less personal sources (pensions, insurance, hospitals, schools) of fulfilling basic needs are growing at the expense of relying on kin. And as other institutions in society grow and diversify, the family becomes relatively less significant.

The policy issues of strategies to reduce boy preference should be seen in this context. If boy preference becomes defined as a new "social problem," this means that development plans will have to consider one more interest group: *women.* Thus if the Korean government is planning a new cluster of apartment buildings in Seoul, it will have to think about how the aspirations of young women for freedom from parents-in-law could be incorporated into the design, without ignoring the problems of elderly parents (especially widows) needing care. The Taiwanese government will have to think twice before putting a quota (as it was considering doing) on the number of female university students it will allow. Korea will have to reform its patriarchal family laws, and countries like India and Taiwan, which already have liberal laws, will have to think about enforcing them. Governments will have to resist the argument that women should get jobs only after all men have jobs. In some instances policies to increase the status of women may conflict with other development policies as when more women want to enter the universities at a time when the government is trying to educate only the number for whom jobs can be found. More often, the policies will be in agreement as for example, when governments want to reduce the number of unwanted children.

To reduce son preference, it is not sufficient to have campaigns against it. The conditions which encourage it must be systematically and persistently undermined as China is now attempting to do. In this book, we have delineated those critical conditions.

If we have alerted more people to these problems, made more available previous work in the area, and stirred up new interest in possible solutions, our efforts have been worthwhile. Perhaps by the year 2000 we will get closer to the goal of every child, a wanted child, regardless of sex. But this will not occur without changes in sex role definitions, the family system, the social security system, and the economy.

REFERENCES

ADDIS, R. S., F. SALZBERGER, and E. RABL (1954) A Survey Based on Adoption Case Records. London: National Association for Mental Health.

ADEY, E. M. (1974) "Population control in China." British Medical Journal, London: No. 5918 (June 8): 548-550.

AGARWALA, S. N. (1962) "Attitudes toward family planning in India." Occasional Paper No. 5, Institute of Economic Growth. Delhi, India.

––– (1961) "A family planning survey in four Delhi villages." Population Studies 15, 2 (November): 110-120.

AGUIRRE, A. (1966) "Columbia: The family in Candelaria." Studies in Family Planning No. 11 (April): 1-5.

AHN, KYE-CHOON and KIM MO-IM (1975) "The second evaluation of the population education program in general education: the case of Yonsei University." Unpublished paper.

AMERICAN PUBLIC HEALTH ASSOCIATION SURVEY TEAM (1970) Family Planning Program of Korea (September). Unpublished paper.

AMMAR, H. (1954) Growing up in an Egyptian Village. London: Routledge and Paul. Reprinted in 1966 by Octagon Books, New York.

ANDERSON, J. E. (1975) "The relationship between change in educational attainment and fertility rates in Taiwan." Studies in Family Planning 6: 72-81.

ANDREWS, F., J. MORGAN, and J. SONQUIST (1967) Multiple Classification Analysis: A Report on a Computer Program for Multiple Regression using Categorical Predictors. Ann Arbor, Michigan: Institute for Social Research, University of Michigan.

ANONYMOUS INDIAN AUTHOR (600 B.C.) "On the importance of having a son," p. 265 in L. A. Coser, Sociology Through Literature. Englewood Cliffs, N.J.: Prentice-Hall, 1963. This poem was translated by A. A. Macdonell.

APTEKAR, H. (1931) Anjea: Infanticide, Abortion, and Contraception in Savage Society. New York: William Godwin, Inc.

ARNOLD, F. (1970) "The relation of parents' educational aspirations for children to fertility in Taiwan," pp. 244-249 in Proceedings of the American Statistical Association, 1970 Social Statistics Section.

ARNOLD, F. and J. T. FAWCETT (1975) The Value of Children: A Cross-National Study. Vol. 3. Honolulu, Hawaii: East-West Population Institute.

AYALA, F. J. and C. T. FALK (1971) "Sex of children and family size." Journal of Heredity 62 (January-February): 57-59.

AYROUNT, H. H. (1963) The Egyptian Peasant. Translated from French by J. A. Williams. Boston: Beacon Press.

BACHI, R. and J. MATRAS (1964) "Family size preferences of Jewish maternity cases in Israel." Milbank Memorial Fund Quarterly 42, 2 (April): 38-55.

BALAKRISHNA, S. and P. N. REDDY (1971) "Preferred family size and composition: an application of paired comparisons." Behavioral Sciences and Community Development 5 (3): 112-115.

BANG, S., M. G. LEE and J. M. YANG (1963) "A survey of fertility and attitude toward family planning in rural Korea." Yonsei Medical Journal 4: 77-102.

BARCLAY, G. W. (1956) A Report on Taiwan's Population to the Joint Commission on Rural Reconstruction. Princeton: Office for Population Research.

——— (1954) Colonial Development and Population in Taiwan. Princeton: Princeton University Press.

BARLOW, P. and C. G. VOSA (1970) "The Y chromosome in human spermatozoa." Nature 226: 961-962.

BARRETT, J. (1973) "Women hold up half the sky," pp. 193-200 in M. B. Young [ed.] Women in China. Ann Arbor: Center for Chinese Studies, University of Michigan.

BEALS, A. R. (1962) Gopalpur: A South Indian Village. New York: Holt, Rinehart, and Winston.

BECK, D. F. (1957) "The changing Moslem family of the Middle East." Marriage and Family Living, XIX, 4 (November): 340-347.

BEILHARZ, R. B. (1963) "A factorial analysis of sex ratio data. A comment on two papers by Edwards." Annals of Human Genetics 26 (June): 355-358.

BELL, B. Z. (1972) "An annotated bibliography of materials on the population of People's Republic of China in the Resource Material Collection of the East-West Population Institute as of June, 1972." Honolulu, Hawaii: University of Hawaii.

BEN-PORATH, Y. and F. WELCH (1972) "Chance, child traits, and choice of family size." Rand Report (December). Santa Monica: Rand Corporation.

BERELSON, B. [ed.] (1970) Family Planning Programs: An International Study. New York: Basic Books.

——— (1964) "Turkey: national survey on population." Studies in Family Planning 5 (December): 1-5.

BERELSON, B. et al. [eds.] (1966) Family Planning and Population Problems. Chicago: University of Chicago Press.

BERELSON, B. and R. FREEDMAN (1964) "A study in fertility control." Scientific American 210 (May), 5: 3-11.

BERNSTEIN, M. E. (1952) "Studies in the human sex ratio. 2. The proportion of unisexual sibships." Human Biology 24 (February): 35-43.

BERNSTEIN, M. E. and M. MARTINEZ-GUSTIN (1962) "Physical and psychological variation and the sex ratio." Journal of Heredity 52 (May-June): 109-112.

BERTON, P. and E. WU (1967) Contemporary China: A Research Guide. Stanford: Hoover Institute.

BHATNAGAR, K. S. (1964) Dikpatura, Village Survey, Monograph. No. 4, Madhya Pradesh, Part 6, Census of India, Delhi.

BLAKE, J. (1961) Family Structure in Jamaica: The Social Context of Reproduction. New York: Free Press of Glencoe.

BOGUE, D. J. (1972) "Korea's family planning situation: accomplishments, problems, and needs for international assistance." University of Chicago, Community and Family Study Center.

BOLLEN, G. (1962) "Bijdrage tot de methode der paarsqewijze vergelijking. Een onderzoek naar de voorkeur voor bapaalde familiesmenstellingen." (Contribution to the method of paired comparisons. An experiment on preference for families.) Unpublished thesis. University of Leuven, Belgium.

BOSERUP, E. (1970) Woman's Role in Economic Development. London: George Allen and Unwin Ltd.

BRAUN, R. A. (1975) "From the stone age to mechanized paradise." Bryn Mawr Now II, 4 (April): 8-9.

BRENNER, R. (1951) A Follow-up Study of Adoptive Families. New York: Child Adoption Research Committee.

BULATAO, R. A. (1975a) "Comparisons of some attitudinal measures of daughter and son preference." Paper presented at the Conference on the Measurement of Preferences for Number and Sex of Children, East-West Center, Honolulu, Hawaii (June 2-5).

––– (1975b) The Value of Children: A Cross-national Study. Philippines. Vol. 2. Honolulu, Hawaii: East-West Population Institute.

BUMPASS, L. L. and C. F. WESTOFF (1970) The Later Years of Childbearing. Princeton, N.J.: Princeton University Press.

BURLING, R. (1963) Rensanggri: Family and Kinship in a Garo Village. Philadelphia: University of Pennsylvania Press.

CARROLL, V. [ed.] (1970) Adoption in Eastern Oceania. Honolulu: University of Hawaii Press.

CERNADA, G. P. [ed.] (1970) Taiwan Family Planning Reader: How a Program Works. Taichung, Taiwan: The Chinese Center for International Training in Family Planning.

CHA, J.-H. (1975) "Alternative approaches to measurement of son preference." Paper presented at the Conference on the Measurement of Preferences for Number and Sex of Children, East-West Center, Honolulu, Hawaii (June 2-5).

CHA, J.-H., C. J. KONG, and E. O. LEE (1973) "Report on construction of a boy preference attitude scale." Research Notes K.I.R.B.S. Seoul: 2: 168-172.

CHA, J.-H, S.-B. LEE, and K. J. KIM (1974) "A historical sketch of son preference in Korea." Psychological Studies in Population/Family Planning 1, 9 (June): 1-47.

CHA, Y. K. (1966) "South Korea," pp. 21-30 in B. Berelson [ed.] Family Planning and Population Programs. Chicago: University of Chicago.

CHANDRASEKHAR, S. [ed.] (1967) Asia's Population Problems. New York: Frederick A. Praeger.

CHANG, J.-J. (1975) "Relationship between parental sex role differentiation, permissiveness to children, and son-preference attitudes." M.A. thesis, Department of Home Economics, Seoul National University, Seoul.

CHANG, Y. (1974) "Ideal family size: the case of Korean women." In Population and Family Planning in the Republic of Korea, Vol. II. Korean Institute for Family Planning, Seoul: 330-343.

CHANG, Y., H. Y. LEE, E.-Y. YU, and T. H. KWON (1974) A Study of the Korean Population 1966. Seoul, Korea: The Population and Development Studies Center, Seoul National University (October).

CHEN, C. S. (1963) Taiwan: An Economic and Social Geography. Taipei, Taiwan: Fu-Min Geographical Institute of Economic Development. Research Report No. 96.

CHEN, P.-C. (1974) "The 'planned birth' program of the People's Republic of China, with a brief analysis of its transferability." Paper presented at the Southeast Asia Development Advisory Group of the Asia Society Seminar on "Implementing a Total National Program for Fertility Reduction" held in Indonesia (August).

––– (1973) "China's population program at the grass-roots level." Studies in Family Planning 4, 8 (August): 219-227.

––– (1972) "The prospects of demographic transition in a mobilized system: China."

Pp. 153-182 in R. Clinton and K. Godwin [eds.] Research in the Politics of Population, Lexington, Mass.: D. C. Heath and Company.

CHIN, A. S. (1970) "Family relations in modern Chinese fiction," pp. 87-120 in M. Freedman [ed.] Family and Kinship in Chinese Society. Stanford: Stanford University Press.

CHINA REPORTING SERVICE (1965) "Peking asks for 'broader view' of Chinese family life." Hong Kong (May 12): 1-4.

CHINA YEARBOOK, 1968-69 (1969) Taipei, Taiwan: China Publishing Company.

――― 1969-70 (1970) Taipei, Taiwan: China Publishing Company.

CHING-LING, S. (1973) "Women's liberation," pp. 201-205 in M. B. Young [ed.] Women in China. Ann Arbor: Center for Chinese Studies, University of Michigan.

CHITRE, K. T., R. N. SAXENA, and H. N. REGUNATHAN (1964) "Motivation for Vasectomy." Journal of Family Welfare 9, 1 (September): 36-49.

CHO, H. (1975) "The kin network of the urban middle class family in Korea." Korea Journal 15, 6 (June): 22-33.

CHOI, J. S. (1966) A Study on Korean Family. Seoul, Korea: Minzoong-suhgwan.

CHOI, T. K. (1972) "The realities of legal consciousness about the equality of the sexes." The Journal of Asian Women 11: 47-92.

CHOW, L. P. (1970) "Taiwan: island laboratory," pp. 35-43 in B. Berelson [ed.] Family Planning Programs: An International Study. New York: Basic Books.

――― (1965) "A program to control fertility in Taiwan: setting, accomplishment, and evaluation." Population Studies XIX, 2: 155-166.

CHOW, L. P. and H. C. CHEN (1968) "Evaluation of the family planning program in Taiwan, Republic of China." Population Index (July-September): 281-282.

CHU, F.-L. (1965) "Can young women in the country side still make progress after giving birth to children?" Selections from China Mainland Magazines, Hong Kong: 476 (May): 18-19.

CHUNG, B. M. (1975) "Thoughts on further research problems in childbearing motivations." Paper presented at the Conference on the Measurement of Preferences for Number and Sex of Children, East-West Center, Honolulu, Hawaii (June 2-5).

CHUNG, B. M., J.-H. CHA, and S. J. LEE (1974) Boy Preference and Family Planning in Korea. Seoul, Korea: Korean Institute for Research in the Behavioral Sciences.

CHUNG, B. M., J. A. PALMORE, S. J. LEE, and S. J. LEE (1973) "Psychological perspectives: family planning in Korea." Psychological Studies in Population/Family Planning, Seoul: 1, 7 (November): 1-43.

CHUNG-KUO FU-NU (Women of China) (1963) "Give the revolutionary task top priority." Selections from China Mainland Magazines, Hong Kong: 364 (April): 40-43.

――― (1963) "Treat the relationship between work, children and household chores in a revolutionary spirit." Selections from China Mainland Magazines, Hong Kong: 394 (November): 23-27.

CLARE, J. E. (1951) "Preference regarding the sex of children and its relation to size of family." Master's thesis, Department of Sociology, Columbia University (June).

CLARE, J. E. and C. V. KISER (1951) "Preference for children of given sex in relation to fertility." Milbank Memorial Fund Quarterly 29 (October): 440-492.

CLIFTON, T. and S. LIU (1971) "They've come a long way." Sunday Star-Bulletin and Advertiser, Honolulu, Hawaii: (October 24).

CODRINGTON, R. H. (1906) "The Melanesians," pp. 317 in W. G. Sumner, Folkways. Boston: Ginn and Company.

COHEN, M. L. (1969) "Agnatic kinship in South Taiwan." Ethnology 8, 2 (April): 167-182.

––– (1967) "Variations in complexity among Chinese family groups: the impact of modernization." Transactions of the New York Academy of Sciences, Series II, 29, 5 (March): 638-644.

––– (1966) "The chia as kinship, property and corporation." Prepared for the Conference on Kinship in Chinese Society, New York (September 15-18).

COLBY, M. R. (1941) Problems and Procedures in Adoption. Washington, D.C.: U.S. Children's Bureau. Publication No. 262.

COLLVER, O. A. (1963) "The family cycle in India and the U.S." American Sociological Review 28, 1 (February): 86-96.

COOK, R. (1940) "Sex control in the news again." Journal of Heredity 31, 6 (June): 265-271.

COOMBS, C. H. (1964) Theory of Data. New York: Wiley and Sons.

COOMBS, C. H., L. C. COOMBS and G. H. McCLELLAND (1975) "Preference scales for number and sex of children." Population Studies (London) 29 (July): 273-298.

COOMBS, L. C. (1975) Table 1, "National Size and Sex Bias Scales. IUSSP Preference Scale Study." Unpublished table. Presented to the Conference on the Measurement of Preferences for Number and Sex of Children, East-West Population Institute, Honolulu, Hawaii (June: 2-5).

––– and C. H. COOMBS (1974) "Measuring conjoint preferences for family composition." Paper presented at the annual meeting of the Population Association of America, New York (April).

––– (1974) "Scales for conjoint preferences for family size and sex composition." Unpublished paper. Ann Arbor: Population Studies Center. University of Michigan (January).

––– (1973) "Problems of contamination in panel surveys: a brief report on an independent sample, Taiwan, 1970." Studies in Family Planning 4: 257-261.

COOMBS, L. C. and R. FREEDMAN (1973) "Preference about sex of children." Unpublished manuscript. Ann Arbor: University of Michigan, Population Studies Center.

CORMACK, M. (1953) The Hindu Woman. Bombay: Asia Publishing House. Also, New York: Bureau of Publications, Teachers College, Columbia University.

COWGILL, U. M. and G. E. HUTCHINSON (1963) "Sex ratio in childhood and the depopulation of the Petén, Guatemala." Human Biology 35 (February): 90-103.

CUNNINGHAM, C. E. (1967) "Soba: an Atoni village of West Timon," in Koentjaraningrat [ed.] Villages in Indonesia. Ithaca, New York: Cornell University Press.

CUTRIGHT, P., S. BELT and J. SCANZONI (1974) "Gender preferences, sex predetermination, and family size in the United States." Social Biology 21 (Fall): 242-248.

DAHLBERG, G. (1948/1949) "Do parents want boys or girls?" Acta Genetica Et Statistica-Medica 1: 163-167.

DANDEKAR, K. (1963) "Vasectomy camps in Maharastra." Population Studies, London: 17 (November): 147-154.

DAVIN, D. (1973) "Women in the liberated areas," pp. 73-92 in M. B. Young [ed.] Women in China. Ann Arbor: Center for Chinese Studies, University of Michigan.

DAWES, R. M. (1970) "Sexual heterogeneity of children as a determinant of American family size." Oregon Research Institute 10 (October): 1-7.

DELA PAZ, D. R. (1975) "Preferences for number and sex of children in the Philippines." Paper presented at the Conference on the Measurement of Preferences for Number and Sex of Children, East-West Center, Honolulu, Hawaii (June 2-5).

Department of Civil Affairs, Taiwan Provincial Government (1970) 1969 Taiwan Demographic Fact Book. Nantou, Taiwan.

——— (1969) 1968 Taiwan Demographic Fact Book. Nantou, Taiwan.

——— (1968) 1967 Taiwan Demographic Fact Book, Nantou, Taiwan.

DE WOLFF, P. and J. MEERDINK (1957) "La fécundité des marriages à Amsterdam selon l'appartenance sociale et religieuse." Population, Paris: 12 (2): 289-318

DIAMOND, N. (1973) "The status of women in Taiwan: one step forward, two steps back," pp. 211-242 in M. B. Young [ed.] Women in China. Ann Arbor: Center for Chinese Studies, University of Michigan.

——— (1969) K'un Shen, A Taiwan Village. New York: Holt, Rinehart and Winston.

DINITZ, S., R. R. DYNES, and A. C. CLARKE (1954) "Preferences for male or female children: traditional or affectional?" Marriage and Family Living 16 (May): 128-130.

DORE, R. P. (1967) City Life in Japan: A Study of a Tokyo Ward. Berkeley, California: University of California Press.

Editorial (1957) "Sex determination." Science 126 (November 22): 1059.

EDWARDS, A. W. F. (1966) "Sex ratio data analyzed independently of family limitation." Annals of Human Genetics, London: 29 (May): 337-347.

——— (1962) "A factorial analysis of sex ratio data: a correction to the article in Vol. 25: 117." Annals of Human Genetics, London: 25 (May): 343-346.

——— (1961) "A factorial analysis of sex ratio data." Annals of Human Genetics, London: 25 (October): 117-121.

——— (1959) "Some comments on Schutzenberger's analysis of data on the human sex ratio." Annals of Human Genetics, London: 23 (November): 6-15.

——— (1958) "An analysis of Geissler's data on the human sex ratio." Annals of Human Genetics, London: 23 (November): 6-15.

EDWARDS, A. S. F. and M. FRACCARO (1960) "Distribution and sequences of sexes in a selected sample of Swedish families." Annals of Human Genetics, London: 24 (July): 245-252.

EILLOV, H. (1967) "Attitudes on family planning in Turkey." Paper presented at the meeting of the International Union for the Scientific Study of Population, Sydney, Australia.

EL-BADRY, M. A. (1969) "Higher female than male mortality in some countries of South Asia: a digest." Journal of the American Statistical Association 64 (December): 1234-1244.

ELDER, G. H. and C. E. BOWERMAN (1963) "Family structure and childrearing patterns: the effect of family size and sex composition." American Sociological Review 28 (December): 891-905.

ELIOT, J. W. (undated) "Attitudes of women attending new family planning clinic at Pamplona Alta, Lima Peru, towards family size and family planning in relation to actual fertility and other related demographic factors." Philadelphia, Pa.: American Friends Service Committee.

——— (1968) "Urban-rural and Berber-Arab differentials in desired numbers of male children and related factors in Algeria." Paper presented at the Population Association of America meeting, Boston (April 18-20).

ENKE, S. and R. A. BROWN (1972) "Old age insurance with fewer children." Prepared for Agency for International Development. Santa Barbara, California: General Electric-Tempo, Center for Advanced Studies (March).

ERBA, P. (1956) "I desideri dei genitori reguardo ai loro figli." (Parents' wishes with regard to their children.) In Attidella 16 Reunione Scientifica della Societa Italiana di Statistica, Rome: 243-286.

ETZIONI, A. (1968) "Sex control, science, and society." Science 161 (September 13): 1107-1112.

Family Planning Perspectives (1975) "Timing intercourse can alter sex ratio but there's a catch." 7 (March-April): 58.

FAN, K. Y. (1969) "Study in the causes of death of the people in Taiwan." Journal of the Formosan Medical Association 68 (April 28): 185-194, 196-206.

FANCHER, H. L. (1956) "The relationship between the occupational status of individuals and the sex ratio of their offspring." Human Biology 28 (September): 316-322.

FARBER, B. and L. S. BLACKMAN (1956) "Marital role tensions and number and sex of children." American Sociological Review 21 (October): 596-601.

FAR EASTERN ECONOMIC REVIEW (1969) "Away from the sink." 66, 51 (December): 591.

FAWCETT, J. T. [ed.] (1973) Psychological Perspectives on Population. New York: Basic Books.

FAWCETT, J. T., F. ARNOLD, R. A. BULATAO, C. BURIPAKDI, B. J. CHUNG, T. IRITANI, S. J. LEE, and T.-S. WU (1974) "The value of children in Asia and the United States: comparative perspectives." Papers of the East-West Population Institute, Honolulu, Hawaii: 32 (July).

FAWCETT, J. T., S. ALBORES, and F. ARNOLD (1972) "The value of children among ethnic groups in Hawaii: exploratory measurements," pp. 234-259 in J. T. Fawcett [ed.] The Satisfactions and Costs of Children: Theories, Concepts, Methods. Honolulu, Hawaii: East-West Population Institute.

FESTINGER, L. (1957) A Theory of Cognitive Dissonance. Evanston, Illinois: Row Peterson.

FINNIGAN, O. D. and T. S. LIU (1973) "The effect of a population text on student knowledge and attitudes: Taiwan." Journal of Family Welfare 19, 4 (June): 30-38.

FINNIGAN, O. D. and T. H. SUN (1972) "Planning, starting, and operating an educational incentives project." Studies in Family Planning 3, 1 (January): 1-7.

FINNIGAN, O. D. and S. M. KEENY (1971) "Korea/Taiwan 1970: Report on the national family planning programs." Studies in Family Planning 2, 3 (March): 37-69.

FLANAGAN, J. C. (1942) "A study of factors determining family size in a selected professional group." Genetic Psychology Monographs 25 (February): 3-99.

FREEDMAN, D. S. (1972) "The relationship of family planning to savings and consumption in Taiwan." Demography 9, 3 (August): 499-505.

FREEDMAN, D. S., R. FREEDMAN, and P. K. WHELPTON (1960) "Size of family and preference for children of each sex." American Journal of Sociology 66 (September): 141-146.

FREEMAN, M. (1971) "A social and ecological analysis of systematic female infanticide among Netsilik Eskimo." American Anthropologist LXXIII, 5: 1011-1018.

FREEDMAN, M. (1970) "Ritual aspects of Chinese kinship and marriage," pp. 163-188 in M. Freedman [ed.] Kinship in Chinese Society. Stanford: Stanford University Press.

FREEDMAN, M. [ed.] (1970) Family and Kinship in Chinese Society. Stanford: Stanford University Press.

FREEDMAN, R. (1975) The Sociology of Human Fertility: An Annotated Bibliography. New York: Irvington Publishers, Inc.

——— (1965) "The accelerating fertility decline in Taiwan." Population Index 31 (October): 430-435.

——— (1964) "Sample surveys for family planning research in Taiwan." The Public Opinion Quarterly 28 (Fall): 373-382.

——— (1963) "The sociology of human fertility: a trend report and bibliography." Current Sociology 20/2: #2, 1961-1962. Oxford, England: Blackwell's.

FREEDMAN, R. and L. C. COOMBS (1974) "Preferences about sex of children."
Cross-cultural Comparisons: Data on Two factors in Fertility Behavior. New York:
An Occasional Paper of The Population Council.

FREEDMAN, R. and J. Y. TAKESHITA (1969) Family Planning in Taiwan: An Experiment in Social Change. Princeton: Princeton University Press.

——— (1964) "Studies of fertility and family limitation in Taiwan." Eugenics Quarterly
4, 4 (December): 233-250.

FREEDMAN, R., L. COOMBS, and M.-C CHANG (1972) "Trends in family size
preferences and practice of family planning: Taiwan 1965-1970." Studies in Family
Planning 3 (12) (December): 281-296.

FREEDMAN, R., A. K. JAIN, A. I. HERMALIN and T. H. SUN (1971) "Fertility after
insertion of an IUCD in Taiwan's family planning program." Social Biology 18, 1
(March): 46-54.

FREEDMAN, R., J. Y. PENG, J. Y. TAKESHITA and T. H. SUN (1963) "Fertility
trends in Taiwan: tradition and change." Population Studies 16, 3 (March): 219-236.

FREEDMAN, R., J. Y. TAKESHITA and T. H. SUN (1964) "Fertility and family
planning in Taiwan: a case study of the demographic transition." American Journal
of Sociology 70, 1 (July): 16-27.

FREEDMAN, R., P. K. WHELPTON, and A. A. CAMPBELL (1959) Family Planning,
Sterility, and Population Growth. New York: McGraw-Hill.

FRIED, M. L. (1966) "Some political aspects of clanship in a modern Chinese city," pp.
285-300 in M. J. Swartz, V. Turner and H. Ruden [eds.] Political Anthropology.
Chicago: Aldine Publishing Company.

FUCHS, F. and P. RIIS (1960) "Fetal sex determination before decision in eugenic
indications for abortion." Nordisk Medicin, Stockholm: 64: 1481-1483.

GALLIN, B. (1969) "Rural to urban migration in Taiwan: its impact on Chinese family
and kinship." In D. Buxbaum [ed.] Chinese Family Law and Social Change. Seattle:
University of Washington Press.

——— (1967) "Mediation in changing Chinese society in rural Taiwan." Journal of Asian
and African Studies 2, 1-2 (January and April).

——— (1966) Hsin-Hsing, Taiwan: A Chinese Village in Change. Berkeley: University of
California Press.

——— (1960) "Matrilineal and affinal relationships of a Taiwanese village." American
Anthropologist 62, 4 (August).

GALSWORTHY, J. (1906) The Man of Property. New York: C. Scribner.

GEISSLER, A. (1889) "Beiträge zur frage des geshlechts verhaltniss der Geborenen."
Z. K. Sachsischen Statistischen Bureaus 35, 1.

GILLE, H. and R. H. PARDOKO (1966) "A family life study in East Java: preliminary
findings" pp. 503-521 in B. Berelson [ed.] Family Planning and Population Programs. Chicago: University of Chicago Press.

GILLESPIE, R. W. (1965) Family Planning in Taiwan 1964-1965. Taichung, Taiwan:
The Population Council.

GINI, C. (1951) "Combinations and sequences of sexes in human families and mammal
litters." Acta Gen. Stat. et Med. 2, 220.

——— (1956) "Esame comparativo di alcuni risultati di inchieste italiani e straniere sui
desiderio dei genitni di avere figli dell' uno 6 piuttosto dell' alto sesso." (Comparative
analysis of some results of Italian and foreign studies on the parents' sex preferences
for their children.) In Atti della 16 Riunione Scientifica della Societa Italiana di
Statistica, Rome: 319-332.

GITTELSOHN, A. M. (1960) "Family limitation based on family composition." American Journal of Human Genetics 12 (December): 425-433.

GIUROVICH, G. (1956) "Sul desiderio dei coniugi di avere figle e di avere figle di un dato sesso." (On the wish of married couples to have children and to have children of a specified sex.) In Atti della 16 Riunione Scientifica della Societa Italiana di Statistica, Rome: 287-317.

GOODALE, J. C. (1971) Tiwi Wives: A Study of the Women of Melville Island, North Australia. Seattle: University of Washington Press.

GOODE, W. J. (1963) World Revolution and Family Patterns. New York: The Free Press.

GOODENOUGH, E. W. (1957) "Interest in persons as an aspect of sex difference in the early years." Genetic Psychology Monograph 55: 287-323.

GOODMAN, L. A. (1961) "Some possible effects of birth control on the human sex ratio." Annals of Human Genetics 25 (May): 75-81.

——— (1953) "Population growth of the sexes." Biometrics 9 (June): 212-225.

GORDON, I. (1930) "Adoptionen als soziologlisches und fuersorgerisches problem" Hamburger Wirtschaft-und Sozialwissent-Schaftliche Schriften. Rostock, Germany: Carl Hinstorffs.

GORDON, M. J. (1958) "The control of sex." Scientific American 199, 5 (November): 87-94.

GOSHEN-GOTTSTEIN, E. (1966) Marriage and First Pregnancy: Cultural Influence on Attitudes of Israeli Women. Mind and Medicine Monographs 11. London: Tavistock.

GOULD, R. A. (1966) "The wealth quest among the Tolowa Indians of Northwestern California." Proceedings of the American Philosophical Society 110, 1 (February): 67-89.

GRANQVIST, H.N. (1950) Child Problems Among the Arabs. Helsingfors: Söderström.

GRAY, E. (1972) "Influence of sex of first two children on family size." Journal of Heredity 65 (March-April): 91-92.

GRAY, E. and N. MORRISON (1974) "Influence of combinations of sexes of children on family size." Journal of Heredity 65, 3 (May-June): 169-174.

GREEN, M. and C. GODFREY (1963) "Contributions of a children's diagnosis clinic to child welfare: services in relation to adoption." Pediatrics 32: 131-140.

GREENBERG, R. A. and C. WHITE (1965) "The detection of a correlation between the sexes of adjacent sibs in human families." Journal of the American Statistical Association 60, 312 (December): 1035-1045.

——— (1967) "The sexes of consecutive sibs in human sibships." Human Biology 39 (December): 374-404.

GUERRERO, R. (1974) "Association of the type and time of insemination within the menstrual cycle with the human sex ratio at birth." New England Journal of Medicine 291: 1056.

GUTTMACHER, A. (1933) Life in the Making. New York: Viking Press.

HA, H. K. (1973) "Boy preference in the Korean history." Research Bulletin K.I.R.B.S., Seoul: 3: 1-10.

HAKIM, K. A. (1967) "Islam and birth control," pp. 46-49 in O. Schieffelin [ed.] Muslim Attitudes Toward Family Planning. New York: The Population Council.

HALDER, A. K. and N. BHATTACHARYA (1970) "Fertility and sex sequence of children of Indian couples." Etudes Demographique Recherches Economique de Louvain, University of Louvain, 36 (4): 405-415.

HAM, P. C. (1971) "A study of the Korean preference for male children." Social Science

Research Institute. Division of Demography. Center for Population and Family Planning. Yonsei University, Seoul.

HAMMER, M. (1970) "Preference for a male child: cultural factor." Journal of Individual Psychology 26 (May): 54-56.

HAN, W. K. (1972) The History of Korea. Seoul, Korea: Eul-Yoo.

HANSEN, F. (1965) "Peking attacks new enemy—'mother love'." Backgrounder on Communism No. 65-SM-17 (February): 1-7. Washington, D.C.: U.S. Information Agency.

HANSEN, F. (1965) "Promote 'revolution' at home, Peking urges party members." Backgrounder on Communism No. 65-SM-25 (March): 1-5. Washington, D.C.: U.S. Information Agency.

HARPER, M. (1936) "Parental preference with respect to the sex of children." Master's thesis, Department of Sociology, University of Chicago (December). Unpublished.

HART, C. W. M. and A. R. PILLING (1960) The Tiwi of North Australia. New York: Holt, Rinehart, and Winston.

HARTLEY, R. E. (1969) "Children's perceptions of sex preference in four culture groups." Journal of Marriage and the Family 31 (May): 380-387.

HARTLEY, R. E., F. P. HARDESTY, and D. S. GORFEIN (1962) "Children's perceptions and expressions of sex preference." Child Development 33: 221-227.

HASSAN, S. (1967) "Religion versus child mortality as a cause of differential fertility." Paper presented to the annual meeting of the Population Association of America, Cincinnati (April).

HAWLEY, A. H. and V. PRACHUABMOH (1966) "Family growth and family planning in a rural district of Thailand," pp. 523-544 in B. Berelson [ed.] Family Planning and Population Programs. Chicago: University of Chicago.

HEER, D. M. (1972) Report on Study: Determinants of Family Planning Attitudes and Practices. Report prepared at conclusion of contract covering field study conducted in Taiwan during 1969-1972 (August).

HEER, D. M., M. O'BRIEN, T. TEIXEIRA, J. WILLIAMSON, and N. WILLIAMSON (1969) "Child mortality, son preference, and fertility. A report with particular attention to the Kentucky pretest." Unpublished paper.

HEER, D. M. and D. O. SMITH (1968) "Mortality level and desired family size." Indian Demographic Bulletin 1, 1: 1-15.

HILL, R., J. M. STYCOS, and K. W. BACK (1959) The Family and Population Control: A Puerto Rican Experiment in Social Change. Chapel Hill, N.C.: University of North Carolina Press.

HIMES, N. E. (1936) Medical History of Contraception. Baltimore: Williams and Wilkins. Rpt. 1963; New York: Gamut.

HINTON, C. (1975) "Women: the long march toward equality." New China (Spring): 26-32.

HOFFMAN, L. W. (1975) "Working paper on measurement of preference for number and sex of children." Paper presented at the Conference on the Measurement of Preferences for Number and Sex of Children, East-West Population Institute, Honolulu, Hawaii (June 2-5).

HOGBEN, L. (1952) "Selective limitation of sibship size." British Journal of Social Medicine 6: 188.

HONG, S.-B. (1971) Changing Patterns of Induced Abortion in Seoul. Seoul, Korea.

HONG, S.-B. and J.-H YOON (1962) "Male attitudes toward family planning on the island of Kangwha-Gun, Korea." Milbank Memorial Fund Quarterly 40, 4 (October): 443-452.

HONG, Y. S. (1962) "Westerner's view of Korean women." The Journal of Asian Women 1: 17-31.

HONG KONG STANDARD (1970) "Mao-thought brides." (March 15).

HONG KONG STANDARD (1971) "Women's lib came to China many years ago." (February 7).

HOOPES, J. L., E. A. SHERMAN, E. A. LAWDER, R. G. ANDREWS and K. D. LOWER (1969) A Follow-up Study of Adoptions (Vol. II): Post-placement Functioning of Adopted Children. New York: Child Welfare League of America Inc.

HSIA, H. S. (1970) "Women: How free are they?" South China Morning Post, Hong Kong (October 11).

HSIEH, C. M. (1964) Taiwan-Ilha Formosa: A Geography in Perspective. Taiwan: Government of Taiwan, Republic of China.

HSU, F. L. K. (1963) Clan, Caste and Club. Princeton, N.J.: Van Nostrand.

––– (1967) Under the Ancestors' Shadow: Kinship, Personality and Social Mobility in Village China. Stanford: Stanford University Press. Originally published in 1948.

HSU, T. C. and L. P. CHOW (1966) "Taiwan, Republic of China," in B. Berelson [ed.] Family Planning and Population Programs. Chicago: University of Chicago.

IMMERWAHR, G. E. (1967) "Survivorship of sons under conditions of improving mortality." Paper presented at the annual meeting of the Population Association of America, Cincinnati (April).

INKELES, A. and D. H. SMITH (1974) Becoming Modern: Individual Change in Six Developing Countries. Cambridge, Mass.: Harvard University Press.

JAFFEE, B. and D. FANSHEL (1970) How They Fared in Adoption: A Follow-up Study. New York: Columbia University Press.

JAIN, A. K. (1969) "Fetal wastage in a sample of Taiwanese women." Milbank Memorial Fund Quarterly 47, 3 (July): 297-306.

JAIN, V. C. (1968) "Some social components of infant mortality in India." Indian Journal of Pediatrics, Calcutta: 35 (February): 109-112.

JAMES, W. H. (1975) "Sex ratios in large sibships, in the presence of twins and in Jewish sibships." Journal of Biosocial Science 7 (April): 165-169.

JONES, R. J. (1973) "Sex predetermination and the sex ratio at birth." Social Biology 20 (June): 203-211.

JUNG, K. H. (1967) Korean Law of Family Relations and Successions: A Study of Its History and Interpretation. Seoul, Korea: Seoul University Press.

KADUSHIN, A. and F. W. SEIDL (1971) "Adoption failure: A social work post-mortem." Social Work 16 (July): 32-38.

KAHN, H. and A. WEINER (1967) Towards the Year 2000: Work in Progress. Daedalus (Summer): 713.

KANG, J. S. (undated) "Mother's Clubs in Korea." Seoul: Korean Institute for Family Planning.

KANG, Y. S. and W. K. CHO (1962) "The sex ratio at birth and other attributes of the newborn from maternity hospitals in Korea." Human Biology 34 (February): 38-48.

––– (1959) "The sex ratio at birth of the Korean population." Eugenics Quarterly 6 (September): 187-195.

KAPADIA, K. M. (1966) Marriage and Family in India. Third edition. London: Oxford University Press.

KATAGIRI, T. (1973) "A report on the family planning program in the People's

Republic of China." Studies in Family Planning 4, 8 (August): 216-218.

KATAGIRI, T. and T. TERAO (1972) "Family planning in the People's Republic of China. Report on the first official IPPF visit." IPPF Medical Bulletin 6, 3 (June): 1-3.

KAZEN, P. M. and H. L. BROWNING (undated) "Sociological aspects of the high fertility of the U.S. Mexican-descent population: an exploratory study." Austin: Population Research Center, Department of Sociology, University of Texas.

KEENY, S. M., G. CERNADA and J. ROSS (1968) "Korea and Taiwan: the record for 1967." Studies in Family Planning 29 (April): 1-9.

KELLER, A. B., J. H. SIMS, W. E. HENRY and T. J. CRAWFORD (1970) "Psychological sources of 'resistance' to family planning." Merrill-Palmer Quarterly 16: 286-302.

KETCHUM, B. (1962) "An exploratory study of the disproportionate number of adopted children hospitalized at Columbus Children's Psychiatric Hospital." Unpublished M.S.W. thesis, Ohio State University.

KEYFITZ, N. (1972) "What mathematical demography tells that we would not know without it." Honolulu, Hawaii: Papers of the East-West Population Institute (March), 72 pp.

––– (1971) "How birth control affects births." Social Biology 18 (June): 109-121.

KHAN, A. H. (1960) "Islamic opinions on contraception." Journal of the East Pakistan Academy for Village Development 1, 3 and 4 (August and October).

KHAN, M. E. (1973) "Factors affecting spacing of births." Journal of Family Welfare, Bombay, 20 (December): 54-67.

KHATRI, A. A. and B. B. SIDDIQUI (1969) "A boy or a girl? Preference of parents for sex of the offspring as perceived by East Indian and American children. A cross-cultural study." Journal of Marriage and the Family 31 (May): 388-392.

KIM, B. S. (1974) "Korean woman and the inequality in employment." Research Notes K.I.R.B.S. Seoul 3: 83-96.

KIM, C. H. (1973) "Sex ratio of children and family planning." Research Notes K.I.R.B.S. Seoul 2: 155-164.

––– and S. J. LEE (1973) "Socio-psychological characteristics of induced abortion repeaters." Psychological Studies in Population/Family Planning, Seoul: 1, 2 (April): 1-19.

KIM, D. H. (1969) A Study on Korean Family System. Seoul, Korea: Seoul National University Press.

KIM, J.-H. (1975) Ten Proposed Revisions to the Korean Family Law. Translated into English. Mimeo distributed by Planned Parenthood Federation of Korea.

KIM, O. K., W. C. KANG, C. O. KIM, J.-H. LEE, K. Y. LEE, C. R. CHUNG, S. K. CHOI, H. K. HA and H. K. HAM [eds.] (1972) A History of Korean Women. Seoul, Korea: Ewha Women's University.

KIM, T. I., J. A. ROSS, and G. C. WORTH (1972) The Korean National Family Planning Program. Population Control and Fertility Decline. New York: The Population Council.

KIRK, D. (1966) "Factors affecting Moslem natality," pp. 561-579 in B. Berelson [ed.] Family Planning and Population Programs. Chicago: University of Chicago Press.

KIRK, H. D. (1964a) "Differential sex preference in family formation: A serendipitous datum followed up." Canadian Review of Sociology and Anthropology 1 (February): 31-48.

––– (1964b) Shared Fate: A Theory of Adoption and Mental Health. New York: The Free Press of Glencoe.

KISER, C. V., W. H. GRABILL and A. A. CAMPBELL (1968) Trends and Variations in Fertility in the U.S. Cambridge, Mass.: Harvard University Press.

KLEIN, H. R. et al. (1950) Anxiety in Pregnancy and Childbirth. New York: Harper.

KLINGER, A. (1975) "The longitudinal study of marriages contracted in 1974 in Hungary." Paper presented at the Conference on the Measurement of Preferences for Number and Sex of Children, East-West Population Institute, Honolulu, Hawaii (June 2-5).

KNODEL, J. and V. PRACHUABMOH (1975) "Preferences for sex of children in Thailand: results from the second round of a National Survey." Paper presented at the Conference on the Measurement of Preferences for Number and Sex of Children, East-West Center, Honolulu, Hawaii (June 2-5).

KNODEL, J. and P. PITAKTEPSOMBATI (1973) "Thailand: fertility and family planning among rural and urban women." Studies in Family Planning 4, 9 (September): 229-255.

KO, U. R. and E. S. KIM (1973) Birth Intervals With and Without Family Limitation in Korea. Seoul, Korea: Korean Institute for Family Planning.

KOCH, G. G., J. R. ABERNATHY, and P. B. IMREY (1973) "On a method for studying family size preferences." Demography 12 (February): 57-66.

KOENTJARANINGRAT [ed.] (1967) Villages in Indonesia. Ithaca, New York: Cornell University Press.

KOH, W. K., M. G. LEE, H. J. LEE and H. Y. LEE (1963) A Study on Korean Rural Family. Seoul: Seoul National University Press.

KOH, Y. B. (1971) "The status of women in Korea." The Journal of Asian Women 10: 1-24.

KONG, C.-J. and J.-H. CHA (1974) "Boy preference in Korea: a review of empirical studies related to boy preference." Psychological Studies in Population/Family Planning 1, 8 (January): 1-30.

Korean Institute for Family Planning (1973) Report on 1971 Fertility-Abortion Survey. Seoul, Korea: Korean Institute for Family Planning.

KORNITZER, M. (1968) Adoption and Family Life. London: Putnam and Company.

——— (1959) Adoption. London: Putnam and Company.

KOYA, Y. (1963) Pioneering in Family Planning. A Collection of Papers on the Family Planning Programs and Research Conducted in Japan. Published with assistance of The Population Council, New York. Printed by Japan Medical Publishers, Inc. Tokyo.

KRANTZ, D. H. and A. TVERSKY (1971) "Conjoint measurement analysis of composition rules in psychology." Psychological Review 78 (March): 151-169.

KRISHNA MURTHY, K. G. (1968) Research in Family Planning in India. Delhi: Sterling Publishers.

KWON, T. H. and H. Y. LEE (1975) "Preference for number and sex of children in a Korean town." Paper presented at the Conference on the Measurement of Preferences for Number and Sex of Children, East-West Center, Honolulu, Hawaii (June 2-5).

KYUNG, S. B. (1973) Women and the Law in Korea. Seoul: Korean League of Women Voters.

LAHIRI, S. (1974) "Preference for sons and ideal family in urban India." Indian Journal of Social Work, Bombay: 34 (January): 323-336.

——— (1973) "Preference for sons and ideal family size: the Indian urban situation." Bombay: International Institute for Population Studies.

LAPPÉ, M. (1974) "Choosing the sex of own children. A dream come true or . . . ?" The Hastings Center Report. Institute of Society, Ethics and the Life Sciences 4 (February): 1-3.

LARGEY, G. P. (1972a) Sociological Aspects of Sex Pre-selection: A Study of the

Acceptance of a Medical Innovation. Unpublished Ph.D. dissertation, State University of New York at Buffalo. (February).

––– (1972b) "Sex control, sex preferences, and the future of the family." Social Biology 19 (December): 379-392.

LAWDER, E. A., J. L. HOOPES, R. G. ANDREWS, K. D. LOWER, and S. Y. PERRY (1971) A Study of Black Adoption Families: A Comparison of a Traditional and a Quasi-Adoption Program. New York: Child Welfare League of America, Inc.

LAWDER, E. A., K. D. LOWER, R. G. ANDREWS, E. A. SHERMAN, and J. G. HILL (1969) A Follow-up Study of Adoptions: Post-placement Functioning of Adoption Families. New York: Child Welfare League of America, Inc.

LEAHY, A. M. (1933) "Some characteristics of adoptive parents." American Journal of Sociology 38 (January): 548-563.

LEE, E. O. (1973) "A study on family planning attitude in high school boys and girls." Research Notes 2 K.I.R.B.S. Seoul: 144-153.

LEE, H.-C. (1972) "A sociological approach to fertility behavior." In Sociological Evaluation of the Family Planning Programs and Research Activities in Korea. Seoul: Korean Sociological Association.

––– (1959) "A sociological study on Seoul family." Nonchong 1: 9-87.

LEE, H.-C. and D.-W. LEE (1974) "Survey of the knowledge and attitudes of Korean University students regarding the two children movement and family planning practices." Women's Resource Development Research Institute, Seoul, Korea, Ewha Woman's University

––– (1972) "A study on urban lower family and their family planning." Younguchongsuh 2: 1-101.

LEE, H. K. (1973) "Sex discrimination as reflected in adages." Research Notes K.I.R.B.S. Seoul, 2.

LEE, H. K., A. ONG, and S. J. LEE (1973) "A comparison of early and late adopters of family planning." Psychological Studies in Population/Family Planning, Seoul: 1, 1 (March): 1-35.

––– (1973) "Boy preference and family planning." Psychological Studies in Population/Family Planning, Seoul: 1, 6 (July): 1-27.

LEE, H. Y. (1975) "Studies on male sterilization." Summer Seminar in Population. Seoul: Ministry of Health and Social Affairs, Korean Institute for Family Planning.

LEE, H. Y., T. W. KWON and J. K. KIM (1966) "A study on the changes in Korean familial value." Jindanhakbo 31: 145-164.

LEE, J. H. (1975) "Information, education and communication activities on family planning and Mother's Club activity in Korea." Summer Seminar in Population. Seoul: Ministry of Health and Social Affairs. Korean Institute for Family Planning.

LEE, J. S. (1972) "Boy preference and family planning." Research Notes 1 K.I.R.B.S. Seoul: 40-54.

LEE, K. T. (1973) "Boy preference in Korean folkways." Research Bulletin 1 K.I.R.B.S. Seoul: 1-14.

LEE, M. Y. (1974) "The effects of boy preference on the adoption rate of family planning and the distribution of family type." Research Notes K.I.R.B.S. Seoul 3: 1-10.

LEE, N. W. (1927) A Consideration on Customs of Cho-sun Women, Kyungsung, Korea: Hon-Nam.

LEE, S. J. (1975) "Korean values and family planning." Summer Seminar in Population. Seoul: Ministry of Health and Social Affairs, Korean Institute for Family Planning.

––– (1974) "Korea." In Population and Family Planning in the Republic of Korea, Vol. II. Korean Institute for Family Planning. Seoul: 294-301.

LEE, S. J. and J. O. KIM (1974) Specific Value of Child: Motives for Having Boy and Its Impact on Attitudinal and Behavioral Aspects of Parents. Unpublished paper.

LEITH, S. (1973) "Chinese women in the early Communist movement," pp. 47-72, in M. B. Young [ed.] Women in China. Ann Arbor: Center for Chinese Studies, University of Michigan.

LEVY, R. (1957) The Social Structure of Islam. Cambridge, England: Cambridge University Press.

LEWIS, O. (1965) Village Life in Northern India. New York: A Vintage Book.

LINDAHL, D. (1958) "Separation of bull spermatozoa carrying X and Y chromosomes by counter streaming centrifugation." Nature 181: 784.

LIU, W. T. and E. YU (1975) "Career goals and home making: implications on fertility behavior in the People's Republic of China." Paper presented at the annual meeting of the Population Association of America, Seattle (April).

LOCKRIDGE, F. (1947) Adopting a Child. New York: Greenberg.

LOYD, R. C. and E. GRAY (1969) "Statistical study of the human sex ratio." Journal of Heredity 60, 6 (November-December): 329-331.

LUM, A. (1971) "Chinese men and women work side by side." Star-Bulletin, Honolulu: (November 9).

MALINVAUD, E. (1955) "Relations between family structure and the sex ratio." Journal de la Société Statistique de Paris, Paris: 96 (1-2-3): 49-63.

MALONEY, J. M. (1972) "Chinese women and party leadership: impact of the Cultural Revolution." Current Scene, Hong Kong: 10, 4 (April): 10-15.

MAMDANI, M. (1972) The Myth of Population Control: Family, Caste, and Class in an Indian Village. New York: Monthly Review Press.

MARKLE, G. E. (1974) "Sex ratio at birth: values, variance, and some determinants." Demography 11 (February): 131-142.

––– (1973) "The potential impact of sex predetermination on fertility." Unpublished Ph.D. Dissertation. Tallahassee: Florida State University.

––– (1969) "An analysis of attitudes and issues concerning the future prospect of sex determination." Master's thesis, Department of Sociology, Florida State University.

MARKLE, G. E. and C. B. NAM (1971) "Sex predetermination: its impact on fertility." Social Biology 18 (March): 73-82.

MARSH, R. M. and A. R. O'HARA (1961) "Attitudes toward marriage and the family in Taiwan." American Journal of Sociology 67, 1 (July): 1-8.

MAY, D. A. and D. M. HEER (1968) "Son survivorship motivation and family size in India: a computer simulation." Population Studies 22, 2 (July): 199-210.

MEAD, M. (1935) Sex and Temperament in Three Primitive Societies. New York: A Mentor Book, New American Library.

MEIER, R. L. (1968) "Modern science and the fertility problem," pp. 406-412 in M. B. Young [ed.] Population in Perspective. New York: Oxford University Press.

MEIJER, M. J. (1971) Marriage Law and Policy in the Chinese People's Republic. Hong Kong: Hong Kong University Press.

MICHELMORE, S. (1968) "Sexual reproduction," p. 412 in L. B. Young [ed.] Population in Perspective. New York: Oxford University Press.

MICHAELS, R. (1963) "Casework considerations in rejecting the adoption application," in I. E. Smith [ed.] Readings in Adoption. New York: Philosophical Library, Inc.

MIDDLETON, J. (1971) "Mothers' Clubs: an example of rural adult education in Korea." Harvard Graduate School of Education.

MILTON, N. (1973) "A response to 'women and revolution'," pp. 179-192 in M. B.

Young [ed.] Women in China. Ann Arbor: Center for Chinese Studies, University of Michigan.

MINISTRY OF HEALTH and SOCIAL AFFAIRS. Republic of Korea (1966) The Findings of the National Survey on Family Planning (December).

――― (1965) The Findings of the National Survey on Family Planning. (December).

MIRO, C. A. and F. RATH (1965) "Preliminary findings of comparative fertility studies in three Latin American cities." Milbank Memorial Fund Quarterly 43, Supplement 2: 36-62.

MITRA, S. (1970) "Preferences regarding the sex of children and their effects on family size under varying conditions." Sankhyā: The Indian Journal of Statistics, Calcutta: Series B 32 (June): 55-62.

MODE, C. J. (1975) "A study of the impact of age of marriage, sex preference, abortion, contraception, and sterilization on population growth in Korea by computer simulation." Philadelphia: Institute for Population Studies, Drexel University.

MOHOPATRA, P. S. (1966) The Effect of Age at Marriage and Birth Control Practices in Fertility Differentials in Taiwan. Unpublished Ph.D. Dissertation.

MONBERG, T. (1970) "Determinants of choice in adoption and fosterage on Bellona Island." Ethnology 9 (April): 99-136.

MONTAGU, M. F. A. (1948) "Sex order of birth and personality." American Journal of Orthopsychiatry 18 (April): 351-353.

MOON, H.-S., S.-H. HAN, and S. CHOI (1974) "Recent trends in ideal family size," pp. 281-293 in Population and Family Planning in the Republic of Korea Vol. II. Seoul: Korean Institute for Family Planning.

MORRISON, W. A. (1961) "Family planning attitudes of industrial workers of Ambarath, a city of Western India: a comparative analysis." Population Studies 14, 3 (March): 235-248.

――― (1957) "Attitudes of females toward family planning in a Maharashtran village." Milbank Memorial Fund Quarterly 35 (January): 67-81.

――― (1956) "Attitudes of males toward family planning in a Western Indian village." Milbank Memorial Fund Quarterly 34, 3 (July): 262-286.

MORSA, J. (1966) "The Tunesian Survey: a preliminary analysis," pp. 581-593 in B. Berelson [ed.] Family Planning and Population Problems. Chicago: University of Chicago Press.

MYERS, G. D. and J. D. ROBERTS (1968) "A technique of measuring preferential family size and composition." Eugenics Quarterly (September): 164-172.

MYERS, R. J. (1949) "Same-sex families." Journal of Heredity 40 (October): 268-270.

McGINN, N. F. (1966) "Marriage and family in middle-class Mexico." Journal of Marriage and the Family 28 (August): 305-313.

McDONALD, J. (1973) "Sex predetermination: demographic effects." Mathematical Biosciences 17 (June): 137-146.

McMAHAN, C. A. (1951) "An empirical test of three hypotheses concerning the human sex ratio at birth in the United States, 1915-1948." Milbank Memorial Fund Quarterly 29 (July): 273-293.

NEWTON, N. (1955) Maternal Emotions. New York: P. B. Hoeber.

NORMAN, R. D. (1974) "Sex differences in preferences for sex of children: a replication after 20 years." Journal of Psychology 88 (November): 229-239.

OKLAND, F. (1932) Will It Be A Boy? Sex-determination According to Superstition and Science. New York: The Century Company.

OOSTERWAL, G. (1967) "Muremarew: a dual organized village in the Memberamo, West Irian," in Koentjaraningrat [ed.] Villages in Indonesia. Ithaca, New York: Cornell University Press.

ORCUTT, G. H., M. GREENSBERGER, J. KORBEL, and A. M. RIVLIN (1961) Microanalysis of Socioeconomic Systems: A Simulation Study. New York: Harper and Row Publishers.

ORLEANS, L. A. (1971) "China: population in the People's Republic." Population Bulletin 27, 6 (December): 1-37.

PAKRASI, K. (1964) "A note on differential sex-ratios and polyandrous people in India." Man in India, Ranchi: 44 (April-June): 161-174.

PAKRASI, K. and A. HALDER (1971) "Sex ratios and sex sequences of births in India." Journal of Biosocial Science, London: 3 (October): 377-387.

––– et al. (1970) "Effect of infanticide on sex-ratio in an Indian population." Zeitschrift Fur Morphologie Und Anthropologie 62 (May): 214-230.

PALMORE, J. A. and R. FREEDMAN (1968) "Perceptions of contraceptive practice by others: effects on family planning acceptance in Taichung, Taiwan." Population Index (July-September): 284-285.

PARK, B. H. (1973) "Boy preference and its relation to family planning: the legal background of boy preferences." Research Bulletin 2 K.I.R.B.S. Seoul: 1-14.

PARK, C. B. (1975) "The third Korean child: son-preference and family building." (Tables only.) Presented at the Conference on the Measurement of Preferences for Number and Sex of Children, East-West Center, Honolulu, Hawaii (June 2-5).

PASTERNAK, B. (1968) "Agnatic atrophy in a Formosan village." American Anthropologist 70, 1 (February): 93-96.

PATHAK, K. B. (1973) "On a model for studying variation in the family size under different sex preferences." Biometrics 29 (September): 589-595.

PEEL, J. (1972) "The Hull family survey. 2. Family planning in the first 5 years of marriage." Journal of Biosocial Science, London: 4 (July): 333-346.

––– (1970) "The Hull family survey. 1. The survey couples, 1966." Journal of Biosocial Science, London: 2 (January): 45-70.

PELZEL, J. C. (1970) "Japanese kinship: a comparison," pp. 227-248 in M. Freedman [ed.] Family and Kinship in Chinese Society. Stanford, California: Stanford University Press.

PETERSON, C. C. and J. L. PETERSON (1973) "Preference for sex of offspring as a measure of change in sex attitudes." Psychology 10 (May): 3-5.

PINCUS, F. L. (1975) "Lin Piao and Confucius: up against the great wall." New China (Spring): 33-43.

PLANNED PARENTHOOD FEDERATION OF KOREA (1975) Family Planning through Non-Family Planning Organizations (June).

POFFENBERGER, T. (1968) "Husband-wife communication and motivational aspects of population control in an Indian village." New Delhi: Central Family Planning Institute.

––– (1967) "Age of wives and number of living children of a sample of men who had the vasectomy in Meerut District, U. P." Journal of Family Welfare 13, 4 (June): 48-51.

POFFENBERGER, T. and S. B. POFFENBERGER (1973) "The social psychology of fertility behavior in a village in India," pp. 135-162 in J. T. Fawcett [ed.] Psychological Perspectives on Population. New York: Basic Books.

POHLMAN, E. (1969) Psychology of Birth Planning. Cambridge, Mass.: Schenkman

Publishing Company, Inc.

——— (1967) "Some effects of being able to control sex of offspring." Eugenics Quarterly 14 (December): 274-281.

——— (1967) "Statistical evidence of rationalization." Psychological Reports 20 (January-June): 1180.

——— and K. RAO (1969) "Why boy babies are preferred for adoption or procreation." Journal of Family Welfare, Bombay: 15 (June): 42-52.

POSTGATE, J. (1973) "Bat's chance in hell." New Scientist (April 5): 12-16.

PRABHU, P. H. (1963) Hindu Social Organization. Bombay: Popular Prakashan.

PRACHUABMOH, V., J. KNODEL, and J. O. ALERS (1974) "Preference for sons, desire for additional children, and family planning in Thailand." Journal of Marriage and the Family 36: 601-614.

PRINGLE, M. L. K. (1967) Adoption Facts and Fallacies. London: Longman's, Green & Co. Ltd.

PROTHRO, E. T. (1961) Child Rearing in the Lebanon. Cambridge, Mass.: Distributed for the Center for Middle Eastern Studies of Harvard University by Harvard University Press.

P'YO, M. D. (1965) The Analects of Confucius. Seoul, Korea: Hyun-Am.

RAHMAN, F. (1964) "Religion and planned parenthood in Pakistan." Paper presented at the Pakistan Population Quake, March, 1964, pp. 86-89 in O. Schieffelin [ed.] Muslim Attitudes Toward Family Planning. New York: The Population Council, 1967.

RAINWATER, L. (1965) Family Design: Marital Sexuality, Family Size, and Contraception. Chicago, Illinois: Aldine.

——— (1960) And The Poor Get Children. Chicago, Illinois: Quadrangle.

RAUCAT, T. (1927) The Honorable Picnic. Translated by L. Cline. New York: Viking Press.

RAUF, A. (1958) "Psychological aspects of family planning." Journal of Family Welfare, Bombay: 4 (March): 85-91.

REE, H. B. (1970) "History of Korean legal system," pp. 123-218 in Korea University, Korea Classic Research Institute [ed.] An Outline of Korean Cultural History. Vol. 2. Seoul: Korea University, Korea Classic Research Institute.

——— (1968) "The legal status of Korean women." The Journal of Asian Women 7: 37-54.

RENKONEN, K. O. (1964) "Problems connected with the birth of male children." Acta Genetica Statistica-Medica 14.

——— (1963) "Decreasing sex ratio by birth order." Lancet 1 (January 5): 60.

——— (1956) "Is the sex ratio between boys and girls correlated to the sex of precedent children?" Annales Medicinae Experimentalis et Biologiáe Fenniáe, Helsinki: 34 (4): 447-451.

———, O. MAKELA and R. LEHTOVAARA (1962) "Factors affecting the human sex ratio." Nature, London: 194 (April 21): 308-309.

RENKONEN, K. O. et al. (1961) "Factors affecting the human sex ratio." Annales Medicinae Experimentalis et Biologiae Fenniae (Helsinki) 39 (2): 173-184.

REPETTO, R. (1972) "Son preference and fertility behavior in developing countries." Studies in Family Planning 3 (April): 70-76.

RIDLEY, J. C. (1972) "The effects of population change on the roles and status of women: Perspective and speculation," pp. 372-386 in C. Safilios-Rothschild [ed.] Toward a Sociology of Women. Lexington, Mass.: Xerox College Publishing.

––– (1971) "Introduction: Women's Changing Status," pp. 189-198 in A. A. Campbell et al. [eds.] The Family in Transition. Round Table Conference sponsored by John E. Fogarty International Center for Advanced Study in the Health Sciences. Washington, D.C.: U.S. Government Printing Office.

RIFE, D. C. and L. H. SNYDER (1937) "The distribution of sex ratios within families in an Ohio city." Human Biology 9 (February): 99-103.

RILEY, M. (1968) Brought to Bed. New York: A. S. Barnes and Company.

RIZK, H. (1963) "Social and psychological factors affecting fertility in the U. A. R." Marriage and Family Living 25 (1) (February): 69-73.

––– (1959) Fertility Patterns in Selected Areas in Egypt. Unpublished Ph.D. dissertation. Princeton University, Department of Sociology.

ROBBINS, H. (1952) "A note on gambling systems and birth statistics." American Mathematical Monthly 59 (December): 685-686.

ROBINSON, W. C. and D. E. HORLACHER (1971) "Population growth and economic welfare." Reports on Population/Family Planning 6 (February): 1-39.

ROGERS, E. M., H. J. PARK, K.-K. CHUNG, S.-B. LEE, W. S. PUPPA and B. A. DOE (1975) "Network analysis of the diffusion of family planning innovations over time in Korean villages: the role of Mother's Clubs." Paper presented at the annual meeting of the Population Association of America, Seattle (April).

RORVIK, D. M. and L. B. SHETTLES (1970) "You can choose your baby's sex." Look Magazine (April). This article was reprinted in Reader's Digest.

RORVIK, D. M. with L. B. SHETTLES (1970) Your Baby's Sex: Now You Can Choose. New York: Dodd Mead and Company, Inc.

ROSALDO, M. and L. LAMPHERE [eds.] (1974) Woman, Culture, and Society. Stanford, California: Stanford University Press.

ROSENBERG, E. M. (1973) "Ecological effects of sex-differential nutrition." Paper presented at the annual meeting of the American Anthropological Association (December).

ROSS, J. (1966) "Predicting the adoption of family planning." Studies in Family Planning 9 (June): 8-12.

ROSS, J. A. and S. BANG (1966) "The AID computer programme, used to predict adoption of family planning in Koyang." Population Studies 20 (1) (July): 61-75.

ROSS, J. A., D. W. HAN, S. M. KEENY and G. P. CERNADA (1970) "Korea/Taiwan 1969: report on the national family planning programs." Studies in Family Planning 54 (June): 1-16.

ROTTER, G. S. and N. G. ROTTER (1972) "Preferred family constellations: a pilot study." Social Biology 19 (December): 401-404.

RUTSTEIN, S. (1970) "The relation of child mortality to fertility in Taiwan." Proceedings of the American Statistical Association: 348-353.

RYDER, N. B. and C. F. WESTOFF (1971) Reproduction in the United States: 1965. Princeton: Princeton University Press.

SACKS, K. (1970) "Social bases for sexual equality: a comparative view," pp. 455-469 in R. Morgan [ed.] Sisterhood is Powerful. New York: Random House.

SALAFF, J. W. (1972) "Institutional motivation for fertility limitation in China." Population Studies, London: 26, 2: 233-258.

––– (1971) "Tilling the land for the revolution: the implications of the ideology of equality for women's fertility goals in China." Paper presented at the annual meeting of the Population Association of America, Washington, D.C. (April).

SALAFF, J. W. and J. MERKLE (1973) "Women and revolution: the lessons of the

Soviet Union and China," pp. 145-178 in M. B. Young [ed.] Women in China. Ann Arbor: Center for Chinese Studies, University of Michigan.

SAMUEL, T. J. (1965) "Social factors affecting fertility in India. Eugenics in India." Eugenics Review 57, 1 (March): 5-15.

SAUNDERS, J. V. D. (1958) Differential Fertility in Brazil. Gainsville, Florida: University of Florida Press.

SAUVY, A. (1968) "Masculinity of the last born of a family and distribution of families by sex." Revue de l'Institute International de Statistique, The Hague: 36 (3): 252-259.

SCHIEFFELIN, O. [ed.] (1967) Muslim Attitudes Toward Family Planning. New York: The Population Council.

SEARS, R. R., E. E. MACCOBY, and H. LEVIN (1957) Patterns of Child Rearing. Evanston, Illinois: Row, Peterson.

SEKLANI, M. (1960) "La fécondité dans les pays Arabs: données numerique attitudes et compartements." Population 15, 5 (October-December): 831-836. Translated and reprinted in Muslim Attitudes Toward Family Planning, edited by O. Schieffelin. New York: The Population Council, 1967.

SEROW, W. J. and V. J. EVANS (1970) "Demographic effects of prenatal sex selection." Paper presented at the annual meeting of the Population Association of America, Atlanta (April). Summarized in Population Index 36 (1970): 319.

SHEPS, M. (1963) "Effect on family size of preferences regarding sex of children." Population Studies, London: 17 (July): 66-72.

SHETTLES, L. B. (1961) "Conception and birth sex ratios: A review." Obstetrics and Gynecology XVIII: 122-130.

SIDEL, R. (1972) Women and Child Care in China: A Firsthand Report. New York: Hill and Wang.

SLOMAN, S. S. (1948) "Emotional problems in 'planned for' children." American Journal of Orthopsychiatry 18 (July): 523-528.

SMITH, D. P. (1974) "Generating functions for partial sex control problems." Demography 11 (November): 683-689.

SMITH, I. E. [ed.] (1963) Readings in Adoption. New York: Philosophical Library, Inc.

SPEARE, A. JR. (1971) "A cost-benefit model of rural to urban migration." Population Studies 25, 1 (March): 117-130.

STINNER, W. F. and P. D. MADER (1975) "Sons, daughters or both? An analysis of family sex composition preferences in the Philippines." Demography 12 (February): 67-80.

STRUNK, M. (1947-1948) "The quarter's poll: Children." Public Opinion Quarterly 11 (November): 641.

STYCOS, J. M. (1971) Ideology, Faith, and Family Planning in Latin America. New York: McGraw-Hill Book Company.

——— (1968) Human Fertility in Latin America. Ithaca, N.Y.: Cornell University Press.

——— (1964) "Haitian attitudes toward family size." Human Organization 23, 1 (Spring): 42-47.

——— (1962) "Experiments in social change: the Caribbean fertility studies," pp. 305-316 in C. V. Kiser [ed.] Research in Family Planning. Princeton, N.J.: Princeton University Press.

——— (1955) Family and Fertility in Puerto Rico. New York: Columbia University Press.

STYCOS, J. M. and K. BACK (1964) The Control of Human Fertility in Jamaica. Ithaca, N.Y.: Cornell University Press.

SUMNER, W. G. (1906) Folkways. Boston: Ginn and Company.

SUN, T. H. (1975) "Measurement of preference for number and sex of children in Taiwan: An application of Coombs' preference scales." Paper presented at the Conference on the Measurement of Preferences for Number and Sex of Children." East-West Center, Honolulu, Hawaii (June 2-5).

SUN, T. H. (1968) "Socio-structural analysis of fertility differentials in Taiwan." Unpublished Ph.D. dissertation, University of Michigan.

SUNG, B. (1975) "Boy or girl? How to make your choice." Singapore Straits Times (April 18).

TAEUBER, I. B. and L. A. ORLEANS (1966) "Mainland China," pp. 31-54 in B. Berelson [ed.] Family Planning and Population Programs. Chicago: University of Chicago.

TALWAR, P. P. (1975) "Effect of desired sex composition in families on the birth rate." Journal of Biosocial Science, London: 7 (April): 133-139.

TAYLOR, W. (1954) "A note on the sex distribution of sibs." British Journal of Preventive Social Medicine, London: 8 (October): 178-179.

TEITELBAUM, M. S. (1972) "Factors associated with the sex ratio in human populations," pp. 90-109 in G. A. Harrison and A. J. Boyce [eds.] The Structure of Human Populations. London: Oxford University Press.

––– (1970) "Factors affecting the sex ratios in large populations." Journal of Biosocial Science, London: Supplement 2: 61-71.

TEITELBAUM, M. S. and N. MANTEL (1971) "Socio-economic factors and the sex ratio at birth." Journal of Biosocial Science 3 (January): 23-41.

TEITELBAUM, M. S., N. MANTEL and C. R. STARK (1971) "Limited dependence of the human sex ratio on birth order and parental ages." American Journal of Human Genetics 23 (May): 271-280.

THEIS, S. V. S. (1924) How Foster Children Turn Out. New York: State Charities Aid Association.

THOMAS, M. H. (1951) "Sex pattern and size of family." British Medical Journal (London) 1 (April 7): 733-734.

TIEN, H. Y. (1973) China's Population Struggle. Columbus, Ohio: Ohio State University.

––– (1969) "Employment and education of women in China: implications for fertility change." Proceedings, International Union for the Scientific Study of Population. Liege: I.U.S.S.P.

––– (1963) "Induced abortion and population control in Mainland China." Marriage and Family Living 25 (1) (February): 35-43.

TURNER, J. E. and A. B. SIMMONS (1975) "Family size attitudes: a comparison of measures." Paper presented at the East-West Population Institute Conference on the Measurement of Preferences for Number and Sex of Children, June 2-5.

UDDENBERG, N., P.-E. ALMGREN, and Å. NILSSON (1971) "Preference for sex of the child among pregnant women." Journal of Biosocial Sciences (London) 3 (July): 267-280.

UNION RESEARCH INSTITUTE (1969) "The role of women in the Cultural Revolution." Union Research Service 55, 2 (April): 15-29.

––– (1966) "The status of women in Communist China." Union Research Service 43, 2 (April): 16-30.

––– (1959) "Emancipation of women in Communist China." Union Research Service 15, 21 (June): 284-295.

UNITED NATIONS (1961) The Mysore Population Study. New York: United Nations.

UNTERBERGER, F. (1931) "Deutsche Med. Wochenschr," p. 1107 in A. Etzioni "Sex control, science and society." Science 161 (September 13, 1968).

U.S. Bureau of the Census (1956) Current Population Reports, Series P-20, No. 67 (May).

VISARIA, P. M. (1963) The Sex Ratio of the Population of India. Princeton University. Ph.D. dissertation. (This dissertation has recently been published in India.)

WAHEED, M. (1973) "Effect on family size of varying sex preference rules." Journal of Family Welfare, Bombay: 19 (March): 35-41.

WAISANEN, F. B. and J. T. DURLAK (1966) A Survey of Attitudes Related to Costa Rican Population Dynamics. San Jose, Costa Rica: American International Association for Economic and Social Development.

WANG, C. M. and S. Y. CHEN (1973) "Evaluation of the first year of the educational savings program in Taiwan." Studies in Family Planning 4 (July): 157-161.

WARREN, J. R. (1966) "Birth order and social behavior." Psychological Bulletin 65 (January): 38-49.

WEILER, H. (1959) "Sex ratio and birth control." American Journal of Sociology 65 (November): 298-299.

WEINSTEIN, E. A. and P. M. GEISEL (1960) "An analysis of sex differences in adjustment." Child Development 31 (December): 721-728.

WELCH, F. R. (1974) "Sex of children: prior uncertainty and subsequent fertility behavior." A Rand Corporation Paper (August). Santa Monica: Rand Corporation.

WESTOFF, C. F. (1959) "The social-psychological structure of fertility," pp. 355-366 in International Population Conference. Vienna: International Union for the Scientific Study of Population.

WESTOFF, C. F., E. G. MISHLER, and E. L. KELLEY (1957) "Preferences in size of family and eventual fertility twenty years after." American Journal of Sociology LXII 5: 491-497.

WESTOFF, C. F. and R. R. RINDFUSS (1974) "Sex preselection in the United States." Science 184 (May 10): 633-636.

WESTOFF, C. F. and R. H. POTVIN (1967) College Women and Fertility Values. Princeton, N.J.: Princeton University Press.

WESTOFF, C. F., R. G. POTTER, and P. C. SAGI (1963) The Third Child: A Study in the Prediction of Fertility. Princeton, N.J.: Princeton University Press.

WESTOFF, C. F., R. G. POTTER, P. C. SAGI, and E. E. MISHLER (1961) Family Growth in Metropolitan America. Princeton, N.J.: Princeton University Press.

——— (1961) "Some estimates of the reliability of survey data on family planning." Population Studies XV 1: 52-69.

WHELPTON, P. K., A. A. CAMPBELL, and J. E. PATTERSON (1966) Fertility and Family Planning in the United States. Princeton, N.J.: Princeton University Press.

WHITEHEAD, R. M. (1971) "Women in China today." China Notes, New York: 9, 2 (Spring): 13-18.

WHYTE, M. K. (1974) Small Groups and Political Rituals in China. Berkeley: University of California Press.

WILLIAMSON, N. E. (1976) "Sex preferences, sex control, and the status of women." SIGNS: Journal of Women in Culture and Society (Summer).

——— (1975) "Future life histories: a method of measuring family size and sex preferences." Paper presented at Conference on Measurement of Preferences for Number and Sex of Children, East-West Population Institute, Honolulu, Hawaii (June 2-5).

――― (1974) "Problems of measuring son preference." Paper presented at the annual meeting of the Population Association of America, New York (April).

――― (1973) Preference for Sons Around the World. Ph.D. dissertation. Department of Sociology, Harvard University, Cambridge, Mass. (March).

WILLIAMSON, N. E., S. L. PUTNAM, and H. R. WURTHMANN (1975) "Future autobiographies: expectations of marriage, children, and careers." Paper presented at the Annual Meeting of the Society for the Study of Social Problems, San Francisco (August). Published as a Paper of the East-West Population Institute, Honolulu, Hawaii, 1976.

WINSTON, S. (1932-1933) "Birth control and sex ratio at birth." American Journal of Sociology 38 (July, 1932-May, 1933): 225-231.

――― (1931) "The influence of social factors upon the sex ratio at birth." American Journal of Sociology 37 (July): 1-21.

WITKE, R. (1973a) "Mao Tse-tung, women and suicide," pp. 7-32 in M. B. Young [ed.] Women In China. Ann Arbor: Center for Chinese Studies, University of Michigan.

――― (1973b) "Woman as politician in China of the 1920s," pp. 33-46 in M. B. Young [ed.] Women in China. Ann Arbor: Center for Chinese Studies. University of Michigan.

WITKIN, H. A., et al. (1962) Psychological Differentiation. New York: Wiley.

WITMER, H. L., E. HERZOG, E. A. WEINSTEIN, and M. E. SULLIVAN (1963) Independent Adoptions. New York: Russell Sage Foundation.

WITTENBORN, J. R. (1957) The Placement of Adoptive Children. Springfield, Illinois: Charles C. Thomas.

WOLF, A. P. (1970) "Chinese kinship and mourning dress," pp. 189-208 in M. Freedman [ed.] Family and Kinship in Chinese Society. Stanford: Stanford University Press.

――― (1966) "Childhood association, sexual attraction and the incest taboo: a Chinese Case." American Anthropologist 68, 4 (August): 883-898.

――― (1964) Marriage and Adoption in a Hokkien village, Cornell University. Unpublished Ph.D. Thesis.

WOLF, M. (1972) Women and the Family in Rural Taiwan. Stanford: Stanford University Press.

――― (1970) "Child training and the Chinese family," pp.37-62 in M. Freedman [ed.] Family and Kinship in Chinese Society. Stanford, Stanford University Press.

――― (1968) House of Lim. A Study of a Chinese Farm Family. New York: Appleton-Century-Crofts.

WOOD, C. H. (1975) Ethnic Status and Sex Composition as Factors Mediating Income Effects on Fertility. Unpublished Ph.D. dissertation, University of Texas, Austin, Texas.

WOOD, C. H. and F. D. BEAN (1975) "Sex composition and fertility: Implications from a comparison of Mexican Americans and Anglo Americans." Unpublished paper.

WOODS, F. J. and A. C. LANCASTER (1962) "Cultural factors in Negro adoptive parenthood." Social Work (October): 14-21.

WU, T. S. (1972) "The value of children or boy preference?" pp. 293-299 in J. T. Fawcett [ed.] The Satisfaction and Costs of Children: Theories, Concepts, Methods. Honolulu: East-West Population Institute.

WYON, J. B. and J. E. GORDON (1971) The Khanna Study: Population Problems in the Rural Punjab. Cambridge, Mass.: Harvard University Press.

WYSHAK, G. (1969) "Intervals between births in families containing one set of twins." Journal of Biosocial Science, London: 1 (October): 337-351.

YANG, J. M., S. BANG, M. H. KIM and M. G. LEE (1965) "Fertility and family planning in rural Korea." Population Studies 18, 3 (March): 237-250.

YANG, J. M., M. G. LEE, S. BANG and J. H. CHOI (1966) Korean Rural Society and Family Planning. Seoul, Korea: Yonsei University Press.

YANG, K.-S. (1975) "An analysis of direct questioning and pictorial thematic interviewing as two methods of measuring ideal family size and son preference." Paper presented at the Conference on the Measurement of Preferences for Number and Sex of Children, East-West Center, Honolulu, Hawaii (June 2-5).

YAUKEY, D. (1961) Fertility Differentials in a Modernizing Country. Princeton, N.J.: Princeton University Press.

YEH, K. C. and C. LEE (1974) "Communist China's population problem in the 1980s." Santa Monica: The Rand Paper Series (May).

YENGOYAN, A. A. and G. H. VITERBO (forthcoming) "Gender and ideology: economic variation and gender preferences in the Central Philippines," pp. in J. F. Marshall and S. Polgar [eds.] Culture, Natality, and Family Planning, Carolina Population Center, University of North Carolina, Chapel Hill.

YOON, J. J. (1967) "Preference to male births by Korean family with its effect on family planning and population growth." Journal of Population Studies, Seoul: 4: 19-29.

YOUNG, M. B. [ed.] (1973a) Women in China: Studies in Social Change and Feminism. Ann Arbor, Michigan: Center for Chinese Studies, University of Michigan.

        (1973b) "Introduction," pp. 1-6 in M. B. Young [ed.] Women in China. Ann Arbor: Center for Chinese Studies, University of Michigan.

YU-LAN, L. (1973) "Liberation of women," pp. 205-210 in M. B. Young [ed.] Women in China. Ann Arbor: Center for Chinese Studies, University of Michigan.

YUN, S. H. (1974) "Effects of programmed self-instructional learning on acquisition of family planning knowledge." Doctoral dissertation. School of Public Health, University of North Carolina. Chapel Hill, N.C.

ZIRKLE, C. (1958) "The knowledge of heredity before 1900," pp. 35-55 in L. Dann [ed.] Genetics and the 20th Century. New York: Macmillan.

INDEXES

AUTHOR INDEX

COUNTRY INDEX

SUBJECT INDEX

ABOUT THE AUTHOR

NANCY E. WILLIAMSON is currently a staff associate of The Population Council, serving as an advisor to a maternal and child health-based family planning project in the Philippines, financed by the United Nations Fund for Population Activities. She is also a visiting lecturer and research associate of the Population Institute of the University of the Philippines. Currently, she is doing research on changes in mortality, fertility, and migration. She received a master's degree in demography and human ecology from Harvard School of Public Health in 1969 and a Ph.D. in sociology from Harvard University in 1973. From 1971 to 1976, she was an assistant professor of sociology at Brown University.

SAGE LIBRARY OF SOCIAL RESEARCH